Bringing Geographical Information Systems Into Business

Bringing Geographical Information Systems Into Business

David J Grimshaw

Longman Scientific & Technical
Longman Group Limited
Longman House, Burnt Mill, Harlow
Essex CM20 2JE, England
and Associated Companies throughout the world

Copublished in the United States with John Wiley & Sons Inc., 605 Third Avenue,
New York NY 10158

Trademarks
Throughout this book trademarked names are used. Rather than put a trademark
symbol in every occurrence of a trademarked name, we state that we are using the
names only in an editorial fashion and to the benefit of the trademark owner with
no intention of infringement of the trademark.

First published 1994

British Library Cataloguing in Publication Data
A catalogue entry for this title is available from the British Library.

ISBN 0-582-22549-3

Library of Congress Cataloging in Publication Data
Grimshaw, David J., 1950-
    Bringing geographical information systems into business / David J. Grimshaw
      p.   cm.
    Includes bibliographical references and index.
    ISBN 0-470-23426-1
    1. Business--Research--Data processing. 2. Marketing research--Data processing.
    3. Geographic information systems. 4. Decision support systems. 5. Management
    information systems. I. Title.
    HF5548.2.G7336   1994
    658.4'038--dc20

                              94-14025
                                CIP

Set by 7 in 10/12 Times
Produced in Malaysia, VVP

For Gill, Catherine and Mark

Contents

Contents

Preface

For many years I worked developing land and property information systems, as part of a corporate – and sometimes inter-corporate – team. At that time the words 'geographical information systems' had not entered my consciousness. We were developing databases and linking them together in order to support various business processes. The maps, where they existed at all, were simple – derived from administrative data. I saw such systems grow and I saw some abandoned, as I wondered why and reflected the inevitable happened and I became an academic.

The potential to use digital maps was present in those days of land and property information systems, but that is precisely what it remained – as potential. As many readers will be aware, this situation changed in the mid to late 1980s as the technology became available at a price where it was economic to use digital maps. The market, the conferences, and the research papers fed from and sustained a rapid growth of geographical information systems in the public sector.

What this personal experience told me was that there could be a similar revolution in other application areas. At the start of the 1990s very few business people had ever heard of GIS. Yet many were using maps – even computer-based maps. There were two problems: firstly, the name GIS actually served to put off business users, and secondly, existing GIS (at that time) were cumbersome and specialist in nature. The potential was building up.

The realisation that there was a book to be written in the area of business applications of GIS occurred to me several years ago. At that time so little was known about the subject that colleagues would greet me on the corridor with blank stares if I dared to mention my favourite topic. Not to be put off I held my counsel until further research and further talking with enthusiasts around the world had been done.

About 18 months ago, after some preliminary research into GIS applications in the financial services sector in the UK, I realised that the time was almost there to write a book. A relatively small proportion of those organisations were using GIS at the time of the survey in 1991. However, when asked about use in the future the majority was overwhelming. Here it seemed was a technology that was poised to make a breakthrough into business use in a variety of industries. Preliminary discussions with publishers met with mixed responses: 'yes, but business regards GIS applications as confidential – where will you get the data from?', or 'yes, but where is the market for such a book?' were typical. One publisher did not even reply to my proposal. A little later, in May 1992, the first conference on GIS in Business was held in Denver. Yes, the market was almost there.

At the European Conference on Geographical Information Systems I happened to be browsing the Longman bookstall when Vanessa Lawrence asked if she could help. Thanks, in no small measure, to Vanessa's enthusiasm and vision this book began to take on real shape.

The main aim of this book is to provide an increased understanding of GIS by seeking to integrate the organisational and business drivers that can make GIS successful. Such an approach is essentially multidisciplinary. I hope it will be read widely by both the GIS community and the business school community, academics and people in business. There are many things that each can learn from the other. Opening the GIS communities' eyes and ears to the lessons of applying information technology in organisations is one of the main drivers in the book. The title, *Bringing GIS into Business*, is a manifestation of the vision to see exciting GIS technology integrated into business of whatever kind for the benefit of that business, its customers and society at large.

The book can be used by practitioners, academics and students. As part of a GIS curriculum the book could provide the basis of a one-term or one-semester course about the organisational and information systems integration issues that face business. Courses in business schools might use the book as a basis of a special course or as part of such courses as market research or marketing and IT.

The development of the ideas for this book has been helped by numerous people. Research seminars and informal discussions at Warwick, Curtin University and NCGIA at Buffalo were particularly helpful – to all those who participated, staff and students – thank you. I would particularly like to thank the University of Warwick for supporting my study leave to give me the time to write the book. Colleagues at Warwick Business School have inevitably taken on extra work because of my absence, you are too numerous to mention but thank you all.

In the course of researching material for the book I have met many interesting and helpful people. First of all this gives me the opportunity to thank those busy people who found time to respond to my postal questionnaire, and often found additional time to talk on the telephone or in person. To all those in the case study organisations mentioned in Part Three of the book I owe a special debt because without your contribution and willingness to talk about your applications there would be no worthwhile book. Some organisations I visited, and for reasons that I respect, have asked to remain anonymous. Your contribution was greatly appreciated. I hope that in some small way that all you have collectively said to me, reflected in these pages, will add up to more than the sum of the parts.

The list of thanks would not be complete without mentioning the academics who have offered stimulating discussion in the period of writing. Special thanks here to Derek Milton of the University of Western Australia, Steve Kessel of Curtin

University of Technology, Perth, WA, Hugh Calkins, David Mark and Paul Densham all of the National Center for Geographic Data and Analysis, State University of New York, Buffalo, and Barry Wellar of the University of Ottawa, Canada, and Richard Hume of the Australasian Spatial Data Exchange Centre. For a crash course in cartography, thanks to Mike Clark and colleagues at the GeoData Institute, University of Southampton.

The act of writing is in itself a rather solitary activity for which my family have given me the freedom and space to create. A very loving thank you to some very special people. A final thank you to April Cottage which you will not find on any map but whose attributes were welcome.

DAVID GRIMSHAW

WARWICK

JULY 1993

Acknowledgements

We are grateful to the following for permission to reproduce copyright material:

Alcoa of Australia Ltd. for Figs 9.2, 9.3, 9.4 and 9.5 and Plate I; Butterworth Heinemann for Figs 1.1 (Grimshaw, 1991), 2.6 (Grimshaw & Hinton, 1992) and 3.1 (Grimshaw, 1991a); CACI Ltd. for Fig. 8.8 from *Marketing Systems Today* Copyright © CACI Limited 1993 and Automobile Association 1992 (Road data) All rights reserved; Professor K Eason for Figs 7.4 and 7.5 (Eason, 1988); GIS World Inc. for Figs 3.7 (Grimshaw, 1993), 5.5 (Wellar, 1993), 6.2 (Maffini, 1993) and 10.9 (Freehling, 1993) and Plates V and VI (Reid, 1993); Oxford University Press for Figs 6.4, 6.5 and 6.6 (Venkatraman, 1991) From *The Corporation of the 1990's: Information Technology and Organizational Transformation*, edited by Michael S Scott-Morton Copyright © 1991 by Sloan School of Management Reprinted by permission of Oxford University Press; School of Industrial and Business Studies, University of Warwick for Fig. 7.2 (Galliers, Grimshaw and Omerod, 1993); Spa Marketing Systems Ltd. for Fig. 8.3 and Plate III; Tactics International Ltd. for Fig. 8.6; The University of Chicago Press for Fig. 8.9 (Monmonier, 1991); John Wiley & Sons Ltd, for Figs 3.5 and 3.6 (Ward *et al.*, 1990) Copyright © 1990 John Wiley & Sons Ltd. Reprinted by permission of John Wiley & Sons Ltd.

Whilst every effort has been made to trace the owners of copyright material, in a few cases this has proved impossible and we take this opportunity to offer our apologies to any copyright holders whose rights we may have unwittingly infringed.

Introduction

1

Business opportunities of GIS

'The most exciting technology since the invention of the map.'

Roger Chorley (1987)

Preamble

It would be easy to imagine that geographical information systems (GIS) were only about helping to solve *geographical* problems. That GIS are to geographers what computer-aided design/computer-aided manufacturing (CAD/CAM) are to engineers. Whilst this statement is true, it only represents part of the truth. As with all things, the whole truth is much more interesting.

Look around your own business, or one you are perhaps familiar with. Think about the information held by that business – how much of that data has a spatial dimension? Some sources claim that as much as 90% of business data is geographic data (Moloney *et al.* 1993). Every business has customers who live somewhere. All manufacturing business has a distribution chain which requires products to be taken to markets by the cheapest route in the least time. All service business choose their location, at least in part, by optimising the spending power in the defined catchment area. And so on. GIS presents an opportunity to solve *business* problems by providing a capability to process the high proportion of business data that is geographic data. The comprehension of this opportunity represents a step in the thought process from perceiving GIS as a specialist *geographical* system to understanding GIS as a *business information* system supporting an organisation's needs.

The shear diversity of technology and applications now under the GIS umbrella is sometimes bewildering. This book takes a new look at GIS from the dual perspective of information systems and the applications of GIS in business. The applications considered are confined to *business* defined as a commercial organisation. However, it must be said that most of the approach outlined in Parts One and Two of the book could be applied to applications in more traditional domains of non-commercial governmental organisations. The concepts, frameworks and indeed the lessons that emerge, although they originate from an information systems perspective, are relevant for everyone concerned with

3

improving GIS: professional and academic from both the information systems and GIS communities. They are most certainly vital for all business people to truly understand.

The wealth of examples illustrating the use and potential use of GIS in business will be discussed in Part Three of this book. But before you can appreciate the business opportunities of GIS you need to know about some of the GIS traditions and how GIS in business is breaking these traditions. This chapter goes on to suggest that the study of GIS could benefit from adopting a completeness paradigm leading to the adoption of a GIS pyramid as a way of structuring the contents of the book.

The GIS tradition

There is now a growing collection of books on the subject of GIS. Many conferences are held around the world to debate GIS technology and the latest applications. In both the USA and Europe there are now specialist conferences dealing with GIS in business. A great deal of commercial sponsorship at these events is evidence of the large market for hardware and software vendors. The number and range of academic journals and professional periodicals specialising in GIS have grown in the late 1980s and early 1990s. All this evidence points to an area of concern that is of growing importance. So much has been achieved that it has been argued that the subject is now mature enough to warrant a reference compendium, and a two-volume set was written in the early 1990s (Maguire *et al.* 1991a).

Some important questions arise. How do GIS differ from other information systems? Why have the information systems community been largely absent from the debates about GIS? The mission of this book is to place GIS firmly within the information systems domain in order to improve the theory and practice of GIS.

Previous writing on GIS has emphasised three different perspectives:

1. *The technology:* for example, the book *Geographic Information Systems: A Guide to the Technology* (Antenucci *et al.* 1991) written by a team of authors working for PlanGraphics Inc. who specialise in the design and implementation of commercial GIS.
2. *GIS applications:* for example, the proceedings of conferences like the European Conference on Geographical Information Systems (EGIS) have papers organised into application themes (EGIS 1992).
3. *The emerging discipline of GIS:* for example, *The Organisational Home for GIS in the Scientific Professional Community* (Morrison 1991).

These perspectives can partly be explained further by discussing the groups of people who have an interest in GIS: the stakeholders (Table 1.1). The first stakeholder group are academic departments of computer science in universities. Research into computer graphics or improving the algorithms of spatial analysis and data retrieval routines are just examples of the interests of this group. The second stakeholder group are a mixture of academics and practitioners who have some problem to solve which involves geographical data analysis. Typically this group of people might work for governmental agencies, with strong environmental concerns. The third stakeholder group are mainly the academic community from university geography departments. The concern with GIS is from a pedagogic, analytical and descriptive point of view. To these three stakeholders we must add the hardware and software vendors who have a commercial imperative to find a market niche for GIS. Each of the stakeholders, if consulted on the business opportunities of GIS, are likely to have a different view. It is important that such differences are taken into account.

Table 1.1   A summary of GIS stakeholders

Perspectives		Stakeholders	
		Academic	**Practitioner/role**
T	Technology	Computer science	Vendor
A	Application	Geography	
		Planning	User
		Environment	
		Business studies	
IS	g Info. System	Information systems	Systems designer
		Systems science	Operational research
O	Organisation	Organisational behaviour	Managers

Note: The stakeholders listed under 'Application' are meant to be illustrative rather than comprehensive.

There has been some debate at conferences and in the literature about the most appropriate academic home of GIS. Morrison (1991) asks the question: where does GIS belong in the traditional professional society or academic department framework? His conclusion is that essentially GIS is the major tool of the discipline of geography. A further perspective on the debate is offered by Unwin (1991) who investigates the curriculum developments in GIS. He concludes that concerns have been with curriculum content rather than knowledge. A reminder from Arnoff (1989) is that if GIS is not to become another technology looking for an application, teaching must include the management of GIS.

Although there are undoubtedly some important technological challenges still remaining, the technology is now at a price which allows a wide range of applications to be economically feasible. The major challenges ahead are in the management of the systems, the organisational settings, and the implementation issues. In other words, all issues that the information systems community have been debating with respect to information systems more generally for many years. Hence it is timely to examine GIS from an information systems point of view.

Applications of information technology (IT) to geographical problems range from automated mapping to the geographical spreadsheet offering sophisticated modelling capability. At the one extreme the objective of automated mapping is essentially to gain efficiency benefits; at the other extreme, the output of geographical models is typically to help the organisation become more effective.

The GIS tradition can be traced back to large-scale land information systems in the 1970s. Models containing geographic variables have been used to assist firms in the location decision since the days of the early gravity models (see for example Lee 1973). Yet applications of IT to the breadth of problems that have some geographical dimension is only just beginning. The potential will be appreciated much more when GIS is seen as simply part of an organisation's wealth of information systems.

Breaking with the GIS tradition

Traditional users of GIS spend 34% of their time using their systems (Hale 1993). Those users who could be described as 'GIS in business' spent about 24% of their time on GIS. The traditional user would typically use an application running under the UNIX operating system whilst the business user would run under DOS (or Windows). These are interesting market statistics because they help to build a picture of the GIS in business user as someone using GIS simply as a part of their data processing role.

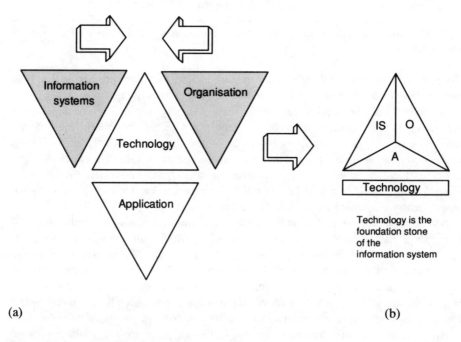

(a)   (b)

Figure 1.1   Building the GIS pyramid

A picture emerges of a business user integrating spatial data with other company data to contribute towards decision making. Using a system for a smaller proportion of working time might also imply that the software needs to be simple to operate and to learn. Many GIS software packages are very complex and offer features that the business user is unlikely to require.

Figure 1.1(a) shows the two traditional perspectives of GIS: technology (T) and applications (A). For GIS technology to deliver the applications needed by the business organisation there must be an additional and complementary two perspectives: information systems (IS) and organisation (O). The shift from the model shown in Figure 1.1(a) to that shown in Figure 1.1(b) represents a paradigm shift in thinking of the GIS community.

Many of the building blocks of the emerging GIS discipline have been cast in a technology or applications mould. All technology and applications are *used* in some organisation or other. The place of technology is one of a foundation stone of the pyramid. To complete the building, greater attention must be given to GIS in its organisational setting.

Towards a completeness paradigm of GIS

What have GIS to do with information systems? You may well ask! A study of the literature might lead you to believe that the answer was 'nothing', since the number of literature citations that deal with the information systems issues of GIS is limited. A search of the ABI/Inform database for the period January 1989 to June 1993 showed 11 499 references to 'information systems' but only 17 references to 'geographical information systems'. One of the reasons for writing this book is to attempt to influence the thinking of the GIS community. To shift the thinking away from a technological preoccupation towards involvement in, and influence by, the information systems community.

A small historical diversion may prove illuminating in helping to explain why an information systems perspective has hitherto been lacking. Some observers (see for example Forrester 1985) have compared the information revolution to the Industrial Revolution of the eighteenth century. The challenge of using technology to manage information can be likened to the challenge of retraining manpower (labour) from agricultural pursuits to manufacturing and employing more capital as substitutes for labour. Information systems have become an increasingly important subject as the information explosion has challenged management with new issues of concern and new opportunities for growth.

During the Industrial Revolution many of the decisions made by the now famous entrepreneurs like Cadbury and Arkwright were based on knowing where there was, for example, a good supply of water, iron ore or a good canal network for transporting finished goods. Although the term would have been alien to those early entrepreneurs, the decisions were made on the basis of 'geographical information'. A knowledge of geography was a crucial input to managerial decision making.

Those early managers had to meet the challenges of setting up their industrial concerns in areas where people had agricultural skills, not industrial ones. The workforce had to be trained in a new technology. This was an era where management of labour and capital were the main challenges. In the information age (Zuboff 1988) the new technology is applied to data as a raw material to transform it into a useful information product. Some influential categories were defined by Zuboff (1988). She recognised that initially the technology is used to *automate*; only later, after some years of experience and organisational learning, will the technology *informate*. The challenge is to use that information to improve decision making. Using GIS to help in the decision-making process is returned to in depth in Chapter 5.

The paradigm of thought influencing the GIS community has originated largely from the discipline of geography, with economics and other subjects contributing at the margins. This is to be expected when we know that most GIS users are geographers. However, it is increasingly being speculated that future users of GIS will be in business and commerce. In these areas of application there is a need to relate GIS ideas to the frameworks of thought already familiar to that community. Furthermore, there is reason to expect that the subject of GIS may be enriched by opening it to the domain of information systems. If the term 'geographical information systems' is written out in full, two-thirds of it is represented by 'information systems'. The subject of how GIS fits into information systems theory is returned to in Chapters 2 and 3.

What is the paradigm that guides the GIS community to date? First, we should have a working definition of a paradigm. Initially a term introduced into scientific literature by Kuhn (1961) a paradigm, even in Kuhn's own writings, has had many different definitions. A good working definition here would be that used by Ritzer (1975 p. 7): 'A paradigm . . . serves to define what should be studied, what questions should be asked, and what rules should be followed in interpreting the answers obtained. The paradigm is the broadest unit of consensus within a science and serves to differentiate one scientific community (or sub community) from another.'

There are parallels with other sub-fields of endeavour within the information systems community. For example, expert systems were originally influenced by the psychology and artificial intelligence traditions. Thought about expert systems became focused on the technology which left the integration of expert systems into the management strategies of the organisations rather isolated.

Information held in a structured way on a computer, or other piece of IT, for subsequent retrieval is commonly referred to as an information system. The use of computers in business is a relatively new subject of study, dating back to the first use of computers in business in the mid 1950s. Much stress in the early literature has been on the technical aspects of systems. Emphasis on the technology naturally followed from the obvious challenges of applying the new IT to difficult and ever-widening problems. Critical literature on the information aspects of IT can only be traced back as far as Ackoff (1967).

However, it is much more appropriate to today's problems to view information systems as a multidisciplinary area. Chapter 2 deals with seeing GIS as information systems. The traditional paradigm in the information systems area has been described by Samuelson (1981) as a substitution paradigm because technology has been used to automate existing processes and substitute capital for labour. This paradigm leads to incremental change, most typically in narrowly defined areas of the business, with an emphasis on technical design. Samuelson (1981) has argued that to gain improvements to the information process of the whole organisation there should be a move to the 'completeness paradigm'. Completeness means analysing the complete socio-technical system. This theme will be returned to in Part Two of the book.

Looking at GIS as information systems is briefly reviewed in the next section, more detail is discussed in Chapter 2.

GIS and information systems

Looking towards the year 2000 Maguire *et al.* (1991b: 324) conjecture that: 'GIS technology may well have disappeared as a 'free-standing' activity in many organisations as its functionality becomes encompassed by business oriented systems, such as those for market analysis, and it becomes part of wider management information systems.' The point is well made that GIS, having been seen as a technology, will in future be seen as a *geographical* information system. It is perhaps unfortunate that the authors chose the term 'management information system' (MIS) because, in the words of Keen and Scott-Morton (1978) MIS is a prime example of a content-free expression which means different things to different people. On a more serious note, MIS tends to be defined as an integrated and comprehensive information system. In these terms, GIS viewed as an information system will certainly become absorbed into the infrastructure of the organisation.

Information systems have been defined as: 'A set of organised procedures that, when executed, provides information to support the organisation' (Lucas 1990: 15). With such a broad definition there can be little doubt that GIS are a special case of information systems. The adjective 'geographical' serves to explain the *purpose* to which the information system is to be applied or some *spatial attribute* of the data upon which the information system is built. A formal definition of a GIS, used as a working definition in this book, is given in Chapter 2.

In the information systems literature there are many examples of adjectives being used as a prefix to the term 'information system'. For example, executive information systems have been defined as: 'The routine use of a computer based system, most often through direct access to a terminal or personal computer, for any business function. The users are either the CEO or a member of the senior management team reporting directly to him or her. Executive support systems can be implemented at the corporate or divisional level' (Rockart and DeLong 1986: 16).

Another similar case would be expert systems. Here the word 'information' is dropped from the description. Consider the following definition of an expert system: 'An interactive system that responds to questions, asks for clarification,

9

makes recommendations, and generally aids in the decision-making process' (Long 1989: 69). It becomes clear that an expert system is an information system containing knowledge and rules such that the user engages in a dialogue with the computer which simulates a consultation with an expert.

In the case of the examples, 'executive' and 'expert' are terms used to denote the applications domain but also the technology. Executive information systems have used technology like touch screens and intuitive user interfaces in order to appeal to a particular market niche. Expert systems have used rule induction algorithms and neural networks which have originated from research in artificial intelligence, often in psychology departments of universities.

The examples of the expert system and the executive information system given above, convey that there are other specialist information systems sponsored by specialists yet now used by a wide business community. The case of GIS is similar in that it was originally sponsored by specialists (geographers) and is now finding general business applications. Chapter 2 deals with this subject in greater depth when GIS is placed into a framework or taxonomy of information systems.

GIS and the organisation

Looking back to Figure 1.1 reminds us that the early concerns about the application of IT were concentrated on the technology issues rather than the information issues. However, it can be argued that with the increasing

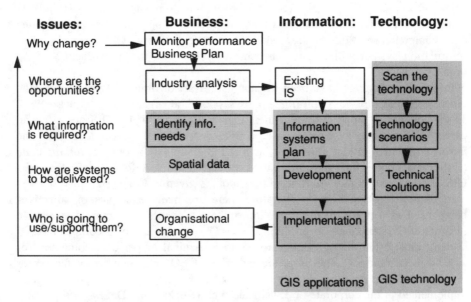

Figure 1.2 GIS in the organisational setting (*Source*: amended from Grimshaw 1991a; first published in *International Journal of Information Management*, **11** (4), December 1991, reproduced here with the permission of Butterworth Heinemann, Oxford)

sophistication of technology and its capability getting faster yet cheaper year by year, there has been a swing towards examining the information issues. Technologies like GIS have had a following of experts who have largely been subject specialists wanting to apply the technology. Not unnaturally this has left a legacy of information issues that have been neglected. This book is aimed at redressing the balance by injecting ideas, concepts and frameworks from the information systems literature into the domain of GIS.

One of the key lessons from earlier applications of new technologies, like expert systems and office automation, is that a vision of the future (dream) is a necessary but not a sufficient condition for success. To be successful the technology needs to be integrated into the business planning process. Not just the information planning cycle, but linked via a two-way bridge to the corporate plan (Earl 1989). More organisations will see GIS as a technological opportunity that can be brought into the business to make a significant impact on profit. The question of how this can be done is returned to in Chapter 3. The underlying trend is for GIS to be increasingly considered as part of the organisation's information management strategy (Grimshaw 1991a).

Figure 1.2 shows that the basic business questions, asked on the left-hand side, relate to three other processes going on in the business. These concern information, systems and technology. This is a useful overall framework to use when it comes to looking in more detail at GIS and the management strategies in Chapter 3. For the moment we should be aware of the wider perspective that this diagram illustrates.

During the next decade, business will be confronted with tough challenges to maintaining market share, and IT will be viewed as the means to attain and increase competitive advantage (Grimshaw 1991b). Specifically, it is likely that GIS will rise to dominate as a key tool for strategic planning. All technologies can be seen as contributing efficiency, effectiveness or strategic transformation depending on the stage of growth attained in a particular organisation (Galliers and Sutherland 1991). The next section of this chapter discusses the stage of growth model. What we will see in the period of the early 1990s is GIS technology maturing so that its application moves from one of achieving efficiency benefits to one of achieving strategic benefit.

In fact, GIS can facilitate high-level decision making, and help in ensuring the integrity and survival of the organisation, particularly as competitive pressures increase. There are two main areas in which GIS technology is likely to have a major impact upon business strategies – competitor analysis and branch rationalisation. In addition, GIS provides a means of examining, in detail, the market share a competitor enjoys.

From the viewpoint of the private sector, GIS applications are currently of an *ad hoc* nature, supporting decision making in functional areas (say) marketing. The major business justifications for developing and using such systems will typically have been to enhance the productivity or effectiveness of the functional area rather than to contribute to the business as a whole. The initiators of early GIS projects would typically be functional specialists. The trend will be for GIS projects to be introduced into companies via a 'top-down' process.

The central concerns of both public and private sector users and potential users of GIS are beginning now to turn towards the corporate needs of the organisation (Maynard and Pearce 1990). At this important stage of thinking the central concern becomes strategic. Managers begin to look for real business reasons for justifying an investment in GIS. The potential of hitherto neglected data sets are realised as data is now regarded as a true corporate resource.

Taking advantage of GIS

We have already observed a rapid increase in the rate at which GIS technology is being developed and marketed. There is a similar explosion in the applications of GIS. At the first conference of GIS in Business and Commerce held in Denver in 1992 it was held that: 'The application of GIS to business and industry problems will be the largest growth area in GIS over the next decade.' As if to reinforce this prediction, the second conference on GIS in Business held in Boston in 1993 was attended by twice as many delegates as that first conference in Denver. The first European Conference on GIS in Business is being held in 1994. During times of expansion, especially times of rapid expansion, stress is introduced into the organisation. The readiness of the particular organisation's ability to be able to cope with this kind of change is an important factor to consider when introducing an information system.

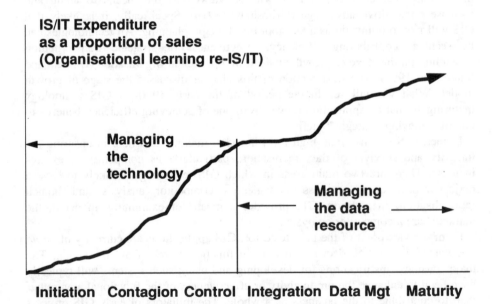

Figure 1.3   The stages of growth (*Source*: amended from Nolan 1979)

A number of studies have been carried out in the field of how organisations respond to increased spending on IT. The first such study, by Gibson and Nolan (1974), has become a classic in the literature. A relatively old piece of work, given the rapid change of technology, it is still referred to as something of a classic because it puts forward a simple idea that has stood the test of time. Essentially, after much empirical work, Gibson and Nolan (1974) found that organisations have variable reactions (go through different stages) as their spending on IT increases. The simple model, as originally put forward by Gibson and Nolan (1974) is shown in Figure 1.3.

The early stage of 'initiation' is where computers and other forms of IT are just beginning to be purchased by the organisation. At this stage the spending rises quickly but most people in the organisation have not learnt how to make the best use of the technology. As people talk to each other about their experiences with using the new computers, experience is shared, ideas are transferred to different working groups and there is a consequently large rise in the demand for yet more technology. This second stage has been dubbed 'contagion' for obvious reasons.

After the steep rise in the spending curve during the contagion stage, management tend to worry that spending is going to get out of control. There follows a period of 'control' when managers try to re-exert their control on spending. Such action may serve to stifle initiative during this stage but it certainly will lead to a slowing down of the spending on IT. When the control mechanisms mature into a set of reasonable mechanisms for maintaining some managerial direction whilst encouraging some initiative in the interests of the basic objectives and mission of the organisation, the firm enters the often elusive stage of 'maturity'.

The basic model has been modified over time to take account of the ever-changing technology (see for example Nolan 1984; Galliers and Sutherland 1991). Further discussion of these later developments of the stages of growth model is left to Chapter 2 in relation to a taxonomy of information systems and Chapter 3 in relation to the planning of information systems. A generic model, called the GIS Starting Grid, is developed in Chapter 3 from some empirical work and forms the basis of discussion of the case studies in Part Three of the book.

Overview of the book

Following this introduction, the book is organised into three parts. The rationale for this structure can best be explained with reference to Figure 1.4. GIS are many things to many people. That they are complex is not in doubt. Maps are complex, yet building them in computer systems is done via simple layers. Similarly, this book adopts a layer approach (represented by the pyramid of Figure 1.1) to building the complexity of GIS.

The four components of the GIS pyramid are all vital and interwoven in practice. For the purpose of explanation and discussion we shall examine, in detail, each component in the three parts that follow.

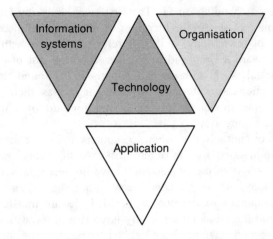

Part I: The Management of Geographical Information

Part II: The Organisational Challenge

Part III: Using Geographical Information in Business

Figure 1.4 The structure of the book

Part One: The management of geographic information

In terms of the pyramid the first part of the book deals with information systems and technology. After defining what GIS are, Part One takes a top-down approach by starting with the business issues that drive the requirement to use information systems to manage data. Some issues concerning spatial data are discussed after outlining an approach to viewing data as a corporate resource for the whole organisation. The emphasis in Part One is to introduce the reader to some specific problems and issues concerning spatial data, to introduce GIS for the non-specialist reader. The traditional GIS specialist reader will find much new material here to provide food for thought about how GIS can be integrated into the business and other information systems.

Part Two: The organisational challenge

The second part of the book looks at the contribution GIS can make to decision making in the business. The role that information plays in the organisation is used as a basis for examining how information systems in general and GIS in particular can be justified. How can the business case be made for investing in GIS? Implementation of information systems is often something tacked on to the end of the information systems development process. Yet we know from research that implementation needs to be a fully integrated part of information systems development. The human and organisational issues are fundamental here.

Part Three: Using geographical information in business

The third part of the book covers a range of applications of GIS. The focus is on how GIS is being used in a variety of organisations to assist in decision making at different organisational levels. Examples and case studies are discussed and brought together from a wide variety of industries and from a number of different countries. The case studies provide real examples of the benefits, costs and issues involved in developing and using GIS in practice. They are included in order to illustrate the principles of GIS outlined in the first two parts of the book and also to provide ample teaching material for courses on GIS in business.

Each chapter concludes with a summary and a section on further reading for those wishing to take a particular topic to a greater depth. A final chapter in the book looks at the important question of 'what makes a successful GIS?' Some future trends are highlighted as being worth watching for as possible ways of enhancing the use of GIS in business.

Summary

This chapter has presented an introduction to GIS, exploring the tradition of GIS to date. Having established that the traditional view of GIS has been dominated by *technology* and functional *applications*, some reasons for the inadequacy of this view were explored. A new paradigm of thought was advanced which views GIS as an information system that works in an organisational setting. This represents a paradigm shift from substitution towards *completeness*.

The technology of GIS presents some exciting opportunities and challenges for business organisations. The challenge is essentially to see the technology as a delivery mechanism for successful applications serving real business needs.

Two 'lenses' with which to view GIS: *information systems* and *organisations* are added to the traditional 'lenses' of *technology* and *applications*. In what follows, the framework represented in Figure 1.4 will be used as a guide to bringing GIS into the business.

References

Ackoff R L 1967 Management misinformation systems. *Management Science* **14**(4), December: 147–56

Antenucci J C, Brown K, Crosswell P L, Kevany M J with **Archer H** 1991 *Geographic Information Systems: A Guide to the Technology* Van Nostrand Reinhold, New York

Arnoff S 1989 *Geographic Information Systems: a Management Perspective* WDL Publications, Ottawa

Department of the Environment 1987 *Handling Geographic Information* Report of the Committee of Enquiry chaired by Lord Chorley, HMSO, London

Earl M J 1989 *Management Strategies for Information Technology* Prentice-Hall, London

EGIS 1992 *Proceedings of the Third European Conference on Geographical Information Systems* Munich, Germany, 23–26 March

Forrester T 1985 *The Information Technology Revolution* Blackwell, Oxford

Galliers R D, Sutherland A R 1991 Information systems management and strategy formulation: the stages of growth model revisited. *Journal of Information Systems* **1**(2): 89–114

Gibson C, Nolan R L 1974 The four stages of EDP growth. *Harvard Business Review* **52**: 74–88

Grimshaw D J 1991a Geographical information systems as part of the corporate information strategy. *International Journal of Information Management* **11**(4): 292–7

Grimshaw D J 1991b The use of GIS by building societies in the UK. *Proceedings of the Third European Conference on Geographical Information Systems* Vol 2, Munich, March, pp 988–97

Hale K 1993 *GIS in business: market trends*. Paper presented at the GIS in Business '93 Conference, 7–10 March, Boston, Mass

Keen P G W, Scott-Morton M S 1978 *Decision Support Systems* Addison-Wesley, New York

Kuhn T S 1961 *The Structure of Scientific Revolution* University of Chicago Press, Chicago, Ill

Lee C 1973 *Models in Planning* Pergamon Press, Oxford

Long L 1989 *Management Information Systems* Prentice-Hall, London

Lucas H C (1990) *Information Systems Concepts for Management*, 4th edn, McGraw-Hill, New York

Maguire D J, Goodchild M F, Rhind D W 1991a Introduction. In Maguire D J, Goodchild M F, Rhind D W (eds). *Geographical Information Systems* Vol 1 *Principles* Longman Scientific & Technical, Harlow, pp 3–7

Maguire D J, Goodchild M F, Rhind D W 1991b Epilogue. In Maguire D J, Goodchild M F, Rhind D W (eds). *Geographical Information Systems* Vol 1 *Principles* Longman Scientific & Technical, Harlow, pp 313–27

Maynard J C, Pearce N J 1990 GIS as part of a corporate IT strategy: a practical approach. *Proceedings of the European Conference on Geographical Information Systems* Vol II, Amsterdam, April, pp 729–36

Moloney T, Lea A C, Kowalchuk C 1993 Manufacturing and packaged goods. In *Profiting from a Geographic Information System* GIS World Books, Inc, Fort Collins, Colo, pp 105–29

Morrison J L 1991 The organisational home for GIS in the scientific professional community. In Maguire D J, Goodchild M F, Rhind D W (eds) *Geographical Information Systems*, Vol 1 *Principles* Longman Scientific & Technical, Harlow, pp 91–100

Nolan R L 1979 Managing the crisis in dataprocessing. *Harvard Business Review*, **57**(2), (March-April): 115–26

Nolan R L 1984 Managing the advanced stages of computer technology: key research issues. In McFarlan F W (ed.) *The Information Systems Research Challenge* Harvard Business School, Boston, Mass

Ritzer G 1975 *Sociology: A Multiple Paradigm Science* Allyn & Bacon, Boston, Mass

Rockart J F, DeLong D W 1986 *Executive Support Systems: The Emergence of Top Management Computer Use* Dow-Jones Irwin, Homewood, Ill, p 16

Samuelson K 1981 InformaticCom and multiway video communications as a cybernetic design and general systems technology. *Proceedings of the Twenty Fifth Annual Conference of the Society for General Systems Research* Toronto, Ontario

Unwin D J 1991 The academic setting of GIS. In Maguire D J, Goodchild M F, Rhind D W (eds) *Geographical Information Systems* Vol 1 *Principles* Longman Scientific & Technical, Harlow pp 81–90

Zuboff S 1988 *In The Age of the Smart Machine* Heinemann, London

Part One

The Management of Geographical Information

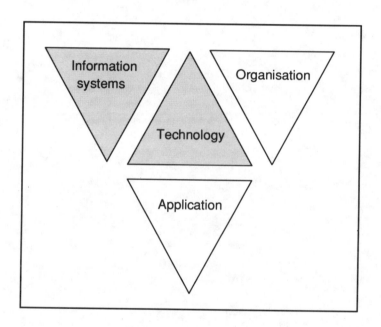

2

What is a geographical information system?

'. . . the most significant development in the management of data since the invention of the computer'.

(Blenheim Online 1993)

Preamble

The purpose of this chapter is to give the reader clear understanding of what GIS are and how GIS relate to other information systems. Currently GIS provide both mapping and analysis capabilities. A simple classification of GIS based on these two features is given. The components of GIS are introduced before discussing the technology, tasks (applications) and timeframe characteristics.

The quote at the head of this chapter captures the essence of what GIS are all about. Simply put, GIS offer management of both spatial and attribute data. Commercially available GIS software packages also often offer the capability to integrate many other types of data such as sound and video.

Another way of viewing GIS is to see it as part of the computer industry. The commercial aspect of GIS is a big business that is growing fast. The size of the GIS market reached $2 billion in 1992 according to Dataquest (Hale 1993). Maguire (1991) predicted a growth rate of between 25 and 35% per year over the next five years 1991–96. This is certainly a remarkable growth and within this the GIS in business market is growing very fast indeed, as is evident from the doubling of the number of delegates at the GIS in Business Conference held in Boston in 1993. However, in a wider context GIS accounts for only a little over 1% of all software revenue.

These are interesting statistics and the precise nature of the figures could be debated endlessly. But what do the statistics mean for the GIS user, the main reader of this book? One important message is that the growth of the GIS industry means increasing choice for the GIS user. There are now more software products to choose from, more consultants to seek advice from and more data agencies to purchase data from.

A review of definitions of GIS

The terms *geographic information systems* and *geographical information systems* are regarded as synonymous, the former having established use in North America and the latter term being more prevalent in Europe. Traditionally geographical information systems (GIS) have been used to help solve problems in the environmental domain. The application of GIS to business problems is interesting because it represents an extension to the original applications domain. The term GIS has taken on many meanings in the literature. What is a GIS? One of the clearest definitions is given in the Chorley Report: 'A system for capturing, storing, checking, manipulating, analysing and displaying data which are spatially referenced to the Earth' (DoE 1987: 132).

The last part of this definition relates to the 'geographical' component. The adjective 'geographical' says something about the data that is used in the information system. So, a GIS is an information system where the data has a geographical dimension (Grimshaw 1989).

One of the main characteristics of the GIS area of interest is that it is multidisciplinary. Contributions to the successful development of GIS theory and practice have come from geography, town planning, computer science, management science and information systems.

Remember, from Chapter 1 that our definition of an information system did not require it to have a computer system driving it. The earliest GIS were paper maps; indeed it is possible to trace geographically based information systems back to the Domesday Book. Information on landownership, collected at a particular point of time and used for the purpose of collecting taxes, certainly falls within our definition of an information system that is related to points on the earth's surface. So, in terms of history, the first GIS is probably 900 hundred years old!

Defining what a GIS is can be done in a number of different ways. We could read all that has been written about the topic, analyse it and present a synthesis of it. We could observe the currency of the term 'GIS' as it has been used. We could adopt the definitions used by well-known and respected authors who have previously written on the subject. Or we could try to ignore the 'G' in 'GIS' and concentrate on information systems. All these alternatives have their attractions. To understand GIS fully we will explore all of these alternative views. Before discussing the formal definitions of GIS that can be used, a mini case study will serve to focus attention on the main features of GIS.

Mini Case Study

A real estate company has a database of residential properties for sale. Clients seeking a new property visit the office and specify their requirements in terms of proximity to schools, price range, number of bedrooms, size of garden and age of property.

The records selected from the database on the basis of the clients' criteria are then displayed on the computer screen showing streets, schools and other geographic features. A further refinement of the search is done interactively by using the map to narrow the search area by specifying proximity to shopping facilities. The resulting list of five properties is still too many to visit on one afternoon so, in addition to the photograph and floor plans displayed for each property, a short video is viewed to simulate a walk-through of the property.

The database contains the attributes of properties (price, age, number of bedrooms, etc.). The display of a map on the computer screen means that there is also a spatial database (distances between points). The GIS has provided a way of using the map to display and retrieve information of value to the client.

The introduction to this book identified three different perspectives on GIS that have been taken in previous books: the technology (Antenucci *et al.* 1991), GIS applications (EGIS 1992) and the emerging discipline of GIS (Morrison 1991). A full chapter discussing the definition of GIS appears in Maguire *et al.* (1991). The technology-led view of GIS would typically define GIS as: 'all automated systems used primarily for the management of maps and geographic data' (Antenucci *et al.* 1991: 6). A wider view of GIS is taken by many authors, most notably to include some organisational issues: 'an institutional entity, reflecting an organisational structure that integrates technology with a database, expertise and continuing financial support over time' (Carter 1989: 3). A view that stresses that GIS are part of the information systems tradition has been put forward by some authors, for example, Devine and Field (1986: 18): 'a form of management information system that allows map display of the general information'.

A precise definition of GIS that everyone could agree on matters less than the understanding gained from reviewing these definitions. Ranging from an emphasis on technology, through applications and information systems perspectives, definitions are, after all, simply a matter of convenient labelling to help with our communications about observable things. A working definition, for the purposes of this book will be returned to later in this chapter.

According to Coppock and Rhind (1991) computer-based GIS have been used since the late 1960s. But were these so-called GIS really full feature, full function GIS? One of the earliest examples, quoted by Coppock and Rhind, was the Oxford System of Automated Cartography. The problems of producing an atlas of Great Britain convinced Bickmore and Shaw (1963) that the computer could provide a cost-effective way of checking, editing and classifying data. This kind of motivating force towards a 'GIS' is typical of what we referred to in Chapter 1 as 'automation'. In other words, the application of computer-based technology to increase the operational efficiency of the organisation. The origins of the term 'GIS' can therefore be traced back to automated cartography.

Automated cartography

Much of the move towards automated mapping in the early 1960s was funded by the military who had the resources to purchase expensive computer equipment (Diello *et al.* 1968). National mapping agencies tried to produce maps, with the aid of computers, that could not be distinguished from those produced manually. Adopting such an approach, Coppock and Rhind (1991) report that the Ordnance Survey could not automate map production on a cost-effective basis until the 1980s.

The term 'GIS' is thought to have first been applied to the Canadian Geographic Information System (Tomlinson 1967) so named in 1966. The system holds maps of the whole of Canada, with a wide range of attribute data about land characteristics which can be used to analyse agricultural potential of marginal farms. Essentially, this is a land information system, originally motivated by the twin aims of efficient map production and inventory resource management.

Land information systems

The term 'land information system' has been used in the literature to refer to systems that relate to specific parcels of land. Often this will be landownership information, officially termed 'cadastral information' in many countries.

In Australia, the term 'land information system' has been given special currency via the National Strategy on Land Information Management (ALIC 1990). The strategy defines a land information system as '. . . essentially a data management approach, usually through a computer system, which enables the sharing of data between a wide range of organisations, ensures land data is consistent and correct and enables its distribution to users' (ALIC 1990: 2). The Australian Land Information Council (ALIC) has determined that within Australasia the term LIS is preferred to describe systems which have been developed to manage land better.

Many examples of land information systems exist. In North America the state of New York sponsored the development of a Land Use and Natural Resource Inventory of New York State (Hardy 1975). Work began on this system in the 1960s but computer-based technology was not advanced enough to apply until the early 1970s.

In the UK most examples arose from the initiatives of local planning authorities. One of the most famous was the National Gazetteer Pilot Study in Tyne and Wear (DoE 1979). This was an attempt to develop an integrated and comprehensive management information system for the whole of the local authority. On the basis that most local authority functions relate to land, the idea was that by creating a central index of land parcels (or addresses) each application could be cross-referenced to the other. In such applications the database management functions are more important than the mapping functions. Indeed, the gazetteer systems rarely had anything but the most basic mapping facilities. Research in the mid 1980s suggested that these systems were declining in their use because of a number of organisational reasons (Grimshaw 1988) such as the need to maintain some central database management team. An important outcome of that research was the realisation that land and property information systems, although designed to provide more management information, were actually used for administrative support.

Spatial analysis

Spatial analysis systems as defined by Johnston *et al.* (1986) are concerned with quantitative (mainly statistical) procedures and techniques applied in locational analytical work. The origins of such work can be traced back to quantitative geography in the 1950s. The term 'spatial analysis' must be distinguished from data manipulation. Most GIS packages on the market today offer many data manipulation features, for example overlays and buffers. However, very few indeed offer much in the way of spatial analysis. In the future, as Openshaw (1991) observed, spatial analysis tools will be absorbed into GIS.

A review of spatial analysis tools will be given in Chapter 5. For the moment, the important thing is to establish that spatial analysis tools are lacking in many commercially available GIS software packages.

Integrated systems

An integrated GIS is distinguished by high levels of mapping capability and spatial analysis. At the moment, in terms of commercially available packages, such a GIS is not widespread; however, with the increasing trend for hardware to become cheaper and more advanced, future GIS will be more integrated systems.

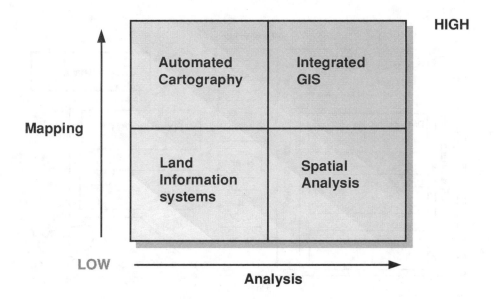

Figure 2.1 Classification of GIS

Figure 2.1 shows diagramatically how the four currently used terms for GIS, automated cartography, land information systems, spatial analysis and integrated systems, can be related to two variables. Taking the degree of analytical capability along the horizontal axis and the degree of mapping capability along the vertical axis, a simple two-by-two box illustrates the range of current GIS.

Working definition of GIS

The GIS pyramid in Chapter 1 illustrates a new paradigm of GIS which depends upon information systems and organisations in addition to technology and applications. These then are the building blocks of a working definition of GIS for the purpose of this book.

● A geographical information system is a group of procedures that provide data input, storage and retrieval, mapping and spatial analysis for both spatial and attribute data to support the decision-making activities of the organisation.

An important part of GIS as used in business is the relationship of GIS to existing information systems like customer databases. The GIS integrates data from a variety of sources and presents information to the decision maker in the organisation.

Components of GIS

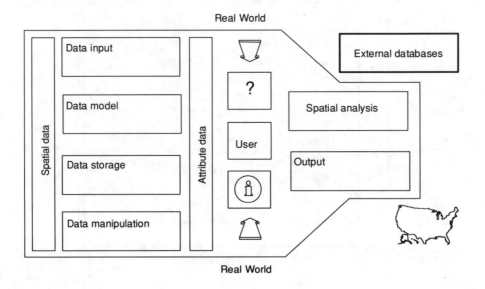

Figure 2.2 Model of a GIS

The components of a GIS are illustrated in Figure 2.2. The model illustrates that both attribute and spatial data are collected from the real world. To input the data into a computer-based information system requires that the data be modelled before it is input and stored in the system. The GIS will exist in an organisation which will interact with the real world. Some data may be purchased from external suppliers rather than being 'collected' in a traditional sense of the word. The output from the system may be in text, table, graph or map form.

Each component is tabulated below, detailed discussion is cross-referenced to the appropriate chapter.

Data input

There are five methods available:

1. Digitising
2. Scanning
3. Remote sensing
4. Global positioning systems (GPS)
5. Photogrammetry

Data model

For a detailed discussion of data models see Chapter 4. In summary, there are two main models:

1. Vector
2. Raster

Data storage

Spatial data will typically require large amounts of storage space, for example the TIGER database is approximately 10Gb and is published on CD-ROM. The US Geological Survey database is over 1Tb in size, which is beyond the current 10^{11} bytes of storage capacity for on-line systems (Goodchild 1991).

1. Hard disk
2. Magnetic tape
3. Compact disc-read only memory (CD-ROM)
4. Write once read many (WORM)
5. Random access memory (RAM)

Data manipulation

Data manipulation is discussed in Chapter 4.

Spatial analysis

See the discussion, earlier in this chapter, about spatial analysis.

Output

During the 1980s two types of output could be distinguished: printer and plotter. This distinction is now disappearing as various forms of electrostatic printing become much cheaper, for example inkjet and laser printers.

Ignore the 'G' in GIS

Some authors, most notably de Meyere (1991) and Waters and Ternouth (1992), have argued the case for dropping the emphasis on 'geographic'. The points put forward by de Meyere (1991) emphasise that GIS are similar to other information systems, that there is nothing sufficiently unique about geographic data to warrant separate treatment. There is a danger, with this view, that it leads to ignoring the special characteristics of spatial data (discussed fully in Chapter 4). The points put forward by Waters and Ternouth (1992) are rather different. They argue that some of the disappointments of failed GIS could be avoided if organisations learned the general lessons of information systems development and implementation.

What is the relationship of GIS to other information systems? The literature contains much debate around the distinguishing features of GIS from other systems like computer-aided design (CAD), cadastral or land information systems, database management systems (DBMS), automated mapping and facilities management (AM/FM), global positioning systems (GPS), spatial information systems, geodata systems, and remote sensing (see for example, Cowen 1987). No

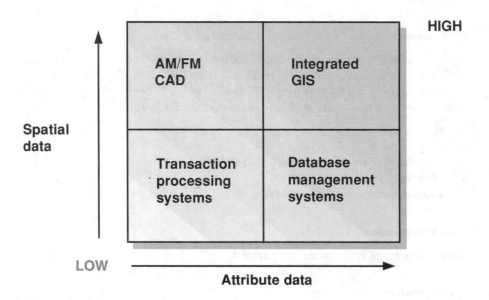

Figure 2.3 Related information systems

doubt the academic debates about definitions will continue at the conferences for many years yet. For practical purposes it matters more that we have a working definition of GIS and that we understand the relationship of GIS to related software products.

Figure 2.3 shows the relationship of GIS to other information systems in terms of two variables: the intensity of the spatial data and the intensity of the attribute data. Systems with little or no spatial data, for example payroll systems, are often referred to as transaction processing systems. More complex attribute data may require the flexibility of a DBMS. Systems with a high intensity of spatial data but limited amounts of attribute data like automated mapping, facilities management or CAD are not fully fledged GIS. Not only are the origins of such systems different and their application functions different but also they contain limited amounts of attribute data. The full GIS is distinguished by an ability to integrate data from a number of sources and by an ability to be able to handle intense amounts of both spatial and attribute data, to map that data and analyse it.

From the review of the literature by Grimshaw (1992a), it is apparent that there is no one commonly agreed framework for discussing information systems. Each contributory discipline has tended to use its own framework for a basis of a study, depending upon whether the study has, for example, an organisational, a technology or a systems perspective. These frameworks all provide a one-dimensional (or at most a two-dimensional) viewpoint on a very complex subject. There are two main problems with such frameworks:

1. They are an oversimplification based upon the relatively narrow view of one discipline. Therefore, the range of concepts are not and cannot be mutually exclusive. Further work is thus required in order to develop a taxonomy which must by definition provide a comprehensive classification system with mutually exclusive categories.
2. The assumption, implicit in the earlier models, is that familiar to the economist, namely *ceteris paribus* (all other things equal). But of course all other things are rarely held constant. It is the nature of the application of IT that there is nothing so constant as change. How can this 'change' element be taken account of in the development of a taxonomy of information systems?

Taking as the starting point three basic questions that have to be answered by anyone concerned to understand information systems we shall then build on existing frameworks.

1. What *t*asks do we have to perform?
2. What *t*echnology can best deliver the systems?
3. What *t*ime frame are we operating in?

These basic questions, characterised as the 'three *T*'s', are used as a starting point.

1. What tasks do we have to perform? The kind of decisions that need to be made (tasks to be performed) are a useful starting point. Under this general question are the issues of what data is required, how this data might be assembled and who is going to use the system? There will usually be a

trade-off between long-run and short-run requirements and the demand to summarise the data.

2. What technology can best deliver the systems? Present and future technologies may be considered. There will usually be a trade-off between flexibility and cost. Over time, the point at which it becomes economic to apply a particular technology will change.

3. What time frame are we operating in? Building on the concept of the stages of growth, the people concerned with information systems will need to place them within the context of the organisational learning and the spending on IT. This dimension recognises that organisations learn as they move from one 'stage' to another.

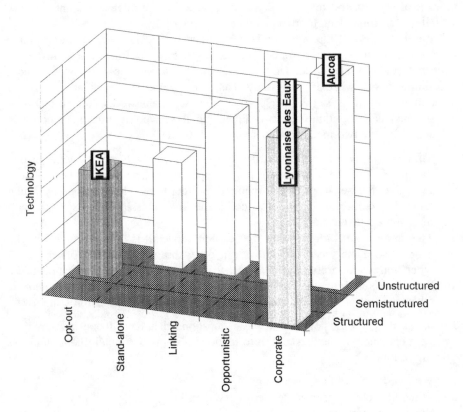

Figure 2.4 A taxonomy of information systems (*Source*: adapted from Grimshaw 1992a)

Figure 2.4 illustrates a three-dimensional presentation of a proposed classification system for information systems using the three T's outlined above. Each of the three T's looked at in isolation would represent two dimensions. Before moving to discuss the concepts in the abstract, some examples are introduced. Three examples of information systems are presented here to illustrate the use of the proposed taxonomy.

Firstly, the simplest case might be that of a utility company using a GIS for operational support. The three-T classification would place a utility GIS as a structured task, using tried and tested technology, developed at a corporate stage of time (Lyonnaise des Eaux).

Secondly, let us take the case of a retailer using GIS to help decide on new locations. The three T's can be applied to place such a system as performing largely semi-structured tasks. With the use of desktop GIS packages a data agency may provide pre-defined reports using customer data and developed in an organisation that has little maturity in terms of IT usage, placing it in the opt-out stage (IKEA).

Thirdly, where would a major GIS project such as a mining company system be placed in the taxonomy? A system initially set up as a stand-alone system for a pilot study is later linked to corporate databases. After a period of time, the system is used by several groups of users for a variety of tasks, including unstructured tasks. Here is the utility of using the x-axis of Figure 2.4 to denote time. So, schematically, the development can be plotted as shown in Figure 2.4.

Each of the three T's is now discussed in more detail and a full classification of each T is given in Tables 2.1–2.3. When applying the taxonomy to a given information system the task, time and technology would need to be classified with reference to these tables.

GIS tasks

The 'task' dimension builds on frameworks based on the work of both Anthony (1965) and Gorry and Scott-Morton (1971) which, as a result of a review of information systems frameworks by Lucas *et al.* (1974) were recommended. Subclasses on this dimension cover the type of decision (task) being supported, for example structured or unstructured, and the level of the task, for example strategic, tactical or operational. A detailed table of the classes in the 'task' dimension is contained in Table 2.1.

Table 2.1   The 'Task' dimension – classification

1	Structured decisions
1.1	Operational control
1.2	Tactical control
1.3	Strategic planning
2	Semistructured decisions
2.1	Operational control
2.2	Tactical control
2.3	Strategic planning
3	Unstructured decisions
3.1	Operational control
3.2	Tactical control
3.3	Strategic planning

Source: Adapted from Grimshaw (1992a).
Adapted from Gorry and Scott-Morton (1971).

To determine the classification the key questions are:

1. Who is to use the system? (operational, middle, or senior management)
2. What decisions are being supported by the system? (structured, semi-structured or unstructured)

The applications of GIS are the *tasks* that organisations use the systems for. Traditionally, classification of applications has been on functional grounds, for example applications for forestry, environmental management, retail location, etc. Applications here will be thought of in terms of the tasks. Remember that information systems generally seek to provide decision makers with information. Thus we might think of 'tasks' as being to do with the types of decisions that managers wish to make to help the organisations manage scarce resources.

Applications of GIS to business can be categorised into a number of different areas. We could classify applications according to subject, for example route planning, mine planning, facilities management or catchment area analysis, or according to industry such as retail, manufacturing, real estate, utilities, financial institutions and transportation.

A more robust and flexible classification of applications according to their relationship to decision making would help to bring the GIS into mainstream information systems debates. On the basis that the very purpose of an information system is to reduce the uncertainty surrounding a managerial decision, we can classify GIS into operational, tactical and strategic systems. Figure 2.5 shows a framework for classifying applications of GIS in business.

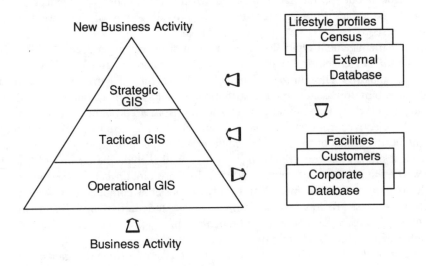

Figure 2.5 GIS applications framework

Operational GIS applications are those which support the operational activities and decisions of the business. For example, operational activities in a public utility company would involve maintaining (say) a gas pipeline. The GIS might be used to plot the course of the pipeline throughout its length. Related to this map information would be various attribute data like the depth of the pipe, its radius, flow, age, material, etc. Such information would typically be used to carry out the day-to-day operations of the company involving, say, decisions about which sections of pipe to renew or what equipment would be needed on site in order to dig up the road and mend a leaking pipe. Examples of operational applications are studied in detail in Chapter 8 where a number of case studies from different industries and different countries are discussed.

The decision-making activities of middle management tend to be described as tactical or semi-structured decisions (Scott-Morton 1967). More external data may be required to provide information for decision making, for example access to commercially available products derived from census variables, like MOSAIC (see the previous discussion on data considerations). 'What if' kinds of modelling would be typical of this kind of GIS application. For example, in a retail organisation a group of specialists searching for new locations for retail outlets would need to assemble base map data containing the urban and rural areas, the road network and perhaps a limited amount of topographical data. Company data would show the expected yield from a given area of floorspace devoted to durable and convenience goods. External data from other companies would be used to provide information about competitors and about the geodemographics of the proposed catchment area of any new outlet. Chapter 9 provides a focus for discussion about the main issues raised when GIS is applied to tactical decision support. Examples from different countries provide a way of illustrating the key issues raised.

Senior management typically make strategic or unstructured decisions. This calls for the *ad hoc* assembly of data to provide relevant and timely information for decision making. The number of branches that a financial institution has on the high street of towns and their distribution by regions of a country would be a strategic decision. This would typically follow from a corporate plan which stated overall objectives, for instance that the bank should increase its market penetration in the north of the country. A GIS might be used by senior executives to help plan the ideal branch network. Such an ideal may well include the closing of branches as well as the opening of some new ones. In these circumstances the ability to be able to model the outcomes of a variety of possible combinations weighted by critical success factors would amply repay the initial investment in GIS technology. Figure 2.6 shows how branch catchment areas can be defined using a number of variables, including drive time to branches.

Operational GIS can be justified on the basis of efficiency gains; GIS for decision support would be justified on the grounds of increased effectiveness.

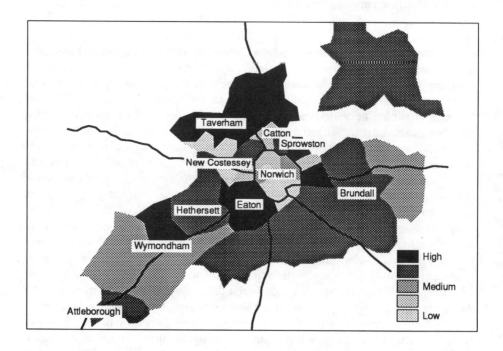

Figure 2.6 Density of potential customers (*Source*: Grimshaw and Hinton 1992; first published in the *Journal of Strategic Information Systems*, **1** (2), 1992, reproduced here with the permission of Butterworth Heinemann, Oxford)

However, GIS used for strategic purposes, which often leads to transformation of the business, must be fully integrated into the information systems of the organisation and should be identified in the information strategy and strongly linked to the business strategy.

Managers who wish to improve the decision-making process will consider a variety of means towards achieving this end. Information systems are one possible means to support decision-making (Scott-Morton 1967). The provision of more information is generally regarded as reducing the uncertainty around making a decision. GIS can be seen as part of the tradition of decision support systems (Grimshaw and Maier 1991).

Although the adoption of GIS by agencies in the public sector of the economy has been widespread (Shand and Moore 1990) the use of GIS by private sector business has only just begun. Part of the reason for this may be that few people in the private sector have thought about the potential of geographical data sets for solving some of their business problems (Grimshaw 1991). A further reason may be that organisations filter information partly on the basis of their professional training. Obermeyer (1990) draws the conclusion that lack of geographical training of professionals in many organisations is a constraint on the development and use of GIS.

An examination of the data held by a typical business reveals that much data has a geographical dimension, for example customer records have a postcode (or zipcode). Examples of such data are given in Chapter 4. Traditional business information systems have, however, not had the capability to do any spatial analysis of the data. De Meyere (1991) suggests that geodata is a misleading concept because geoinformation does not exist. He asserts that geodata is only locational and topological attributes. This view is an oversimplification. The power of a GIS comes from the ability to link attribute data to spatial data. Viewed in this way GIS, used by managers, can reveal patterns within existing data sets, like customer records, that they were previously unaware of.

Most of the current applications of GIS by people in marketing functions of companies is to solve problems in the consumer market. Knowing where existing and potential markets are is crucial to any business. After all, if you are trying to sell lawn mowers to people who live in high-rise flats you are not going to be very successful. Additionally, there are potential gains to be made by applying GIS to industrial markets (Grimshaw 1992a).

GIS over time

The 'time' dimension builds on frameworks based on the work by Gibson and Nolan (1974) modified by Galliers and Sutherland (1991) and adapted to the GIS context by Grimshaw (1993). Subclasses on this dimension cover the six stages of growth. A detailed table of the classes in the 'time' dimension is contained in Table 2.2. To determine the classification the key question is: where is the organisation now in terms of the seven 'S's'? (Pascale and Athos 1981).

Table 2.2   The 'time' dimension – classification

1	Opt-out		4	Opportunistic
1.1	Strategy		4.1	Strategy
1.2	Structure		4.2	Structure
1.3	Systems		4.3	Systems
1.4	Staff		4.4	Staff
1.5	Style		4.5	Style
1.6	Skills		4.6	Skills
1.7	Shared values		4.7	Shared values
2	Stand-alone		5	Corporate
2.1	Strategy		5.1	Strategy
2.2	Structure		5.2	Structure
2.3	Systems		5.3	Systems
2.4	Staff		5.4	Staff
2.5	Style		5.5	Style
2.6	Skills		5.6	Skills
2.7	Shared values		5.7	Shared values
3	Linking			
3.1	Strategy			
3.2	Structure			
3.3	Systems			
3.4	Staff			
3.5	Style			
3.6	Skills			
3.7	Shared values			

Source: Adapted from Grimshaw (1992a).
Adapted from Galliers and Sutherland (1991).

Applications of GIS in business, in common with many other areas of the application of IT, experience what has come to be known in the literature as 'stages of growth' (Gibson and Nolan 1974). An outline of the Gibson and Nolan (1974) model was given in Chapter 1. The idea of a growth model is essentially simple, that over time the level of spending on IT of any given business will go through stages. The utility of this essentially simple idea is that the model can be used as a diagnostic tool which helps managers to understand where their organisation is now in terms of use of IT. A major limitation of the model is that it provides a 'snapshot' view which gives no insight into what changes over time might be expected. An adaptation of the static growth model idea by Wiseman (1985) suggests three eras of IT. Grimshaw and Maier (1991) used this model to explain the use of GIS within a business unit over time.

The first era of IT has come to be known as the era of data processing, when the emphasis of information systems was on operational support. Grimshaw and Maier refer to this as the 'first-wave GIS'. 'Second-wave GIS' would then be characterised by a move towards integrating GIS into the corporate information systems of the organisation. The benefits of data integration are more clearly seen at this stage and the skills required to make this happen are all available to the business. In the third era of IT the needs of the business drive the applications. IT is seen as having the potential to change, or transform, the business. There is very little evidence to suggest that companies have gone beyond the second wave in their applications of GIS.

It is worth considering how GIS might be used in the third era. Considering the strategic applications of GIS was one of the central concerns of a paper by Grimshaw (1991) where four ways of applying GIS were put forward:

1. Using GIS to identify and target customers as a first step towards linking with customers and/or suppliers through technologies like electronic data interchange.
2. Providing strategic decision makers with information that has come from a geographical analysis of company and competitors' data.
3. GIS technology as a major component of a new product. There are a number of car navigation systems that essentially rely on GIS technology as being the 'new' part of the product.
4. Integration of GIS within the value-adding process of a product. For example, many data agencies sell geographical data sets. To add value to these data sets and differentiate the market many agencies, for example Pinpoint Analysis, offer their own GIS, for example GEOPIN2.

The move towards such strategic usage of GIS is characterised by the increasing realisation that data is a corporate resource of tremendous value. The business then takes seriously the process of identifying information systems that could contribute to critical aspects of the business success. The question about how this can be done is discussed in Chapter 3.

The fact that three eras have been discussed is not meant to imply that a particular business will have to start at the beginning and develop through all three eras. The question of how organisations learn to cope with technology and use it to best business advantage is a complex area of study and one that is discussed fully in Chapter 3. The time-frame dimension provides a richer view of systems over time than that provided either by the Gibson and Nolan (1974) model or the Grimshaw and Maier (1991) model.

GIS technology

The 'technology' dimension builds on frameworks based on the work of Burns and Caldwell (1990), Earl (1989) and Istel (1988). Subclasses to this dimension cover computers, communications, data and tools. Some organisations who need to collect and analyse information about new technology as it becomes available and the opportunities that might be available tomorrow from exploiting that technology have developed their own 'in-house' taxonomies (Istel 1988). A detailed table of the classes in the 'technology' dimension is contained in Table 2.3.

Table 2.3   The 'technology' dimension – classification

1	Computers		2	Communications
1.1	Digital		2.1	Computer intraconnect
1.1.1	General purpose		2.2	Computer system interconnect
1.1.1.1	Mainframes		2.2.1	DEC DECNET
1.1.1.2	Minicomputers		2.2.2	IBM 3270
1.1.1.3	Microcomputers		2.2.3	IBM SNA
1.1.2	Experimental		2.2.4	OSI
1.1.2.1	Optical computers		2.3	LANS
1.1.2.2	Data flow computers		2.4	MANS (metropolitan area networks)
1.1.2.3	Parallel computers		2.5	WANS
1.1.2.4	Database engines		2.6	GANS (global area networks)
1.1.3	Special purpose			
1.2	Analogue		3	Data
1.2.1	General purpose		3.1	Data model
1.2.2	Experimental		3.1.1	Vector
1.2.3	Special purpose		3.1.2	Raster
1.3	Hybrid		3.2	Data dictionary
1.3.1	General purpose		4	Applications
1.3.2	Experimental		4.1	Operating systems software
1.3.3	Special purpose		4.2	GIS tools
			4.3	Database management systems

Source: Adapted from Grimshaw (1992a).
Adapted from Istel (1988) and Earl (1989).

Any discussion about specific commercial products would rapidly become out of date and it is not the intention of this book to discuss them. There are a number of sources of up-to-date information about software products, for example see GISWorld (1993) or AGI Yearbook (Green *et al.*1993). However, some of the principal features of GIS technology are worth discussing from a user's point of view.

Computer technology

Most of the hardware vendors have machines that are suitable for running GIS. The computer technology itself is not GIS specific, although some of the peripherals like scanners, digitisers and plotters may be heavily used by some GIS applications. Some trends that may be worth watching for include parallel processing (Lake 1992) and database engines (Haworth 1992).

Communications

GIS, as we have seen earlier, are systems that are likely to require data from a variety of sources. Also they are likely to be used by more than one user group within an organisation. Therefore, the ability of systems to communicate is important. The GIS industry does not have particularly unique communications issues, although there are a number of nationally and internationally agreed spatial data transfer standards.

The trend towards more open systems is likely to continue which means that proprietary communication protocols will have a limited life. Whatever vendor is used to supply communications, the important thing is to make sure that your communications network conforms to open systems standards.

Applications

Applications software is often supplied by the market in generic GIS. To make such systems useful for applications in marketing or retail location planning someone needs to adapt the programs. This can be done by the software vendor, a specialist software house, or the end user.

The trend towards generic software products has spawned a number of businesses who will customise a GIS for your organisation. Many of these companies also add value to the original software product by packaging it with data sets that are specifically useful for an industry or set of applications. For example, in the UK market Pinpoint Analysis has tailored the ARC/INFO package for the financial services and retail sectors and sell this as a product called GEOPIN2. As a specific data set for the financial services customers may purchase FINPIN. In the North American market Equifax have tailored ARC/INFO to produce a package called Infomark for Windows.

Data

Major sources of national cartographic data are often government agencies, for example the Ordnance Survey in the UK. The range of other data products that can be supplied by adding value to basic cartographic data or by adding value to census data has given rise to a specialist sector of the GIS industry which we shall refer to as data agencies.

The taxonomy of information systems suggested in this chapter is based on tried and tested components. Each dimension has already been applied in practice and found to be useful. The thrust of this chapter has been to advance arguments in favour of using a multidimensional framework to provide a classification system (or taxonomy) that reflects a dynamic environment.

Summary

This chapter has reviewed a range of different meanings given to GIS. The working definition arrived at emphasises the role of GIS in integrating spatial and attribute data in a way which supports the decision making of the organisation. Related information systems such as AM/FM, CAD/CAM, transaction processing and DBMS are analysed in terms of the degree of spatial and attribute data they process. Similarly, when reviewing closely related terms like land information systems, spatial analysis and automated cartography, the interrelationship of mapping and analysis capabilities was used as a way to differentiate the systems.

The applications of GIS to business tasks has been related to decision making. Since the purpose of information systems is to reduce the level of uncertainty in the decision-making process GIS have been classified as operational, tactical and strategic systems. This is the application classification which will be followed through the examination of case studies in Chapters 8–10.

A conceptual model of a GIS is introduced (Figure 2.3) to provide a framework for discussion of the components of GIS. Other views of GIS are introduced, for example the GIS industry perspective and the GIS as an academic discipline perspective. The final section of the chapter looked at GIS as an information system and applied a taxonomy of information systems to GIS. The main advantage of using the three T's framework of, time, task and technology is that it provides a way of visualising the relationships between these three concepts. This framework will be used in Chapters 4 and 5 and again in Chapters 8–10.

Further study

The ideas presented and discussed in this chapter are followed up in other parts of this book. Therefore the references given at the end of the chapter provide adequate reading in themselves.

References

ALIC (Australian Land Information Council) 1990 *National Strategy on Land Information Management* ALIC, Belconnen, Australia

Antenucci J C, Brown K, Croswell P L, Kevany M J with **Archer H**, 1991 *Geographic Information Systems: A Guide to the Technology* Van Nostrand Reinhold, New York

Anthony R N 1965 *Planning and Control Systems: a Framework for Analysis* Harvard Business School Press, Boston, Mass

Bickmore D P, Shaw M A 1963 *Atlas of Great Britain and Northern Ireland* Clarendon Press, Oxford

Blenheim Online 1993 What do you mean – GIS? *Preview GIS '93* 18–20 May 1993, Blenheim Online, London, p 2

Burns J, Caldwell E 1990 *Management of Information Systems Technology* Alfred Waller Ltd, Oxfordshire

Carter J R 1989 On defining the geographic information system. In Ripple W J (ed) *Fundamentals of Geographic Information Systems: A Compendium* American Society of Photogrammetry and Remote Sensing, Falls Church, Va, pp 3–7

Coppock J T, Rhind D W 1991 The history of GIS. In Maguire D J, Goodchild M F, Rhind D W (eds) *Geographical Information Systems* Vol 1 *Principles* Longman Scientific & Technical, Harlow, pp 21–43

Cowen D J 1987 GIS vs CAD vs DBMS: what are the differences? In *Proceedings of the GIS '87 Symposium* American Society of Photogrammetry and Remote Sensing, Falls Church, Va, pp 46–56

de Meyere J C 1991 The confusing concept of geo information. Paper presented at the Second European Conference on Geographical Information Systems, Brussels, April

Devine H A, Field R C 1986 The gist of GIS. *Journal of Forestry*, August: 17–22

Diello J, Kirk K, Callander J 1968 The development of an automated cartographic system. *Cartographic Journal* 6: 9–17

DoE (Department of the Environment) 1979 *Property Systems for Government: A Report of the National Gazetteer Pilot Project* Research Report No 30, HMSO, London

DoE 1987 *Handling Geographic Information* Report of the Committee of Enquiry chaired by Lord Chorley, HMSO, London

Earl M J 1989 *Management Strategies for Information Technology* Business Information Technology Series, Prentice-Hall: London

EGIS 1992 *Proceedings of the Third European Conference on Geographical Information Systems* Munich, Germany, 23–26 March

Galliers R D, Sutherland A R 1991 Information systems management and strategy forumulation: the stages of growth model revisited. *Journal of Information Systems* 1(2): 89–114

Gibson C, Nolan R 1974 Managing the four stages of EDP growth. *Harvard Business Review* January–February 52: 74–88

GISWorld 1993 *1993 GIS International Sourcebook* GISWorld, Fort Collins, Colo

Goodchild M F 1991 The technological setting of GIS. In Maguire D J, Goodchild M F, Rhind D W (eds) *Geographical Information Systems* Vol 1 *Principles* Longman Scientific & Technical, Harlow, pp 45–54

Gorry G A, Scott-Morton M S 1971 A framework for manament information systems. *Sloan Management Review* 13: 55–70

Green D R, Rix D, Cadoux-Hudson J (eds) 1993 *Geographic Information 1994: The Source Book for GIS* Taylor & Francis, London

Grimshaw D J 1988 Land and property information systems. *International Journal of Geographical Information Systems* 2(1): 67–79

Grimshaw D J 1989 Geographical information systems: a tool for business and industry? *International Journal of Information Management* 9 119–26

Grimshaw D J 1991 Geographical information systems as part of the corporate information strategy. *International Journal of Information Management* 11(4): 292–7

Grimshaw D J 1992a Towards a taxonomy of information systems: or does anyone need a TAXI? *Journal of Information Technology* 7: 30–6

Grimshaw D J 1992b The transformation of customer databases. *Proceedings of the Fourth Conference of the Association for Geographical Information Systems* 24–26 November, Birmingham, UK, pp 1.7.1–6

Grimshaw D J 1993 Corporate GIS stage by stage. *Proceedings of the GIS in Business '93 Conference* 7–10 March, Boston, Mass, GIS Books Inc, Colo, pp 133–7

Grimshaw D J, Hinton M A 1992 Taking technology opportunities to the business. *Journal of Strategic Information Systems* 1 (2): 106–10.

Grimshaw D J, Maier J R 1991 *The Integration of GIS into a Marketing DSS* Warwick Business School Research Papers No 33, ISSN 0265–5976, Warwick Business School Research Bureau, Coventry: University of Warwick

Hale K 1993 GIS in business: market trends. Paper presented at the GIS in Business '93 Conference, 7–10 March, Boston, Mass

Hardy E E 1975 The design, implementation, and use of a statewide land use inventory: the New York Experience. In *Proceedings of the NASA Earth Resources Survey Symposium* Vol 1C National Aeronautics and Space Administration, Washington, DC, pp 1573–7

Haworth G 1992 Database engines for geographical information systems. In Cadoux-Hudson J, Heywood I (eds) *Geographic Information 1992/93: The Yearbook of the Association for Geographic Information* Taylor and Francis, London, pp 436–48

ISTEL 1988 A taxonomy of information technology. Internal Paper presented on business management systems course, University of Warwick, July

Johnston R J, Gregory D, Smith D M (eds) 1986 *The Dictionary of Human Geography* 2nd edn, Blackwell, Oxford

Lake T 1992 Parallel computing for geographical information systems. In Cadoux-Hudson J, Heywood I (eds) *Geographic Information 1992/93: The Yearbook of the Association for Geographic Information* Taylor & Francis, London, pp 431–5

Lucas H C, Clowes K W, Kaplan R B 1974 Framework for information systems. *INFOR* **12**: 245–60

Maguire D J 1991 An overview and definition of GIS. In Maguire D J, Goodchild M F, Rhind D W (eds) *Geographical Information Systems* Vol 1 *Principles* Longman Scientific & Technical, Harlow, pp 9–20

Morrison J L 1991 The organisational home for GIS in the scientific professional community. In Maguire D J, Goodchild M F, Rhind D W (eds) *Geographical Information Systems* Vol 1 *Principles* Longman Scientific & Technical, Harlow, pp 91–100

Obermeyer N J 1990 Bureaucratic factors in the adoption of GIS by public organisations: preliminary evidence from public administrators and planners. *Journal of Computing, Environment and Urban Systems* **14**: 261–71

Openshaw S 1991 Developing appropriate spatial analysis methods for GIS. In Maguire D J, Goodchild M F, Rhind D W (eds) *Geographical Information Systems* Vol 1 *Principles* Longman Scientific & Technical, Harlow, pp 389–402

Pascale R T, Athos A G 1981 *The Art of Japanese Management*, Penguin, Harmondsworth

Scott-Morton M S 1967 *Decision Support Systems. An Organisational Perspective* Addison-Wesley, Reading, Mass

Shand P J, Moore R V (eds) 1990 User sites. In *The Association for Geographical Information Yearbook 1990* Taylor & Francis, and Miles Arnold, Oxford, pp 325–48

Tomlinson R F 1967 *An Introduction to the Geographic Information System of the Canada Land Inventory* Department of Forestry and Rural Development, Ottawa

Waters R, Ternouth P 1992 Kill the 'G' in GIS! In *Proceedings of the Fourth National Conference of the Association for Geographic Information* Birmingham, UK, pp 2.5.1–4

Wiseman C 1985 *Strategy and Computers* Dow Jones-Irwin, New York

3

GIS and information strategies

*'Firms need information (management) strategies which link the exploitation of
information technology to business needs and also identify new business
opportunities.'*

Michael Earl (1989:37)

Preamble

The previous chapters have established that business enterprises have an
abundance of geographic data. The release of this untapped data resource to
support business decision making is now possible with the recent developments in
GIS technology. How does a business assess the potential worth of GIS? Where
might the idea to use GIS come from? What kind of GIS data and application is
appropriate?

These are the essential questions that can best be answered by managers
engaging in the process of developing an information management strategy. The
quote at the head of this chapter from Michael Earl (1989) stresses that the
questions asked above in relation to GIS are ones that might apply to any kind of
IT. The exploitation of that technology must be in relation to current business
needs and new business opportunities. The important questions for the business to
face are thus those about its business strategy, such as how can links with
customers be strengthened? Or which market can our new product be launched in?

Linking GIS to the information strategy

The link between information systems and the business strategy is a two-way one.
The technology has to be scanned for opportunities that may be possible at given
price/performance levels. On the other hand the key business goals have to be
examined with the objective of identifying information systems that can contribute
to their achievement.

Evidence from surveys of practice suggest that many organisations do not have
an information strategy (Galliers 1987a). Indeed, many of the classic examples of
companies gaining competitive advantage from IT seem to have been brought

about more by accident than deliberate policy. Many more opportunities are missed because the company does not have a systematic approach to the use and development of the corporate information resource.

You may be wondering what an information strategy is. Well, in common with many terms in the business information systems field there is no accepted and commonly used definition. It may be helpful to think of the information strategy as a planning process involving the thinking of *what* information systems are required by the business, *how* these systems are to be delivered to the users, and *who* is going to use and support them.

The components of the strategy will therefore be an interrelated mixture of information systems, IT and the management of the systems and technology in the organisation as a whole. Approaches to the planning process have differed in the past. However, it is possible, if an oversimplification, to classify information strategy approaches into a continuum ranging from technology-led through to business-led.

How does GIS fit into the information strategy? Essentially there are two ways. Firstly, as a piece of technology GIS is an opportunity. Secondly, as a delivery mechanism of information GIS provides a way of investigating the geographical dimension of internal and external data. Many items of data collected and used by industry generally have a geographic dimension. Using this geographical dimension of data can add substantial value to information. It is the main thrust of this chapter that the major impact of GIS on business will be to aid decision making. To maximise the potential of this still relatively new technology organisations must plan for its use by integrating GIS within their planning process for an information strategy.

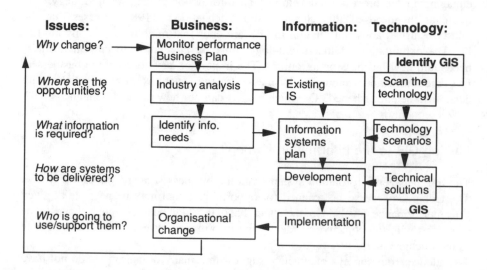

Figure 3.1 Framework for an information strategy (*Source*: amended from Grimshaw 1991a)

New technology, such as GIS, has first of all to be viewed as an opportunity – rather than simply a cost. Many managers are unaware of the opportunities that GIS or indeed other new technologies may bring to their business. The suggested framework, outlined in Figure 3.1, is aimed at raising management awareness of the *issues*, integrating the *business* plan with the *information* requirements and identifying gaps in the current information systems, and scanning new *technology* for opportunities. Each of these four parts of the framework is considered separately in the following subsections; however, in practice the four parts would be part of an iterative process.

Issues

The process of developing an information strategy is based on five fundamental issues of concern to management:

1. *Why change?* The awareness of managers needs to be raised in relation to the opportunities in the industry concerned. For example, there may be a threat from new entrants to the industry – so that the organisation needs to increase the barriers to entry in order to sustain its market position. The classical approach here is to use the five forces model of competition developed by Porter (1985) (see Figure 3.2). Various other frameworks, reviewed by Ward *et al.* (1990), can also be used.
2. *Where are the opportunities?* The business opportunities in relation to the technology available are discussed later in the chapter in terms of four ways in which GIS can be used as a strategic tool.
3. *What information is required?* The information requirements arising from the business plan need to be identified and compared to the existing information systems to determine the information systems plan. The tools and techniques available for identifying information requirements have been well documented (Galliers 1987b). Some specific questions need to be asked here about the requirements for geographic information. The geographic information intensity matrix (see Figure 3.3) may be a useful tool to use in the debate about the geographic aspects of data.
4. *How are systems to be delivered?* Having identified what systems need to be developed to fulfil the business requirements it remains to identify the technology which can best deliver these systems. There are few well-accepted methods here. It is likely that some form of scenario building, perhaps using Delphi questionnaires, will be useful. Full consideration of these issues are discussed in the subsection on technology.
5. *Who is going to use/support them?* In most cases, the development of new information systems in the organisation will lead to the need to review the organisation itself. Typically there will be a need to restructure the organisation and redefine job roles.

Business

It has previously been argued that GIS are simply part of the manager's toolbox. A manager, concerned to improve the decision-making process, will naturally consider a variety of means towards achieving this goal. Information systems to support decision making have a long established tradition (Scott-Morton 1967) and in many ways GIS should be seen as part of the tradition of decision support systems (Grimshaw and Maier 1991).

As operational support systems GIS can be justified on the basis of efficiency gains; as decision support systems GIS might be justified on the grounds of increased effectiveness. However, GIS used to transform the business must be fully integrated into the information systems of the organisation and should be identified in the information management strategy and strongly linked to the business strategy. The focus of this section is on the use of GIS in this latter sense. GIS as a potentially strategic tool is now explored further.

Is GIS just another business tool? The answer is both 'yes' and 'no'! 'Yes', because GIS is at its simplest level a technology which enables decision makers to explore the geographical dimension of data. In this way GIS is a tool to be used by managers in the right place at the right time (Grimshaw 1991b). On the other hand, the answer to the question could be 'no' because the GIS tool can be used in a pervasive way. If GIS is integrated into the organisation and used as a corporate resource then the importance of GIS extends beyond that of 'just another tool'. It is then a tool of significance to the organisation. In these circumstances, the selection, development and implementation of a GIS will be a large and significant project. To such a business, GIS would be a strategic tool. Such a project needs to be firmly rooted in the business strategy. The business strategy then needs to provide a bridge to the information management strategy so that there may be two-way traffic (Earl 1989).

The central concerns of both public and private sector users and potential users of GIS are beginning now to turn towards the corporate needs of the organisation (Maynard and Pearce 1990). At this important stage of thinking the central concern becomes strategic. Managers begin to look for real business reasons for justifying an investment in GIS. The potential of hitherto neglected data sets are realised as data is now regarded as a true corporate resource.

Strategic business planning is about thinking ahead, anticipating environmental changes, and understanding the strengths, weaknesses, opportunities and threats (SWOT) in a particular industry. The business planner may use a number of different frameworks available to help this process.

The Porter (1980) five-forces model is one of the most well-known frameworks and can be useful in helping to indicate where there is a potential for IT to help gain competitive advantage. The model in Figure 3.2 is helpful because it provides a framework for thinking about the dynamics of competition and especially the changing external environment. Further reading on the topic of business strategy is given at the end of this chapter.

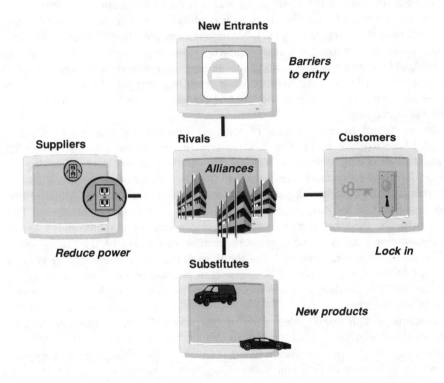

Figure 3.2 Forces of industry competition (*Source*: adapted from Porter (1980) and Earl (1989))

Suppose, as a result of applying the five-forces model, your business faces a threat from the strong bargaining power of customers. Information technology generally may be used, for example, to lock in customers by raising switching costs. The classic example of this is American Hospital Supplies (AHS) who placed 3000 order entry terminals in hospitals. It became very easy and convenient to order from AHS. Changing to other suppliers would have involved switching costs associated with purchasing new terminals. Some examples of how this Porter model may be used to pinpoint strategic GIS applications is given in the next section.

Is GIS a *strategic* business tool? To answer this question we need to explore two related ideas that have sometimes been confused: strategic and competitive. According to a generally accepted definition put forward by Munro and Huff (1985), 'strategic' is something which directly supports the creation and implementation of an organisation's strategic plan, whilst 'competitive' is something which directly supports the strategy by improving the value/cost relationship of the firm in its competitive environment.

Towards the end of the 1980s there was a body of literature and thinking built up to suggest that IT, used in the right way, could provide competitive advantage (for example Benjamin *et al.* 1984). Numerous examples, like Thompson Holidays and American Airlines, are often quoted. However, recent research has cast considerable doubt on the validity of gaining competitive advantage from IT (Hochstrasser 1990). There may be some transitory competitive advantage to be gained by using IT but after a short period competitors catch up, essentially via a process of copying.

So we return to the question of strategic information systems. It might be helpful here to think of IT uses in three eras first suggested by Wiseman (1985) and later adapted by Ward *et al.* (1990). The first era, that of data processing was where information systems were generally used to support operational needs of the organisation. In the terms applied to GIS earlier by Grimshaw and Maier (1991), the first era of IT roughly equates to the 'first-wave GIS'. The second era of IT is often characterised by a move towards more corporate systems and a greater integration of data. This equates to the earlier discussion of the 'second-wave GIS'. Many observers have said that the third era of IT is where the organisation uses IT to redefine its essential business. Here the use of IT is very much driven by the needs of the business and the corporate plan. IT is no longer a necessary evil in this third era.

In terms of GIS applications what insights does this brief diversion into the historical development of IT have to offer? As applications of GIS grow, particularly in the private sector where there is a profit imperative, there will increasingly be uses of GIS which are strategic for a particular business. How can these strategic applications of GIS be identified? In a study by Meyer and Boone (1987) four ways in which IT could be used strategically were put forward. So the question of GIS being a strategic tool can be reformulated into a question of whether GIS can be used in any of the four ways discussed below.

1. *Linking with customers and/or suppliers.* Manufacturing and retail companies in particular are often the examples given of linking with suppliers by using technologies like electronic data interchange (EDI). Links with customers can be strengthened by using GIS to identify and target marketing efforts.
2. *Integration of information usage within the value adding process.* By increasing customer loyalty, for example by offering a customer order-entry system, companies have successfully added value to their product by adding an information service.
3. *Development, production, marketing and delivery of new information-based products or services.* Traditional examples, so frequently used in the literature, quote new financial services and products that depend upon IT to be delivered to customers. Most of these examples rely on using communications technology to offer customers direct links to some kind of central database. GIS is much more likely to be used in the marketing of new information products. Such products may offer opportunities of market segmentation that can be directed and targeted much more effectively using a GIS.

4. *Provision of information to support strategic decision making and implementation of strategy*. This is the area where intuitively there appears to be more scope for the application of GIS. Often a geographical analysis of company data will give insights that were not readily available previously.

The key to developing a strategic information system is identifying the contribution that can be made to key business goals.

Information

In the field of information systems there are some frameworks designed to assess the way in which information can be exploited. The Porter and Millar (1985) information intensity matrix can be used to assess the potential for exploiting IT in a particular industry sector. Adapting this model, in Figure 3.3, gives a framework for assessing the contribution of GIS to particular industries. The vertical dimension measures the geographical information intensity of the value chain. Briefly put, the value chain represents the products and services that are inputs to the operations, decisions behind the operations, production, distribution and consumption of goods and services (Porter 1985). The horizontal dimension represents the extent to which geographic information and information products are the goods and services to be sold.

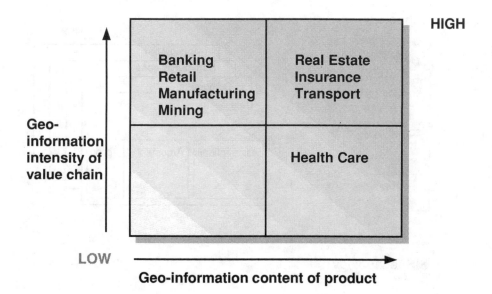

Figure 3.3 Geographical information intensity matrix

The value of this particular model is that it allows managers to focus on geographical information. Most managers will naturally think mainly about products or services. Information generally and geographical information specifically is rather intangible and difficult to pin down. This kind of framework is useful in raising the awareness amongst managers about the possibilities of applying GIS in their industry.

In addition to an examination of information requirements, the range of existing information systems needs to be reviewed. In particular, the role of geographic data in such systems needs to be studied. For example, customer databases are rich in geographic data and are prime candidates for linking to GIS.

Technology

The selection of the appropriate technology to fit the needs identified in the business strategy needs to be considered in the context of the applications that have been identified. Some of the definitions of GIS that we have reviewed rely on technology – computer systems are assumed. Our working definition of GIS does not explicitly say anything about technology. But this is not to deny the importance of IT. If you are in any doubt about this, pause to think of the common questions asked of an expert. What system would you recommend? What system do you use? What are the advantages of system 'x' over system 'y'?

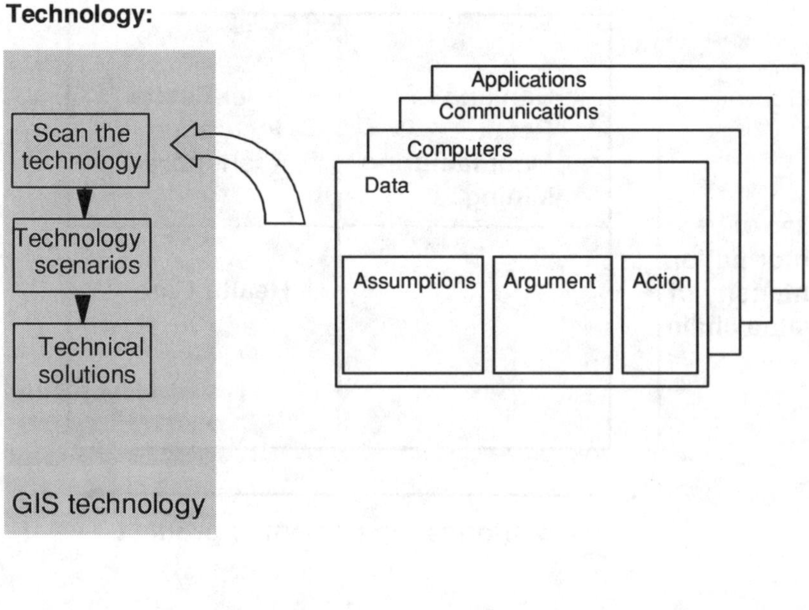

Figure 3.4 GIS technology scanning

All these questions refer to 'system' in the sense of software and hardware combinations. The total GIS is much more than any such combination as our definition makes clear. The GIS pyramid outlined in Chapter 1 has technology as the base of the pyramid – a fitting place for technology, essentially a platform to build on, yet hidden, for most of the time, from the user.

Taking technology as a delivery mechanism for a GIS is the starting point of this section. Looked at in diagrammatic terms, Figure 3.4 shows an expanded view of the 'GIS technology' part taken from Figure 3.1. Scanning the available technology for the appropriate solution that fits the organisational needs is the first step in the process of IT planning.

Here our concern is to establish a framework for understanding GIS technology as a fundamental part of the GIS pyramid. The theoretical concerns are about establishing principles that will stand the test of time in a rapidly changing technological environment. The practical concerns are about collecting sufficient information about new and emerging technologies in order to make a new purchase decision, or an upgrade decision.

Mini Case Study

A financial institution has a dominant market position in some regions but has little presence in others. Over the past four years a package called PROSPEX from GEOMATRIX has been used, running on a stand-alone personal computer. The package has provided clear business benefits for modest cost. However, more recently problems with upgrading the software, general support of the package and 'user-unfriendliness' have constrained progress. An opportunity has arisen, on the recommendation of a consultant, to change to another GIS software package called TACTICIAN.

All IT services are managed in-house. A number of transaction processing systems run on mainframe computers. Small applications have often been developed on stand-alone personal computers with limited data transfer capabilities.

The problem, in essence, is whether to change to this recommended package, or consider some other solution. Can the organisation simply accept the advice of the consultant? Should the organisation study the available technology, making an informed decision based upon a match between business requirements and the facilities of the particular package? How, in limited time, can the organisation compare the 'technology' of different products on the market?

The answer to these issues is not simple. There are many facets of the presenting problem. Organisational and personnel issues need some consideration. Excluding, for the purpose of discussion, all such factors, this chapter focuses on the technology aspect of the problem. A framework is required for collecting market information about new technologies, for analysing that information and for relating it to the technology platform of the business as a whole.

The framework illustrated in Figure 3.4 provides the basis for a technology architecture. This is a similar concept to that of data architecture which will be introduced in Chapter 4. The technology architecture encapsulates the principles

Table 3.1   Technology architecture framework

	Data	Computers	Communications	Applications
Assumptions	Data integration	Central mainframe	Local area network	OS/2 or UNIX
Argument	Internal and externally held data will be required by different groups	High volume of transactions demand central processing with distributed access	Business requires local accountability	Multi-tasking on LAN, with good applications software choice
Action	Agree data ownership and custodianship principles	Central processing with decentralised control of data	Adopt open standards to provide flexible connections	Choose application packages that will run on the workstation

upon which the technology platform is designed. Conceptually, we can think of four parts to the technology architecture: data, computers, communications and applications (Earl 1989).

Table 3.1 illustrates how some of the cells might be filled in as part of an organisation's preparation of a technology plan. Market scanning data can then be kept in a filing system similar to that suggested in Table 2.3. The features of particular applications packages then need to be compared with the principles contained in the architectural table. John Ward *et al.*'s (1990) approach to formulating the way in which information systems can be delivered to the business is to suggest that the IT infrastructure will have different characteristics according to the position of the organisation on the strategic grid (McFarlan 1984).

We should also be aware here that different applications within the same organisation may well be placed in different quadrants of the strategic grid. Each of the quadrants will have different requirements for technology. Examples of how the technology considerations will differ according to the segment of the portfolio are given in Figure 3.5.

The Ward *et al.* (1990) approach, by comparison, is descriptive. To that extent it is less of a methodology, perhaps his approach could be classed as guidelines. The ideas are based on the strategic grid and so can be used easily where that grid has been employed to assist with the development of an information systems portfolio.

The challenge of the rapid change of IT was one of the driving issues identified at the beginning of this chapter. In the methodology proposed by Earl (1989) new technology opportunities are identified in the updating stage. There are a whole set of techniques concerned with how to forecast technology change, for example scenarios, environmental scanning, and brainstorming.

Like other products, IT has a life cycle. If you look at the pattern of employment of IT within an industry there is a standard path identified by Little (1981). Such a path may be different in different industries, for example point of sale systems are

Strategic	Turnaround
. Flexible architecture . Relational database . Tailored packages	. Prototype development . New technology . R & D
. Integrated architecture . Mandatory standards . Incremental technology	. Avoid obsolescence . Packages . Disinvestment
Factory	**Support**

Figure 3.5 Guidelines for IT infrastructure (*Source:* adapted from Ward *et al.* 1990)

well established in grocery retailing but not in builders' merchants. Monitoring the use of technology in related industries can thus be helpful in the identification of technology opportunities.

Ward *et al.* (1990) has related the technology life cycle to the strategic grid to suggest how the IT strategy needs to be related to the technology type. The following technology types defined by Little (1981) are illustrated in Figure 3.6.

1. *Emerging.*
   Definition: Technology under development by vendors but not yet used in industry.
   Implication: Monitoring of vendor developments of new products and emerging technologies is an important aspect of building an IT infrastructure.
2. *Pacing.*
   Definition: Trial applications, often developed in cooperation with vendors.
   Implication: Does the business wish to be a technology leader? If so it may have to invest in research and development activity and the development of prototype systems.
3. *Key.*
   Definition: Leaders in the industry adopt systems that use the technology.
   Implication: The key technologies must be mastered. Otherwise the business will fall behind its competitors.

4. *Base.*

    Definition: Technology is now widely used in the industry.

    Implication: The main challenge here is likely to be avoiding freezing the technology too much in the past. Obsolescent technology needs to be identified as part of the strategy and policies for the divestment of that technology should be formulated.

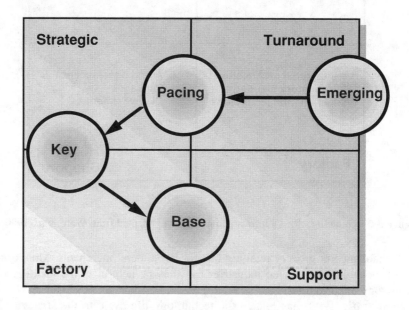

Figure 3.6   Impact of technology life cycle on strategy (*Source*: adapted from Ward *et al.* 1990)

However, it is not only technology which changes over time but also organisations. Of crucial importance to the acceptability and use of new technology in organisations is the experience of that organisation with IT.

GIS stage by stage

A search of the literature revealed one previous piece of work which has used the stages of growth idea to describe the development of GIS applications. Crain and MacDonald (1984) suggest that GIS goes through three stages. The observations leading to these stages were made of the Canadian Geographic Information System. The first stage is described as 'inventory applications' where GIS is used to organise and store data relating to entities of interest. In the business world this would be the equivalent of using GIS for facilities management. The second stage is reached when GIS is used for analysis, for example using spatial modelling to determine potential site locations. The second stage, dubbed 'management applications', is where the information system becomes a decision support rather than simply a transaction processing system.

According to Dickinson and Calkins (1988) it will be three to five years before most inventory systems move to stage-two applications. It is interesting to note that the main reason given for this length of time is the lack of spatial analysis routines in GIS packages. The technology focus of these attempts to use stages of growth ideas to describe GIS developments is a weakness. Technology is important but it is only part of the story. Since more information systems fail for organisational reasons than for technology reasons (Grimshaw 1988) it is important that the analysis brings into focus some organisational factors in addition to the technological ones. Additionally we need to be aware that these applications of the stages of growth idea were observed in the domain of environmental applications. In a number of important respects business applications of GIS are different (Grimshaw 1989).

A new attempt to apply stages of growth ideas to the field of GIS in business would be worth while if it included an analysis of organisational factors and was rooted in observations made in the business domain. Obermeyer (1990) concluded that a lack of geographical training was a constraint on the development and use of GIS. Grimshaw and Maier (1991) in the context of using GIS in marketing, talked in terms of first and second 'wave' GIS. The classification here was in terms of operational and decision support systems. A classification of applications can be useful in a specific context; however, the organisation that is using a GIS will change and evolve over time. Therefore some classification that makes use of the dynamics of growth is required.

The Galliers and Sutherland (1991) model makes a useful starting point for examining the dynamics as far as they relate to the application of GIS in business. The model provides a framework of how an organisation develops its use of computer technology. It has proved to be useful in IT strategy formulation and can be adapted to be a useful tool for those concerned with the introduction of GIS.

The stages of growth model and its principles tells us that there is a certain order of IT progress, although it does not say anything about the speed or time-scales of implementation (Zhao and Grimshaw 1991).

Figure 3.7 shows a modified stages of growth model which fits the circumstances of GIS (Grimshaw 1993). The model is essentially modified to show five stages. Many organisations will indeed travel the road through all stages sequentially. However, this is not a requirement. The utility of the model is in terms of the diagnosis of an organisation. The main question to have in mind when using the model is 'where are we now?'

Having established what the main characteristics of your organisation are you are in a much better position to determine what you need to do in order to get where you want to be. A better understanding of the model will be gained by explaining the source of the model. Where is the empirical evidence for the model presented in Figure 3.7?

A study of the financial services sector in the UK found a number of generic

Stage Element	Opt out	Stand-alone	Linking	Opportunistic	Corporate
Strategy	Ad hoc	Audit	Top-down	Technology led	Integrated
Structure	Informal	Finance led	Centralised	Coalition	Cooperative
Systems	Operational	Duplication	Decision support	Strategic	Comprehensive
Staff	Non-technical	MIS Manager	Business analysts	IS planners	IS Director
Style	What is GIS?	Do your own thing	Partnership	Run with it!	Team building
Skills	Scarce	Technical	Project mgt	Marketing	Innovative
Shared Values	Efficiency	Indeterminate	Effectiveness	Strategic	Transformation

Figure 3.7   The GIS starting grid

strategies employed (Grimshaw 1992a). Analysis of a survey followed by detailed case studies showed five very distinctly different ways of introducing GIS into a building society. Such financial institutions may be unfamiliar to readers outside the UK; however, since the Financial Services Act 1988 many restrictions have been lifted and these bodies are now all-purpose financial institutions in competition with banks and insurance companies. In principle, similar deregulation of the financial market-place has occurred in many countries, including the USA. The main business issues and background to the study are inset as a mini case study.

Mini Case Study

A study to examine the value of GIS as a corporate support tool and identify factors affecting the relationship between GIS and the information strategy of the organisation (Grimshaw 1989) was carried out by a survey of all UK building societies to find out who used, or had plans to use, GIS.

In order to understand the findings of the survey it is necessary to have a broad understanding of the building society sector and its demand for geographical data. The advantages and disadvantages of these different approaches are then discussed before the chapter closes with some management and organisational issues arising out of the study.

At the time of the survey, in May 1991, there were 100 members of the Building Societies' Association. The societies range in size from those having over 2000 branches (including agencies) to those having only one office. Some societies have a nationwide spread of branches, others are rather more regionally concentrated. The largest 30 societies conducted over 90% of the business in the sector.

Moves in Europe to create a single market from 1992 have offered an opportunity for the larger societies to think across traditional national boundaries. However, financial services are not like physical products (e.g. cars) that can be sold in any country. The institutional and cultural background of the country is likely to affect the market for some financial services. Under the provisions of the Building Societies Act 1986 societies can only operate in other states of the European Community by means of a subsidiary.

The Building Societies Act 1986 paved the way for building societies to offer a range of financial products and services. This increased competition, at a time when the housing market suffered a downturn, creating a business environment in which customer information became a crucial factor in the sustained marketing of successful financial services.

The legislative framework and the competitive environment have, according to research by Capello *et al.* (1990), influenced the structure of the building societies in the following ways.

1. There has been an increase in the number of mergers.
2. An increase in the number of branches, and an increase in the number of estate agencies owned by building societies.
3. A concentration of assets in the largest building societies.

Table 3.2 summarises the main characteristics of the building society sector, showing the assets, branches, and agencies of the largest 30 societies.

Table 3.2   Key characteristics of the largest societies

Name	Assets (£m.)	Branches	Agencies
Halifax	47 920.8	760	1 700
Nationwide	26 647.2	814	249
Woolwich	15 327.2	546	1 684
Alliance & Leicester	13 552.6	407	1 151
Leeds	13 447.9	482	570
National & Provincial	8 465.1	321	
Cheltenham & Gloucester	7 270.3	175	8
Bradford & Bingley	7 155.8	250	456
Britannia	6 298.2	255	300
Bristol & West	4 682.6	171	71
Birmingham Midshires	3 160.5	135	115
Yorkshire	3 063.5	141	140
Northern Rock	2 794.6	125	506
Town & Country	2 155.0	77	219
Chelsea	1 820.3	55	238
Skipton	1 662.3	57	10
Coventry	1 645.9	65	45
Leeds & Holbeck	1 489.2	75	70
Regency & West	1 254.7	80	33
Leamington Spa	1 180.7	63	
Derbyshire	1 043.2	60	37
Norwich & Peterborough	1 018.0	67	7
Portman Wessex	962.5	49	123
West Bromwich	873.8	80	17
Principality	769.2	50	62
Heart of England	766.0	54	62
Portsmouth	760.8	19	57
North of England	759.6	52	222
Newcastle	731.8	54	301
Cheshire	694.7	56	13

Source: Building Societies Association (1990).

The business environment has thus made it ever more important to understand who the customers are, in terms of where they live, and their socio-demographic characteristics. In common with other financial services organisations the major information systems issue currently is the conversion of account-based data into customer information. Most of the large societies and banks are investing heavily to convert their traditional accounts databases into customer information.

The sample frame was compiled from the list of members of the Building Societies Association (BSA). In the *1990 Yearbook* (BSA 1990) there are 100 members listed. A letter, questionnaire and reply paid envelope were mailed to all 100 members in May 1991. Letters were all addressed by name to the head of the IT function. These names were all taken from the *Yearbook* or found from a simple telephone call to the head office.

Overall, 52 replies were received. Two of these stated that it was company policy not to respond to any questionnaire survey. One response was from a building society that had recently merged. So there were 49 usable responses out of 99 building societies, which makes a 50% response rate. The responses were, however, skewed towards the large societies. So if the largest 30 societies are taken, there was a 90% response. These response rates are very high when compared to other studies employing a similar research method. The findings of the study can therefore be taken to be representative of the building society sector as a whole.

Main findings

Data processing (DP) budgets

It has been reported by Stares (1990) that the building society industry is expected to spend more than 1 billion on IT in the next three years. The DP budget question was answered by 71% of respondents. The budgets range in size from 10 000 to 69m. As expected there is a good correspondence between size of society and the amount of money spent on DP.

Who runs IT?

The job title of the person responsible for IT varied widely. However, 60% of the largest 10 societies had a director responsible for IT. Whilst amongst the smaller societies responsibility for IT was still part of the finance department.

IS/IT strategy

Around 90% of respondents stated that they had an IS/IT strategy. Most of these societies regularly reviewed their strategy. In fact, only 11% of strategies were over one year old. It might have been expected that the smaller societies, with a more stable business, would review strategy less frequently. However, this is not the case. Amongst the largest 30 societies, 15% have an IS/IT strategy that is more than 18 months old. In fact one of the top 10 societies has a strategy that is nearly three years old.

A very interesting finding is that 10% of respondents stated that GIS is part of their IS/IT strategy. Taking the largest 30 societies, 15% said GIS was part of their IS/IT strategy.

Use of GIS

The main purpose of the questionnaire was to establish who was using GIS. The fundamental finding, is therefore, that some 34% of building societies have or will have a GIS. If the top 30 societies are taken then this proportion rises to 52%.

Looking in more detail at the current situation, we find that 20% of respondents have a GIS. This proportion rises to 33% of the largest 30 societies. Those considering using GIS in the future were a further 14% of respondents or 18% of the largest 30 societies.

The survey reveals that GIS is a significant application in the building societies, especially amongst the larger ones. Furthermore, it is apparent that those considering using GIS in the future represent a 70% increase over current users. This is ample demonstration of the timeliness of the current research.

The earliest recorded use of GIS by a building society was in 1976. Two more have been using GIS since the early 1980s. The other GIS users are much more recent users, with 40% implementing their GIS within the last two years. The early implementations of GIS, at a time that the term was not in widespread use, was on mainframe hardware. This is in contrast to all the recent examples of GIS being implemented on personal computer hardware platforms. Overall it could be concluded that each building society with a GIS has decided on its own best route to choosing a system. All current users have different software products driving their systems.

As expected, there is a considerable consensus about what GIS is used for. Table 3.3 shows, for societies that currently have a GIS, the uses by percentages. It is interesting to note that 70% of GIS users employ their systems to perform three or more of the tasks shown in the table.

Table 3.3   Current use of GIS by building societies

Use	Building societies (%)
Target mailing	80
Market potential	70
Catchment area	50
Branch location	40
Other	30
Insurance rating	20
Credit assessment	10

There is also a consensus about who the main users of GIS are. The marketing department are the main users in 70% of the cases. Geographical data sets are purchased by 70% of the societies who have a GIS.

Of those societies using GIS at the present time, an overwhelming (70%) consider it to be a decision support (tactical) rather than an operational tool. This finding is in direct contrast to the empirical studies undertaken in the public sector where the majority of organisations regard GIS as an operational information system.

The initial questionnaire was intended to be an exploratory one. Further, more detailed information was sought from those organisations that do have a GIS or who intended to implement one shortly. Follow-up interviews were conducted on a semi-structured basis building a number of case studies.

The essence of the five stages is discussed below in relation to the industry case study reported in the mini case.

'Opt-out stage': purchase GIS service from a data agency

Given that the information systems agenda of most societies is a very busy one, especially with the conversion of accounts data to customer data, it is not surprising that many societies have gone outside their own organisations for GIS. Data from customer records are typically sent to the data agency either once or twice per year. Analysis is then returned to the society on a fixed fee basis. With a typical fee of around 10 000 to 15 000 per annum, many societies clearly have judged that it is not worth bringing the services in-house.

In terms of the model, such an organisation is clearly devoting much of its energy to the development of operational (customer databases) information systems. Overall goals are likely to be expressed in terms of increasing efficiency. Only a small number of people in the organisation may be aware of GIS at all, let alone its enormous potential. These organisations are at the 'opt-out' stage.

'Stand-alone stage'

Often following a successful period of 'opt-out' an organisation has found GIS to be useful, especially for some specific tasks. Frustration with the ability of the central IT service to provide analysis of customer information on a geographic basis, it is typical in the stand-alone stage for enthusiasts (possibly in the marketing department) to 'do their own thing'. These circumstances are most likely to occur when the head of the IT service is an MIS manager reporting to (say) the head of finance. In this scenario there is a lack of corporate strategy informed about IT opportunities and the possible role of information systems in the organisation.

The stand-alone philosophy will typically result in data duplication. A stand-alone application must be fed with data from many sources, some of which will be internal databases such as customer information. When this is first extracted from the corporate database the data will be up to date; however, there is a likelihood that it will become out of date because of a failure to extract the data at regular intervals from the corporate database.

'Linking stage': in-house development

Those societies that profess to have had GIS for a 'long time', that is since the 1970s, have typically developed their own systems. These systems are characterised by strong links to the customer databases run on the mainframe computers. Development costs for such systems are likely to have been high but systems will have been tailor made to the particular requirements of the user.

In terms of the stages of growth model such an organisation would typically be at the 'linking' stage. The strategy is being driven from the top, and there is a strong tradition of central computer systems with well-developed project management skills. Often the rational given for developing a system will be to enhance effectiveness.

'Opportunistic stage': strategic technology opportunity

The evidence suggests that many building societies consider GIS to be a strategic information system. Those that take this view would be unlikely to invite a data agency to run their geographical analysis. The typical hardware platform used here is relatively small and cheap: a powerful personal computer with good graphics and a GIS package. With this route towards GIS the major decision to be taken is which GIS package to purchase and which external data sets to use.

There are examples in this category of user who see GIS as being a technological opportunity (Grimshaw and Hinton 1992). Ideas generated by enthusiasts may be marketed to other users and the organisation culture here would foster a coalition spirit typified by the phrase, 'run with it'. In terms of our model, these organisations are clearly in the 'opportunistic' stage.

'Corporate stage'

The overriding strategic objective of an organisation at the corporate stage is to use IT to transform the business. The applications of IT to achieve efficiency and effectiveness benefits have already been implemented. The strategy of the business and the strategy of the IT services are integrated. Typically the IS director will be a member of the board and will be fully involved in discussions of business strategy. In order to bring about such fundamental change there will be a cooperative staff structure where there is an emphasis on team building and systems are comprehensive.

The first section of this chapter has discussed the usefulness of a stages of growth model to organisations embarking on using GIS. A model, based on earlier work by Galliers and Sutherland (1991), has been simplified and adapted for use in the GIS environment. The model advanced is one to be recommended for use by any organisation thinking about using GIS for the first time or starting a large GIS project. With the basic question of 'where are we now?' in mind, the model can be used to diagnose what needs to be done in order to get to the target.

It is worth noting that, for any one organisation, the answer to the question 'where are we now?' will not necessarily fall into one neatly defined stage for all the elements. For example, an organisation broadly at the 'stand-alone' stage may lag on the style element because knowledge of GIS is not widespread in the organisation. This would indicate that if the organisation wishes to move to a 'linking' stage there would be more effort required to develop the organisational style. A further point worth stressing is that asking different people about 'where we are now?' will mostly result in different answers. Often the differences will reflect stakeholders in the process of using IT.

Summary

This chapter has drawn some parallels between the eras of information systems and the 'waves' of GIS that have been observed in practice. The increasing importance of GIS to organisations is evidence that we are observing a movement from the dawn of operational systems to the maturity of strategic systems. Such strategic systems need to be born of the business strategy in order to be fully integrated with the other information resources of the organisation.

A framework advanced in this chapter is a useful starting point for a business which may find that GIS is a technology that can deliver information resources to the decision makers. By concentrating on five key issues faced by managers, the framework can be applied in real business situations. The framework should be used for guidance in setting up the process of developing an information strategy. The final product of a strategy is less important than setting in motion a healthy debate that becomes a continuous process. Involvement of key managers in that process is a key factor in the success of the information strategy.

In the future, as the technology of GIS matures, there may well come a time when debate about GIS turns from a technology focus to an information and organisational focus. It is hoped that the ideas here will make a contribution to that debate by identifying the major issues and advancing a framework that can be used in those organisations endeavouring not only to come to terms with new technology like GIS but also to develop a coherent approach to the management of information in their organisations.

The model discussed in this chapter is based on theoretical work in the information systems field and empirical work concerned with the use of GIS in the financial services sector of the economy. The use of GIS in the financial services sector is a rapidly growing applications area. To date, publication of case studies has been anecdotal. This chapter takes a critical look at the process of identifying the technology, the business requirement, piloting GIS and the benefits gained.

GIS, like many ITs before it, is experiencing a period of rapid growth in applications. Some businesses, through the natural enthusiasm of one or two individuals, embark on GIS projects on an *ad hoc* basis, others embody geographical information into their other information systems generally. The main argument in this chapter has been that planning for the use of GIS will bring the maximum benefits to the business as a whole. This planning activity is best carried out as part of the organisation's information management strategy process.

A variety of approaches to GIS have been examined empirically in order to derive a stages of growth model. The main purpose of the stages of growth model is to enable business to answer the important question of where they are now in terms of their use of IT. Using the stages of growth model as a diagnostic tool then provides a way of understanding where the organisation needs to develop policies in order to bring about the change required in order to use GIS effectively.

The information management strategy process is itself only part of the wider strategic planning process of the business as a whole. Information strategy should be rooted in the business strategy. That is where the organisational objectives are set and where the competitive forces are examined. A framework (Figure 3.1) has been used to show how the business strategy is linked to the information management process. The discussion in this chapter has also shown how the business, information and technology components of the information strategy formulation process are linked together and how each part of that process can be tackled in a practical way. At the heart of the matter is the issue of how GIS can contribute to the decision-making activity of the organisation. The next chapter tackles the issues around information and data for GIS as a precurser to a discussion of GIS for supporting decision makers, dealt with in Chapter 5.

Further study

In a single chapter there has inevitably been a restricted amount of material that could be presented and discussed in relation to information strategies. For those readers who wish to study information strategies in more depth there are a number of books and courses available. The following books are recommended starting points for further study:

Earl M J 1989 *Management Strategies for Information Technology* Prentice-Hall, New York

Gunton T 1989 *Infrastructure: Building a Framework for Corporate Information Handling* Prentice-Hall, Hemel Hempstead, UK

Scott-Morton M S (ed) 1991 *The Corporation of the 1990s: Information Technology and Organisational Transformation* Oxford University Press, New York

Ward J M, Griffiths P M, Whitemore P 1990 *Strategic Planning for Information Systems* Wiley Series in Information Systems, John Wiley & Sons, Chichester

Some understanding of business strategy would also be helpful for readers who wish to further their understanding of the material covered in this chapter. A good starting point can be made with the following three books:

Johnson G, Scholes K 1993 *Exploring Corporate Strategy*, 3rd edn, Prentice-Hall, New York

Porter M E 1985 *Competitive Advantage: Creating and Sustaining Superior Performance* Free Press, Macmillan, New York

Whittington R 1993 *What is Strategy and Does it Matter?* Routledge Series in Analytical Management, London

References

Benjamin R I, Rockart J F, Scott-Morton M S, Wyman J 1984 Information technology: a strategic opportunity. *Sloan Management Review* Spring **25**(3): 3–10

Building Societies Association 1990 *Building Societies Yearbook 1990, Official Handbook of the Building Societies Association* Franey & Co Ltd, London

Capello R, Taylor J, Williams H 1990 Computer networks and competitive advantage in building societies. *International Journal of Information Management* **10**: 54–66

Crain I K, MacDonald C L 1984 From land inventory to land management. *Cartographica* **21**: 40–6

Dickinson H, Calkins H W 1988 The economic evaluation of implementing a GIS. *International Journal of Geographical Information Systems* **2**: 307–27

Earl M J 1989 *Management Strategies for Information Technology* Prentice-Hall, New York

Galliers R D 1987a Information technology planning within the corporate planning process. In Berry A D, Duhig T (eds) *Controlling Projects within an Integrated Management Framework* Pergamon Infotech State of the Art Report, 27–38

Galliers R D (ed) 1987b *Information Analysis* Addison-Wesley, Sydney

Galliers R D, Sutherland A R 1991 Information systems management and strategy formulation: the 'stages of growth' revisited. *Journal of Information Systems* **1** (2): 89–114

Grimshaw D J 1988 The use of land and property information systems. *International Journal of Geographical Information Systems* **2**: 57–65

Grimshaw D J 1989 Geographical information systems: a tool for business and industry? *International Journal of Information Management* **9**: 119–26

Grimshaw D J 1991a Geographical information systems as part of the corporate information strategy. *International Journal of Information Management* **11** (4): 292–7

Grimshaw D J 1991b GIS – a strategic business tool? *Mapping Awareness and GIS Europe* **5** (2), March: 46–8

Grimshaw D J 1992a The use of GIS by building societies in the UK. *Proceedings of the Third European Conference on Geographical Information Systems* Vol 2, 23–26 March, Munich, Germany, pp 988–97

Grimshaw D J 1992b The transformation of customer databases. *Proceedings of the Fourth Conference of the Association for Geographical Information Systems* 24–26 November, Birmingham, UK, pp 1.7.1–6

Grimshaw D J 1993 Corporate GIS stage by stage. *Proceedings of the GIS in Business '93 Conference*, Boston, Mass, 7–10 March, GIS World Books Inc, Fort Collins, Colo, pp 133–7

Grimshaw D J, Hinton M A 1992 Taking technology opportunities to the business. *Journal of Strategic Information Systems* **1** (2): 106–10

Grimshaw D J, Maier J R 1991 *The Integration of GIS into a Marketing DSS* Warwick Business School Research Papers No 33, ISSN 0265–5976, Warwick Business School Research Bureau, Coventry: University of Warwick

Hochstrasser B 1990 Evaluating IT investments – matching techniques to projects. *Journal of Information Technology* November: 1–12

Little A D 1981 *Strategic Management of Technology* Report to European Management Forum, Boston, Mass

McFarlan W F 1984 Information technology changes the way you compete. *Harvard Business Review* **62** (3), May–June: 98–102

Maynard J C, Pearce N J 1990 GIS as part of a corporate IT strategy: a practical approach. *Proceedings of the First European Conference on Geographical Information Systems* Vol II, Amsterdam, April, pp 729–36

Meyer N D, Boone M E 1987 *The Information Edge* McGraw-Hill, New York p 333

Munro M C, Huff S L 1985 Information technology and corporate strategy. *Business Quarterly* Summer

Obermeyer N J 1990 Bureaucratic factors in the adoption of GIS by public organisations: preliminary evidence from public administrators and planners. *Journal of Computing, Environment and Urban Systems* **14**: 261–71

Porter M E 1980 *Competitive Strategy* Free Press, Macmillan, New York

Porter M E 1985 *Competitive Advantage: Creating and Sustaining Superior Performance* Free Press, Macmillan, New York

Porter M E, Millar V E 1985 How information gives you competitive advantage. *Harvard Business Review*, July–August: 149–60

Scott-Morton M S 1967 *Decision Support Systems: An Organisational Perspective* Addison-Wesley, Reading, Mass

Stares C 1990 Controlling expenditure on information technology. In *Building Societies Yearbook 1990, Official Handbook of the Building Societies Association* Franey & Co. Ltd, London pp 167–70

Ward J M 1988 Information systems and technology: application portfolio management – an assessment of matrix-based analysis. *Journal of Information Technology*, **3**(3), December: 205–15

Ward J M, Griffiths P M, Whitemore P 1990 *Strategic Planning for Information Systems* Wiley Series in Information Systems, John Wiley & Sons, Chichester

Wiseman C 1985 *Strategy and Computers* Dow Jones-Irwin, New York

Zhao P, Grimshaw D J 1991 *A Comparative Study of the Application of IT in China and the West: Culture and the Stages of Growth Model* Warwick Business School Research Bureau Paper, No. 32, ISSN 0265-5976, Warwick Business School Research Bureau, Coventry: University of Warwick

4

The nature of geographical data

'Transfer from paper map to electronic format invites many inconsistencies especially when many sets of features can be related in a geographical information system.'

Mark Monmonier (1991:56–7)

Preamble

The previous two chapters in this part of the book have defined GIS and placed them within the context of more general information systems, stressing the importance of serving the business need. Taking a top-down approach to defining information requirements based on business need, this chapter examines the nature of data, distinguishing between data and information.

The differences and similarities between spatial (geographical) and non-spatial data are discussed. Information is examined as a key resource, alongside land, labour and capital. What is different about information that requires special management? Sources of data to be found in a typical business are used to the illustrate the potential of internal data sets, e.g. customer data, when combined with external data.

The economics of information is briefly explored (more detailed discussion is left until Chapter 6) to illustrate the cost and value of information. Some general data issues concerning quality, ownership, validity and data protection are explored from a management point of view via a comparison of approaches in different countries, using a case study to illustrate some of the practical issues.

The nature of data and information

Data is the raw material of an information system. An item of data given to a manager without a context, for example the number '1.5', fails to convey information. By the addition of meaning, for example, by telling the manager that '1.5' represents the average percentage of turnover that a company in the UK spends on IT, data has been converted into information. The idea of information having a context related to a decision area of concern to the manager is returned to in more detail in Chapter 5. This process has been described by Checkland (1981) in the simple formula:

$$\text{Information} = \text{data} + \text{meaning}$$

A more formal definition of data is given by Galliers (1987 p. 4) as: 'That collection of data, which when presented in a particular manner and at an appropriate time, improves the knowledge of the person receiving it in such a way that (s)he is better able to undertake a relevant activity or make a relevant decision.' Information is often used, in conversation, as being interchangeable with the word 'data'. For the purposes of this book the above definitions will be used. This chapter goes on to explore some of the specific issues relating to the geographical nature of data.

All businesses have a mix of data: the geographical and the non-geographical. Understanding that data and modelling the relationships between data is one approach to building information systems. It has been argued that the data used by an organisation is much more stable over time than the business processes used (Avison and Fitzgerald 1989). In today's rapidly changing business environment this has never been more true because computer technology is being used to change the business processes, or to use the jargon – re-engineer the business (Scott-Morton 1991).

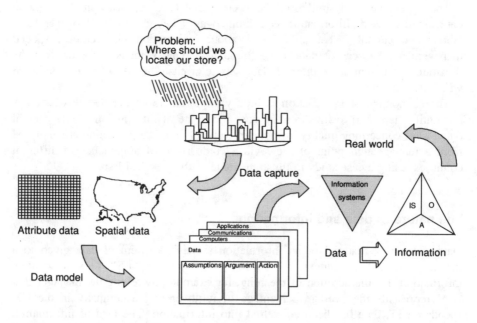

Figure 4.1 From data to information

Taking a simplistic view of a GIS as comprising hardware, software and data, it has been estimated that data replacement is only done on a 25–50 year cycle and data costs represent some 80% of total system costs (Coote and Rackham 1992). If you have any doubt about the size of such figures, reflect upon the financial services sector where recent effort has gone into translating account-based data into customer based data. The point is well made that without data, information is often not available to the right people at the right time and in the right place. The process of transforming data into information is a complex one and worth discussing in some detail.

Figure 4.1 shows that data must be captured from the real world in order to solve or help to solve a specific problem like where to locate a store. In outline, the data captured will be both attribute and spatial data. To use the data effectively in an information system requires the data to be modelled and a data architecture to be defined. The data architecture, together with architectures defined for computers, communications and applications (as discussed in Chapter 3) provide the IT platform upon which the information system can be built. The information system then provides information to the managers of the organisation.

Unlocking the geographical data in business

All information systems involve the storage and retrieval of data. What is different about 'geographical data Much of the literature stresses the differences between spatial and non-spatial data. First of all we will look at the differences and then examine the similarities.

Studies have shown that 90% of business data is geographical (Moloney *et al.* 1993). Some examples of business data with a geographical component are given in Table 4.1. All companies have customer files, with street names and often zip codes or postcodes. For many years the potential of such data has remained hidden. To unlock the geographical data requires a code (often termed a geocode) to be attached to each record in your customer file. The appropriate geocode depends upon the application, it may include census enumeration area or tract, postcode, or latitude and longitude. There are a number of data products available which will help to geocode internal company data. An example of such a product is AddressPoint, marketed in the UK by Ordnance Survey, which translates an address to a grid reference. In turn the grid references may easily be converted into area codes such as postcodes or census areas.

Any geographical feature, for example a bauxite mine, can be subdivided into: where is the mine, what is the mine, when did the mine exist, and what is the relationship of the mine to other spatial features (for example a river or a road). The first fundamental question is 'where is it? Locations are recorded using a system of coordinates like latitude and longitude. For any study area defined by a GIS it is essential that the same coordinate system is used for all the data sets. The data may be stored to different levels of accuracy depending on the use to which it will be put. For example, the location of retail outlets in a given study area used to

Table 4.1   Business geographical data

File or database	Data fields	Geocodes
(a) Internal data		
Customer files	Name Address Purchases	Postcode Census
Facilities file	Location name Address Size Product range	Latitude/longitude Postcode
Product file	Product type Sales by location	Postcode
(b) External data		
Physical maps	Points Lines Polygons	Addresses Road network Postcode boundaries
Retail maps	Floorspace Retailer name Products	Shopping centre boundaries Latitude/longitude
Geodemographics	Lifestyles	Census areas Postcode areas

model the impact of opening a new outlet would be satisfactory to an accuracy of 10 m. But a gas utility company wishing to map the location of a gas pipeline would require accuracy down to at least 1 m.

The second fundamental question is 'what is it'? For example, if the feature is a mine then the mine planner would probably want to store a number of attributes including landownership, date first licensed, quality of mineral deposit, output per annum, etc. These *attributes* are all non-spatial. A number of spatial attributes might also be kept in a database, for example details relating to depth, quality, thickness at specific points in space.

The third fundamental question is 'what is its relationship to other spatial features'? For example, the store location planner needs to know not only the proposed location but also the relationship of that location to other existing competitive stores. This may be expressed in terms of distance or drive time or some combination of the two.

The fourth question relates to 'when' the feature existed. The mine planner may be responsible for restoration of the site once mineral extraction is completed. To do this data about the original landscape is required. This will probably include its topography, and natural ground cover.

The level of geographical *specificity* is another important consideration in determining the utility of geographical data. The following sets of questions illustrate increasingly specific information (Brusegard 1989):

1. The number of cars sold by General Motors (GM) in North America this year.
2. The number of cars sold by GM in Montreal.
3. The number of cars sold by GM through dealer 'A' in Montreal.
4. The number of cars sold by GM through dealer 'A' in Montreal to people living within four miles of the dealership.
5. The number of cars sold by GM through dealer 'A' in Montreal to people living within four miles of the dealership who have purchased a GM vehicle from that same dealer within the last five years.
6. The number of cars sold by GM through dealer 'A' in Montreal to people living within four miles of the dealership who have purchased a GM vehicle from that same dealer within the last five years and whose workplace is within one mile of the dealership.

These questions illustrate not only increasing specificity but also illustrate that turning geographical data into geographical information requires data on points and spatial relationships. Geographical data, by definition, has a locational identifier. The data is fundamentally about *where* facilities, resources, services or activities are. The description of such geographic data is normally done in terms of three characteristics that mark it as different from other data the business is familiar with (such as lists and tables).

Geographical position

Locations are recorded in terms of a coordinate system such as latitude and longitude (for example the Ordnance Survey grid reference). All data sets used together in a study should have a common coordinate system. An appropriate level of accuracy should be chosen. This will depend on the purpose for which the data is being used. For example, the location of automatic teller machines (ATM) in a bank system will have different accuracy requirements from the location of underground pipelines in a utility facilities management system.

Spatial relationship

Whilst it is important to know the location of (say) ATMs, the bank is also likely to want to know how close the ATMs are to shopping and commercial properties. In more formal terms the spatial relationship describes adjacency, proximity and connectivity of map entities.

Time

Geographical entities change over time. Therefore it is sometimes important to know for which period of time the data was collected. Clearly the road and other transportation networks change, as do retail and other land uses. Time is difficult to handle in a sophisticated way and is an area requiring further research.

The translation of these geographical characteristics into geographic entities in a spatial database can be conceptualised into points, lines and polygons. The logical description of these geographical entities in a spatial database can be thought of in terms of one of the data models discussed later in this chapter.

Points

A point, as defined in the Standards for Digital Cartographic Data, is a zero-dimensional object that specifies a geographical location through a set of coordinates. Practically, a point can be thought of as a site of interest to the business such as a retail store or a property for sale.

Lines

A line represents links between points. Practically, lines may be roads, pipelines, cables, etc.

Polygons

Polygons are areas or zones. In reality they may be postal areas, census districts, shopping centres, catchment areas or any other zone of interest to business decision making.

Data architecture

Spatial data representation and manipulation are much more complex than standard textual or numeric data. A GIS will contain both types of data, commonly referred to as *spatial* data and *attribute* data. The ability of GIS to integrate different data types is one of its strengths. Using this integrating ability to the full requires thought to be given to the data architecture.

The concept of data architecture is related to the computing, communications and applications architectures discussed in Chapter 3. The data architecture of an organisation may be expressed at different levels of detail. An architect of the built environment asked to design a new university would make assumptions about, amongst other things, the volume of traffic, occupancy rates of each building, and environmental screening. After a dialogue with the client the architect translates the assumptions into the action required to make the building work and to be physically strong. Any design made by the architect is dependent on these assumptions. Taking a design out of the context in which it was developed often fails. A good example of this came on a recent visit to the State University of New York at Buffalo which houses part of the National Center for Geographical Information and Analysis. The Amherst campus at Buffalo was originally designed for the University of Arizona, consequently lots of open corridors and balconies were embodied into the design to provide shade from the strong sunshine. During a March snowstorm these features of design were not appreciated. In a similar way, the data architect starts by knowing why the organisation is collecting data and what it is to be used for.

Some assumptions relating to the data need to be made as a first step in the design process. Data modelling is generally undertaken in the systems development process. There are some considerations which specifically relate to spatial data and others which do not. In business applications geographical data is generally being used in conjunction with attribute data. Since the attribute data is likely to reside already in a hierarchical or relational database it is important to consider spatial data assumptions. Can your existing customer file held in a relational database be linked to your preferred GIS package without data duplication? Spatial data assumptions need to be considered in the areas described in the sections below.

Geographical data model

Generally the term 'data model' means the conceptual organisation of the database. Most business information systems use either a hierarchical, network or relational data model. Representation of the geographical feature in a computer system is done by using one of two spatial data models: raster or vector. The raster data model is essentially the simplest of the two and may well be sufficiently detailed for the purposes of most business applications. A summary of the advantages and disadvantages of the two data models is given in Table 4.2, and Figure 4.2 illustrates how data is modelled by raster or vector.

Table 4.2   Geographical data models

Raster characteristics	
Each feature in the real world is represented as a cell	
Raster: advantages	**Raster: disadvantages**
Simple	Data redundancy
Efficient for digital images	Topology is difficult to represent
Efficient for map overlays	Output of maps do not have a smooth appearance
Vector: advantages	**Vector: disadvantages**
Less storage space used	More complex data structure
Efficient for topology	Overlays are difficult
Output of maps is of good-quality images	Cannot manipulate digital images

Vector characteristics
Each feature in the real world is represented as a line, point or polygon via a set of coordinates

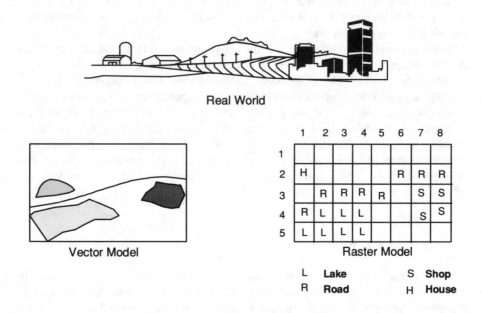

Figure 4.2   The real world as represented by vector and raster models

Most software packages on the market use a particular spatial data model for holding and displaying data. For example, ARC/INFO uses a vector model and SPANS uses a raster model. Many utility programs are available to translate vector data into raster format and vice versa. Critical decisions about which kind of GIS to buy and use depend partly on the data sources used and partly on the kind of analysis that the GIS is to be used for. Much of the digital source data in the UK from, for example Ordnance Survey or Bartholomew's, is in vector format although their range of products include raster data. Data collected via remote sensing will typically be collected in raster format. As Table 4.2 shows, the raster format has advantages for spatial analysis. One of the disadvantages of the raster model, that it is less compact, can be overcome by the quadtree data model which uses a variable size grid. Large geographical areas such as a retail branch catchment area can use a large cell size except for the finer detail required at the boundary.

Map projections and map scale

Data integration implies the combining of data from different sources. One of the important sources of incompatibility might be the map projection used. The choice of map projection will often be straightforward. The most obvious choice is to use the projection of the national survey, usually the Universal Transverse Mercator

(UTM) or the Lambert Conformal Conical projection (Maling 1991). Issues of choice are more likely to occur when the study area goes beyond national boundaries, or where it covers a large geographical area, such as Canada. The degree of accuracy required for business applications of GIS is not great enough to be concerned about projections for their own sake; however, the assembly of data from a variety of sources makes it important to be aware of the possibility of combining different map projections.

Integrating maps from different sources may also bring with it the problem of differing map scales. Whilst a GIS will technically be able to transform maps to the same scales, the process will involve some generalisation of map features. So the business user needs to decide what level of generalisation is acceptable for the application being considered.

Data quality

Quality can have many definitions, and recently attention by managers to the quality issue has led to its embodiment in standards, for example the BS 5750 standard for quality information systems. One useful accepted definition of quality of data is that it is 'fitness for use' (Chrisman 1983). Such a definition of quality follows on well from our earlier definition of information being data plus meaning, which is always dependent on the context that the data is required for. Various bodies responsible for data standards and the exchange of spatial data have adopted this definition, for example the US National Committee Digital Cartographic Data Standards Task Force (DCDSTF 1988).

Data error

Any representation of the earth is bound to contain error. Data free of error is therefore a misnomer. The critical question is how much and what kind of error is acceptable. By acceptable, we mean for the purpose to which the data is to be used ultimately. Chrisman (1991) puts forward a taxonomy of error with the following classifications:

1. *Positional accuracy* is traditionally the chief accuracy concern of the cartographer; however, for most business purposes the accuracy of a point may be acceptable with some degree of latitude. A critical feature of accuracy is whether it can be measured. One test of positional accuracy is published in Vonderohe and Chrisman (1985).
2. *Attribute accuracy* can be thought of as statistical significance. For example, the attributes assigned to a particular postcode area by the MOSAIC database depends upon the assumptions made when the cluster analysis of the raw census data was performed.
3. *Logical consistency* can sometimes be checked by the computer. For example, is there a missing boundary line making an incomplete polygon? Or does each

object have a label? Such errors may be checked using a topological model (White 1984).

4. *Completeness* relates to knowing that all the data you expect to be present is in fact there. For example, it is straightforward to check a list of census districts against a map to determine if they are all coded.

Data format standards

Data standards is a wide-ranging topic. It is an important one because agreed standards can promote the effective and efficient transfer and use of data. The US Standard which has been adopted in North America and Australasia is based on a conceptual model of spatial objects, spatial phenomena and spatial features. Some examples of these concepts are given in Table 4.3.

Table 4.3   Basic concepts of the Spatial Data Transfer Standard

Concept	Example 1	Example 2	Example 3
Phenomena	Cash machine	M1 motorway	Sainsbury's store
Class (entity type)	ATM	Road	Store
Attribute	Name of bank	Speed limit	Floorspace
Object	Point or node	Line	Area
Feature	Phenomena + object		

In the UK there are currently a number of *de facto* standards used to allow the transfer of geographical information. Some common ones include DXF (copyright of Autodesk), SIF (copyright of Intergraph) and OSTF (Ordnance Survey Transfer Format). Ordnance Survey has recently decided to stop supplying OSTF. Rowley (1992) estimates that the way is now clear for NTF (a *de jure* British Standard, BS 7567 : 1992) to become accepted and move from its current 40% of the market to near 100%.

Data exchange standards

Considering what assumptions to make about data exchange standards depends upon what data and how much data is to be exchanged with other organisations. In a business environment the point has already been made that data will need to be bought from external agencies. Data exchange can be done either in the traditional form of magnetic tape or other media being physically purchased by the data user or by electronic transfer. Electronic data transfer has traditionally been constrained by a lack of technical and organisational procedures (Calkins 1992). However, the technical constraints are rapidly being removed with the advances in network technology.

For data to be successfully exchanged there needs to be common definitions and standards for spatial data. Some very basic standards are needed. For example, the vector data model stores points, lines and polygons. These entities do not have standard definitions although efforts have been made in this direction (Moellering 1987).

The demand for more data brings with it associated costs. However, there is evidence to suggest that sharing data is very cost-effective: 'GIS operations able to share data between different organisations received benefits at least four times greater than their costs' (Schmidt *et al.* 1990). Calkins (1992) envisages that spatial data sharing could take two organisational forms:

1. A centralised data sharing operation; or
2. A distributed data sharing operation where each participating organisation retains responsibility for maintaining and controlling the data.

Whatever the organisational features are that support data sharing and exchange there are a number of issues worth resolving:

1. *Data access* will need to be limited to authorised users and somebody must have responsibility to ensure data integrity.
2. *Data documentation* needs to adequately describe the data to the potential user, including liability of the data owner and such documentation must be maintained.
3. *Cost recovery* of the data, including any support unit via direct sales or by barter.

Availability of data

Any GIS application will require data. This data is often the most expensive part of any system so it is worth considering data that is available in the public domain. Most business applications will not require topographical data which is the largest, most complex, and expensive data set. However, basic data like the road and rail network, administrative boundaries and the extent of urban areas will be essential for most applications. Business applications typically use socio- demographic data from the census and other sources.

Sources of data vary depending on the country concerned. In addition to data availability, copyright, price, and data format are important issues to consider when choosing data sets for a GIS (for a debate of these issues see Glickman 1992). The choice of data will depend on factors like the type of application, geographical area required, data formats that can be read by your software packages and the ability to link the spatial data sets to attribute data already held in business databases.

The United States Bureau of the Census makes available TIGER (Topologically Integrated Geographical Encoding and Referencing) files relating to the 1990 census (US Department of Commerce 1989). TIGER files contain the following attribute data: political and statistical geographical area codes (for example census tract) and zip codes. Spatial data includes transportation and hydrological networks. Attribute data contained in the census such as housing values, income, occupation, and population counts can be related to the geographical area codes contained in the TIGER files.

Statistics Canada make available a similar file of boundary data called CARTLIB for use with census data. In the UK the 1991 census can be linked to a geographical area boundary file called ED91. For marketing purposes the postcode is perhaps the most often used geographical area. A cross-reference file is now available called PostED. This provides for matching customer postcode records to census demographics which should result in improved target marketing (Raper *et al.* 1992).

A subclass of geographical data that has become known as *geodemographics* is concerned with the development of area typologies that can be used to discriminate consumer behaviour (Brown 1991). Data sets that fall within this subclass are essentially derived by cluster analysis of census variables.

Some commercially available data products in the UK are derived from the census, for example SuperProfiles, ACORN and MOSAIC (see Beaumont 1991 or Brown 1991 for a detailed discussion). SuperProfiles, for example, may be purchased as a data set (to be used in the company GIS) or alternatively with a market analysis package called SOLUTIONS which can be installed on a personal computer. Other software packages like INSITE may be used for retail branch planning.

Companies who are starting to explore geographical data often purchase the service of data agencies who will take their customer data together with geodemographic data and produce standard output. When the business has found sufficient benefits from this approach they will typically bring the GIS in-house so that modelling may be done on an *ad hoc* basis at any time.

Geographical Data Management

Europe

In the industrial society manufacturing was the dominant sector and capital the key strategic resource. In the emerging post-industrial society or information economy it is information which is becoming the key strategic resource. Information can be traded, exchanged, owned and manipulated by many users (Openshaw and Goddard 1987). In other words it is the commodification of information which is transforming the economic base of society (Hepworth 1986).

If these statements are taken as a workable premise then we can go on to discuss the implications for GIS. It is already evident that much geographical data is currently collected by government. Can this data become more readily available to those in the private sector?

The *Government Guidelines*, published by the Department of Trade and Industry (1986), state that the principle of charging should be what the market will bear. However, government may also charge on a marginal cost basis where they are releasing information which has not been previously exploited. The Chorley Report (DoE 1987: 78) recommended that: 'Charges for data should be at marginal cost, and only at a higher rate if the market will bear it. For some users – such as educational establishments – reduced charges will be appropriate, as will be quid pro quo arrangements in some circumstances.' The government's response (DoE 1988) was favourable to a whole range of recommendations aimed at increasing the availability of data. When the appropriate action, following the publication of the government's response to the Chorley Report, is taken the public should have access to a National Register of Title (giving details of ownership of land and property), all spatial data will be referenced to the National Grid and where it refers to properties it will contain a reference to the postcode, and all public sector bodies will be encouraged to make their data available on a commercial basis.

The government have also recognised that it is desirable to keep archives of digital mapping and key digital data sets. A number of departments have been asked to investigate the costs of establishing and maintaining these archives and the arrangements for charging access to them.

Given the potential uses of GIS by the private sector, it seems that the future shape of GIS will involve using data held in some sort of database external to the company, for example, census data or a National Title Register. This will be in addition to internally generated data sets, for example customer records that have been given a spatial reference. These data sources are likely to be held in different formats and perhaps at different geographical scales.

Table 4.1 illustrated the diverse nature of the typical data sources. Broadly, three groups of externally held data can be identified: census data, digital mapping and facilities data. The characteristics of each of these groups is shown in the table. Whilst changes in available technology are likely to affect how these data sources are used (for example, digital maps may become available relatively cheaply on optical disk) the simple fact will remain that such diverse sources of data will require integration into some kind of decision support system.

The design of an appropriate 'software engine' to allow for analysis of the data so assembled in order to provide management with appropriate decision support is a crucial task. The extent to which industry rises to this challenge of developing such a software engine will determine how quickly GIS technology will really be of benefit outside of the public agencies currently investing their time and energy.

A survey of large users' business requirements reported by Rowley (1992) showed that the greatest need (on standards) was for geographical information management. That is, a coordinated approach to provide high quality data sets. Examples of such an approach in the UK would be: *The National Street Gazetteer* developed by the Local Government Management Board, *The Computerised Street and Road Works Register* coordinated by the Department of Transport, and the *National Land and Property Gazetteer* by the Local Government Management Board.

Within the European Community a recent report recommended the setting up of an umbrella organisation for geographical information (DGXIII 1992). One of the prime functions of such a body would be to promote standards for data exchange.

North America

The market for GIS applications in business is perhaps the most advanced in the USA. One of the prime contributing reasons for this is that data is available relatively cheaply. The TIGER files referred to earlier are available broadly at the cost of distribution. The philosophy of the US government is that the taxpayer has paid for the collection and analysis of data therefore it should be available to all. One of the most marked examples of the impact of this policy is the extent to which a US street index is available in most downtown software stores in a shrink-wrapper for about $100. Various value added data agencies have taken the original TIGER files and updated and validated them before resale. The result is an external data file, with geocoding, which can be linked to internal customer files to unlock real business information.

Australasia

The most expensive part of a GIS is the data. With a GIS it is not only the cost of data capture but also the cost of data purchase, since most GIS users will purchase at least some of the data. Recent studies have also shown that the data will typically have the longest life. One user's data is another user's information. Therefore, in terms of promoting the use of geographical data sets, governmental attitudes and policies are critical.

In Australia, at the federal level, the Australian Land Information Council (ALIC) was created in 1986 to be responsible for the coordination of land information policies and activities. One of the ways in which this is done is through the national strategy which was first produced in 1988 (ALIC 1988) and subsequently revised in 1990 (ALIC 1990a). In November 1991 the name was changed to the Australia New Zealand Land Information Council (ANZLIC). The strategy covers a number of key issues with respect to data. The need for the strategy was stated as: 'In particular, it has been realised that issues such as land resource management, environmental monitoring, and economic development require land information from both the public and private sectors' (ALIC 1990b: 2). Recognising that land information impacts on all sectors of the community the strategy promotes the wider interaction of public and private sectors to ensure use and exchange of data. Critical issues here include data use, data custodianship, charging, and access to government-held land information.

One of the central planks of the land strategy is that land information is a corporate resource. This means that the data needs to be shared and therefore transferred between organisations (ANZLIC 1992a). The key concept used to translate this objective into practice is that of custodianship. All data is considered to be corporately owned by the state land information system participants and managed by the custodians. It is the custodians' responsibility to ensure data is accurate, timely, reliable and complete, in consultation with other users. The selection of a data custodian may sometimes be problematical and in recognition of this the paper suggests a number of possibilities including 'the agency which has the greatest operational need for the data item', or 'the agency which is the first to record changes to the data item' (ANZLIC 1992b).

The related concept of data owner is protected by the law of copyright. ANZLIC (1992b) recommend that a licence agreement be made between the supplier of land information and the end user for a fixed licence fee. Under such agreements the supplier is under obligation to supply data of a quality that will meet the client requirements.

A licence agreement begs the question of the level of fee. A third issues paper (ANZLIC 1992c) makes some recommendations for developing a charging policy. One of the basic key issues here is 'what product is being charged for?' Basic data products can have value added to them many times. There is a tension here between the desire of organisations to introduce land information systems with a view to reducing costs and on the other hand to view information as a commercial product. Yet information has many unique attributes, making it difficult to apply commercial pricing rules; for example, information can be sold and kept at the same time. One of the suggested bases for charging is as a reciprocal arrangement for data exchange between data custodians.

At the heart of these issues is the fundamental issue of whether information is being collected for public benefit or commercial gain. A fourth issues paper (ANZLIC 1992d) discusses the case for each of these extreme views and concludes in a non-committal way by suggesting that there is no best approach.

Whatever the source of data and however much was charged for it, the data will need to be integrated into other systems within your own organisation. To do this successfully requires the data to be transferred from vendor to user in a format that can be used. A Spatial Data Transfer Standard (SDTS) was adopted in the USA as a Federal Information Processing Standard on 29 July 1992. To encourage the adoption of this standard, to supersede Australian Standard AS 2482, in Australia and New Zealand ANZLIC have established an Australasian Spatial Data Exchange Centre (AUSDEC 1992). The remit of this group is to help users and suppliers to implement the new spatial data transfer standard.

The SDTS requires the data custodian to label the quality of the data being transferred according to five measures. These record lineage, positional accuracy, attribute accuracy, logical consistency and completeness (Clarke 1992). It is then the responsibility of the users to determine if these characteristics are suitable for the type of use for which the data is required.

Evidence for the significance of data transfer activity has been collected by a recent survey conducted by Miller (1992). This shows that 55% of current GIS users undertake frequent data transfer. In the future this is forecast to rise to 80% of respondents expecting to undertake frequent data transfers.

The federal model of Australasia may at first sight seem inappropriate to a

Europe that seems destined to safeguard subsidiarity. However, a European Directive requires that all official agencies of member states must make available all their environmental holdings of information to the general public at reasonable cost (CEC 1990).

Two specific issues arising from the Australian experience are worth consideration. Firstly, from a management point of view there is a need to define the framework for deciding on data ownership, custodianship and price. Secondly, from a technical point of view there is a need to adopt standards of data exchange that facilitate data transfer both within Europe and between Europe and the rest of the world.

The differences between ·what happens in Europe and elsewhere is not simply a matter of academic interest, it is fundamentally important in influencing the spread of GIS. As Rhind (1992) claimed, the primary determinant of different rates of take-up of GIS in different countries is the conditions on which data is available.

Returning to the theme of applicability of GIS, data is an important determinant of the spread and type of GIS. Figure 4.3 shows how the notions of data *depth* and *breadth* can be used to illustrate the applicability of GIS to different aspects of business strategy. For applications of GIS that support the operational aspects of the business, such as facilities management, detailed data is required (the data has a high degree of depth). The data sources are likely to depend on the organisation for collecting them, therefore the data breadth is said to be narrow. This places operational systems in the upper left quadrant of the diagram. Applications of GIS

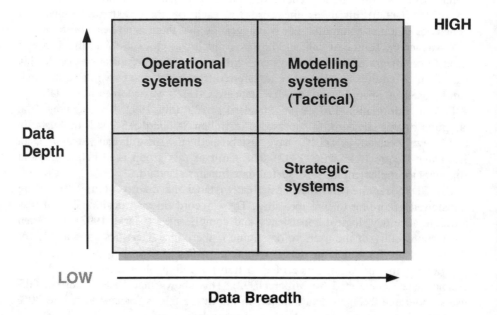

Figure 4.3 Data characteristics and GIS

that require detailed data but from a broad range of sources fall into the lower right quadrant of the diagram, labelled modelling systems. Modelling requires a wide range or breadth of data (typically from both internal and external sources). Systems to provide managers with information to run the business require a relatively narrow range or breadth of data, yet also rely on summarising the operational data. In other words the data is not 'deep'. In terms of the diagram such systems are in the upper left quadrant. Strategic systems are those that contribute to the strategic objectives of the business and require broadly based summary data.

Earlier in this chapter the availability of geographical data was considered (see Table 4.1) in terms of internal and external data sets. It may seem paradoxical that customer files are, especially in financial service organisations, not readily available. Account-based data is no substitute for customer data. However, when available the customer file is likely to be the most accurate source of information about who buys products. Geocoded segmentation data such as MOSAIC or ACORN, whilst having high availability, will have lower accuracy than internal customer files. This is an important trade-off to be aware of when using geographical data. Broadly, the value to the organisation will decline as accuracy declines, even though data may be more readily available and therefore tempting to rely on. Figure 4.4 illustrates the relationship between accuracy and data availability.

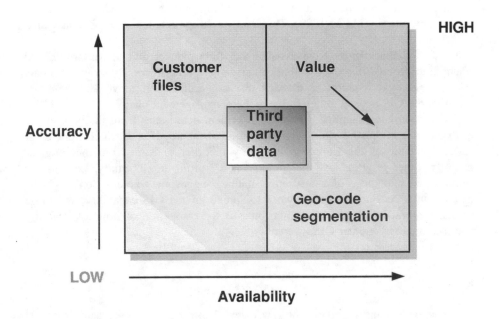

Figure 4.4 Data accuracy vs availability

Case study

A case study of one company is taken to illustrate how GIS, initially used as a tool for operational management, is now successfully part of that company's strategic planning. The case shows how the applicability of GIS within one company has changed. The reasons for this change are discussed and some general lessons are suggested. A more detailed review of this case is given in Chapter 9.

Alcoa of Australia mines bauxite in the jarrah forest of Western Australia. GIS has been used for mine planning purposes which is essentially an operational system. Recent developments of the applicability of GIS in the company have been for environmental management. Such activity, it is argued, moves GIS from an operational system into a strategic one. The role of data that is used by the company is pivotal in the success of the system.

The strategic business issue facing the company is that in order to gain licences to mine bauxite the company must satisfy the government that the environment will be protected and returned in a healthy state after mining operations. Many of the plants in the jarrah forests have developed a disease called 'dieback'. Briefly, this disease can result in the death of the jarrah by infection with a fungal root pathogen called *Phytophthora cinnamomi* (Batini 1973). Recently, mining operations have entered areas of the forest that are largely free of the disease (Elliott and Wake 1989).

Basic land information in Western Australia is available from the Integrated Land Information Programme (ILIP 1992). Data required for mine planning purposes is collected from many different locations out in the field by Alcoa. Additionally, environmental data is collected by employees of CALM who are paid for by Alcoa (CALM 1989). This data, at a very detailed level, is then shared with ILIP.

Maps of dieback areas have assisted the mine planner and the environmental scientist to provide improved dieback management procedures. By overlaying data such as geology, location of dieback disease, access, soil movements and ore location, the GIS is used to determine dieback management plans.

The section has examined a number of critical data issues from the perspective of experience in Australasia. Facing up to one of the key 'European challenges' of looking outside of the European boundary in order to learn from the progress made by other geographical 'federations' is a fruitful area of study. Lessons are summarised into those of a theoretical nature, suggesting where action might be taken within the European framework to spread greater GIS capability; and those of a more practical nature that contribute to the discussion of how applicability may be spread by greater GIS awareness.

Summary

This chapter set out to explore the raw material of all GIS, namely data. We have traced how data is transformed into information for use in a specific context within an organisation. Data represents about 80% of the cost of a GIS and replacement is on a relatively long timescale. When GIS users are asked about common problems with their systems, the most common response is the difficulty experienced in reading in different data sets.

Data is a key component of all information systems and for GIS, where typically many data sets are used, the availability of data that is accurate, timely and in a format that is readily transferable is crucial. The wider applicability of GIS will be governed by the availability of data in the two critical dimensions examined in this chapter, namely their depth and breadth.

Some important data issues have been covered, including data models, map projections, data quality, data error, data format standards and data exchange standards. These issues have all been discussed within a framework of developing a data architecture representing a sound policy framework for the organisation using GIS.

Data management policies differ throughout the world. Some of the most important issues and policy frameworks in Europe, North America and Australasia have been reviewed in an effort to distil best practice.

Further study

From a practical point of view the availability of data is something that is constantly changing, and will continue to change for the foreseeable future. The picture varies between different countries. Therefore, it is important to be aware of data sources for the areas of study. One of the best sources available is the annually updated:

1993 International Sourcebook GIS World Books Inc, Fort Collins, Colo.

From a more theoretical point of view the area of data analysis and data modelling as a stage in the development of information systems is a whole subject of study in its own right. There are many specialist books in this area. A good starting point would be:

Howe D R 1983 *Data Analysis for Data Base Design* Edward Arnold, London

Specialist books on GIS have specific chapters dealing with the particular features of spatial data, for example:
Arnoff S 1989 *Geographic Information Systems: A Management Perspective* WDL Publications, Ottawa
Masser I, Blakemore M (eds) 1991 *Handling Geographical Information: Methodology and Potential Applications* Longman Scientific & Technical, Harlow

References

ALIC (Australian Land Information Council) 1988, Land information systems – the ALIC definition, ALIC, *ALICNEWS* Newsletter of the Australian Land Information Council, 1(1): 8, Belconnen, ACT, Australia

ALIC (Australian Land Information Council) 1989 *National Strategy on Land Information Management* ALIC, Belconnen, ACT, Australia

ALIC (Australian Land Information Council) 1990a *Land Information Management in Australasia Status Report 1988–1990* ALIC, Belconnen, ACT, Australia

ALIC (Australian Land Information Council) 1990b *National Strategy on Land Information Management* ALIC, Belconnen, ACT, Australia

ALIC (Australian Land Information Council) 1990c 31 January–1 February 1990, *Report of the Second National Workshop on Natural Resources Data Management* ALIC, Adelaide, Australia

ANZLIC (Australia New Zealand Land Information Council) 1992a *Data Custodianship/Trusteeship* ALIC, Australia, Issues in Land Information Management Paper No 1, Belconnen, ACT

ANZLIC 1992b *A General Guide to Copyright, Royalties, and Data Use Agreements* ALIC, Australia, Issues in Land Information Management Paper No 2, Belconnen, ACT

ANZLIC 1992c *Charging for Land Information* ALIC, Issues in Land Information Management, Paper No 3, Belconnen, ACT, Australia

ANZLIC 1992d *Access to Government Land Information Commercialisation or Public Benefit?* ALIC, Issues in Land Information Management Paper No 4, Belconnen, ACT, Australia

AUSDEC (Australasian Spatial Data Exchange Centre) 1992 *Mapping Your Data Into Spatial Data Transfer Standard* Australasian Spatial Data Exchange Centre, Victoria, Australia, Transfer, *The Newsletter of the Spatial Data Transfer Standard Support Group* **1**(1): 2–3

Avison D E, Fitzgerald G 1989 *Information Systems Development*, Blackwell Scientific, Oxford

Batini F E 1973 *Jarrah Dieback – A Disease of the Jarrah Forest of Western Australia* Bulletin No 84, Forest Department, Perth, WA, Australia

Beaumont J R 1991 Managing information: getting to know your customers. *Mapping Awareness* **5**(1): 17–20

Brown P J B 1991 Exploring geodemographics. In Masser I, Blakemore M (eds) *Handling Geographical Information: Methodology and Potential Applications* Longman Scientific & Technical, Harlow, pp 221–58

Brusegard D 1989 Research progress in the use and value of GIS information. In Calkins H W, Osrud H J, Obermeyer N J (eds), *Use and Value of Geographical Information: Initiative 4 Specialist Meeting Summary Report and Proceedings* Technical Paper 89-7, National Center for Geographical Information and Analysis, State University of New York at Buffalo, pp 11–13

Calkins H W 1992 Institutions sharing spatial information. In Newton P W, Zwart P R, Cavill M E (eds) *Networking Spatial Information Systems* Belhaven Press, London, pp 283–92

CALM 1989 *Manual of the Forest Priority System and Developmental Prescriptions for Dieback Control in Good Quality Forest during Bauxite Mining* February, Department of Conservation and Land Management, Perth, WA, Australia

CEC 1991 *Directive on Public Access to Environmental Information*, EN 5222/90, Commission of the European Community, Brussels, Belgium

Checkland P B 1981 *Systems Thinking, Systems Practice*, John Wiley & Sons, Chichester

Chrisman N R 1983 The role of quality information in the long-term functioning of a GIS. *Proceedings of AUTOCARTO6*, Vol 2, ASPRS, Falls Church, pp 303–21

Chrisman N R 1991 The error component in spatial data. In Maguire D J, Goodchild M F, Rhind D W (eds) *Geographical Information Systems* Vol 1 *Principles* Longman Scientific & Technical, Harlow, pp 165–74

Clarke A L 1992 Spatial data standards. In Newton P W, Zwart P R, Cavill M E (eds) *Networking Spatial Information Systems* Belhaven Press, London, pp 77–87

Coote A M, Rackham L J 1992 Handling update: issues in spatial data maintenance. *Proceedings of the Conference of the Association for Geographical Information* 24–26 November, Birmingham, pp 2.30.1–9

DCDSTF 1988 The proposed standard for digital cartographic data. *The American Cartographer*, **15**: 9–140

Department of Trade and Industry 1986 *Government Held Tradable Information: Guidelines for Government Departments in Dealing with the Private Sector* Department of Trade and Industry

DGXIII 1992 EUOGI, *Report of the Committee for Investigating the Feasibility of Creating a European Umbrella Organisation* Commission of the European Communities Directorate General XIII-E2 (Information Technology), Luxembourg, 14 December

DoE (Department of the Environment) 1987 *Handling Geographical Information, Report to the Secretary of State for the Environment of the Committee of Enquiry into the Handling of Geographical Information Chaired by Lord Chorley* DoE, HMSO, May

DoE, 1988 *Handling Geographical Information: The Government's Response to the Report of the Committee of Enquiry Chaired by Lord Chorley* HMSO, February

Elliott P E, Wake G W 1990 The integration of environmental management into mine planning using a geographical information system: the Alcoa experience. Internal paper, Alcoa of Australia, Applecross, WA, Australia

Galliers R D (ed) 1987 *Information Analysis: Selected Readings* Addison-Wesley, Sydney, Australia

Glickman V 1992 Common responses to common challenges: towards a charter for the marketing of geographical information. *Proceedings of the Fourth National Conference of the Association for Geographical Information* 24–26 November, Birmingham, UK, pp 1–8

Hepworth M E 1986 The geography of technological change in the information economy. *Regional Studies* **20**: 407–24

ILIP (Integrated Land Information Programme) 1992 *State Land Information Capture Programme 1991–92* ILIP, Perth, Western Australia

Maling D H 1991 Coordinate systems and map projections for GIS. In Maguire D J, Goodchild M R, Rhind D W (eds) *Geographical Information Systems* Vol 1 *Principles* Longman Scientific &Technical, Harlow, pp 135–46

Miller D R 1992 *An Analysis of Spatial Data Transfer Activities in Australia and New Zealand* Technical Report 2, Australasian Spatial Data Exchange Centre, Victoria, Australia

Moellering H 1987 *Issues in Digital Cartographic Data Standards* Numerical Cartography, University of Ohio, Columbus, Ohio

Moloney T, Lea A C, Kowalchuk C 1993 Manufacturing and packaged goods. In *Profiting from a Geographical Information System* GIS World Books, Inc, Fort Collins, Colo, pp 105–29

Monmonier M 1991 *How to Lie with Maps* University of Chicago Press, Chicago

Openshaw S, Goddard J 1987 Some implications of the commodification of information and the emerging information economy for applied geographical analysis in the United Kingdom. *Environment and Planning A* **19**: 1423–39

Raper J F, Rhind D W, Sheppard J 1992 *Postcodes: The New Geography* Longman Scientific & Technical, Harlow

Rhind D W 1992 Data access, charging and copyright and their implications for geographical information systems. *International Journal of Geographical Information Systems* **6**(1): 13–30

Rowley J 1992 A strategy for geographical information standards. *Proceedings of the Conference of the Association for Geographical Information.* 24–26 November, Birmingham, pp 2.21.1–7

Schmidt A, Huxhold W, Calkins H (eds) 1990 *Urban GIS/Data Sharing Guidebook* National Computer Graphics Association and Urban and Regional Information Systems Association, Washington

Scott-Morton M S 1991 *The Corporation of the 1990's: The Transformation of the Organisation by Information Technology* Oxford University Press, New York

US Department of Commerce 1989 *TIGER Update* 2, October

Vonderohe A P, Chrisman N R 1985 Tests to establish the quality of digital cartographic data: some examples from the Dane County land records project. *Proceedings of AUTOCARTO7* American Society for Photogrammetry and Remote Sensing, Falls Church, pp 552–9

White M 1984 Technical requirements and standards for a multipurpose geographical data system. *The American Cartographer* **11**: 15–26

Part Two

The Organisational Challenge

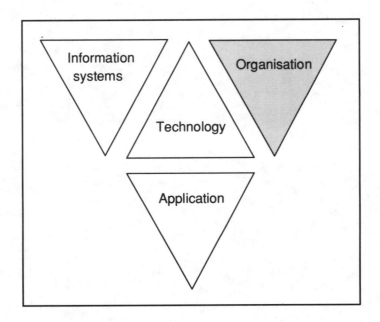

5

GIS for decision support

'. . . you can't put a value on information, on its own it's worthless. Its only value is the use people make of it'

Kit Grindley (1991)

Preamble

Part One has been concerned with establishing what a GIS is, how to incorporate GIS into the information management strategy, and the nature of geographical information. We now turn to the crucial issues around the challenge to the organisation. Information systems generally rarely fail because of technological factors, rather they fail for organisational reasons (Grimshaw 1988b). In the many conferences, academic papers and books on GIS there is currently a dearth of discussion on the organisational issues. Yet the institutional and organisational aspects ultimately determine the value of the technological (Wellar 1993a).

As Kit Grindley (1991) in the quotation above aptly points out, information is only of value to the people who make use of it. Why do some people ignore information? What makes managers ask for the wrong information? Why are policies decided without knowledge of the full facts? This chapter will focus on the role of information in the organisation, particularly in the decision-making process. Spatial and attribute data is collected both inside (internally) and outside (externally) the organisation (as was discussed in Chapter 4). Turning that data into useful information was explained in Chapter 4 as adding meaning to the data. Such meaning depends upon the *context* or decision for which the data is required. All decisions take place within an organisational context.

The subject of information – what is it? etc. – has been covered by Chapter 4. The perspective here is to focus on whether different 'information systems', 'technology' or 'applications' are required to deliver information to different levels or people in the organisation.

The role of information in the decision-making process

For meaning to be attached to data the data has to be understood in the context of decision making. One of the best ways of explaining this idea further is to see what might happen if data is taken in an inappropriate context, or 'out of context'. The following extract from *The Return of Heroic Failures*, by Stephen Pile (1988: 94–5), makes the point in a succinct way.

'The most important book review in our field was penned by Mr Ed Zern of *Field and Stream*. In the 1950s he told his editor that the countryside magazine would benefit from a books department.

Impressed by this idea, the editor commissioned him to select a good outdoor book and review it. Missing the point with a wholeheartedness that boarders on genius, Mr. Zern chose *Lady Chatterley's Lover* which, unknown to him had been banned throughout the Commonwealth and tried for obscenity because of the unending scenes of outdoor carnality involving the gamekeeper and his employer's wife.

Mr Zern's review:

Although written many years ago, *Lady Chatterley's Lover* has just been reissued by Grove Press, and this fictional account of the day to day life of an English gamekeeper is still of considerable interest to outdoor-minded readers, as it contains many passages on pheasant-raising, the apprehending of poachers, ways to control vermin, and other chores and duties of the professional gamekeeper. Unfortunately, one is obliged to wade through many pages of extraneous material in order to discover and savour these sidelights on the management of a Midland shooting estate, and in this reviewer's opinion this book cannot take the place of J.R. Miller's *Practical Gamekeeping*.'

Hopefully few people made decisions on the basis of information in this book review.

Managers and others responsible for making decisions clamour for information. For the politician the absence of information is often given as reason for delaying the decision or for making the 'wrong' decision (Wellar 1990). It is all too easy for lack of information to be the political 'fall guy'. Unfortunately IT is often seen as the way to get information to decision makers – it can also be the fastest way of getting irrelevant, untimely, inaccurate information, leading to information indigestion. The solution is easily stated but less easily implemented. Improved decisions require improved information which in turn depends upon defining information requirements. This depends on the information user knowing what they need and being able to communicate that need to the analyst developing the information system.

The predominant assumption has been that making geographical information available to decision makers will improve the decision-making process. Calkins (1989) questions this assumption and calls for a study of the use, costs and benefits of geographic information. The use of geographic information in relation to the decision making process will be examined in this chapter. The issue of costs and benefits is left until Chapter 6 to explore.

Friend and Jessop (1969) took an operational research approach to the study of the process of decision making. They observed that in any situation where it was difficult to choose between alternative policies there would be demands for further forms of exploratory activity. These could be analysed into three distinct classes which were related to the perception of different sources of uncertainty. Figure 5.1

illustrates that the call for 'more investigative research' is because of a high level of uncertainty about the operating environment. The results of the research would typically be fed to the manager in the form of more information.

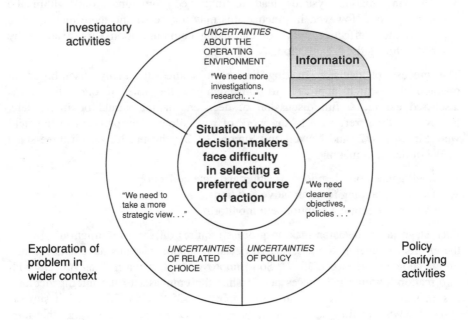

Figure 5.1 The role of information within the framework of decision making (*Source*: adapted from Bardon *et al.* 1986)

One of the very basic assumptions of information systems is that more information leads to better decisions. This assumption has been questioned many times in the academic literature, for example by Ackoff (1967). In his classic paper, Ackoff (1967) argued that the traditional approach to the development of information systems contained some fallacious assumptions. In particular, five assumptions were questioned:

1. That more information leads to better decisions. Unfortunately, in practice managers often suffer from information overload or too much irrelevant information.
2. That managers need the information they want. In practice managers will typically suggest a long 'wish list' of information wanted but this is rather different from the information needed to run the business.
3. That managers are able to model the decision they wish to make. In practice there is seldom a clear model available where all the relevant variables and their relationship to other variables are properly understood.

4. That managers do not need to understand the information system. However, if a manager does not understand the information system it will be difficult to control and monitor the use of that system. In practice the full participation of the manager is required in the development of any information system to ensure that the organisation gains the appropriate benefits.
5. That information systems lead to improved communications within the organisation. However, in practice this may not be so and there may well be other, more effective, ways of enhancing communications, for example by restructuring the organisation.

The process of decision making has been studied by many disciplines: an operational research approach to understanding the role of uncertainty was discussed earlier. A full discussion of decision making would be incomplete, however, without reference to the work of psychology. The pioneers in the field were Simon (1972) and Newell and Simon (1972) who put forward a three-stage model of decision making:

1. Intelligence: problem identification and data collection.
2. Design: planning for alternative solutions.
3. Choice: selecting a solution and monitoring.

Each stage in the decision-making process requires different information. Most of the efforts to develop computer-based decision support systems have concentrated on the choice stage (Keen 1977). So to improve the decision-making process with information systems it is necessary to shift the emphasis to the intelligence and design stages. In terms of using geographical DSS (or spatial decision support systems, SDSS, as they have come to be known) Densham (1989) argues that they must be iterative, integrative and participative. These issues will be returned to in Chapter 7 in the discussion about implementation.

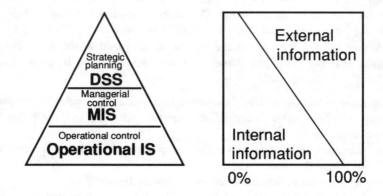

Figure 5.2   Types of decision (*Source*: adapted from Nichols 1987)

For the moment, let us take the traditional assumption as given and proceed to examine the types of decision in order to see if there is any relationship between the type of decision and the characteristics of information required. Some of the earliest and most widely regarded work in the management science field was undertaken by Anthony (1965) who proposed a triangle of decision types as shown in Figure 5.2. The types of decision can be explained as follows:

1. *Strategic planning*. Concerned with developing objectives and allocating resources, for example the decision to develop a new product. Such decisions are most typically made by high-level managers in the hierarchy of the organisation.
2. *Managerial control*. Concerned with the use of resources in the organisation, for example investigating the reasons for the difference between actual and budget cost. These decisions are most frequently made by middle-level managers.
3. *Operational control*. Concerned with the day-to-day operations of the business, for example the control of the day's production in a manufacturing plant. These decisions are typically made by lower-level managers.

So, different levels of managers in an organisation would typically be making different levels of decisions. How does this affect the kind of information that is required by them?

Characteristics	Operational control	Managerial control	Strategic planning
General:			
Time frame	Historical	⟶	Predictive
Expectation	Anticipated	⟶	Surprise
Source	Largely internal	⟶	External
Scope	Detailed	⟶	Summary
Frequency	Real time	⟶	Periodic
Organisation	Highly structured	⟶	Loose
Accuracy	Highly accurate	⟶	Tolerable
Spatial:			
Resolution	High	⟶	Low
Relationship	Spaghetti	⟶	Topological

Figure 5.3 Information characteristics and types of decision (*Source*: adapted from Keen and Scott-Morton 1978 p 82)

From Figure 5.3 it should be clear that operational decisions require much more detailed, accurate, structured and internally generated data. At the other end of the spectrum, strategic decisions require summary, tolerably accurate, data from both inside and outside of the organisation. Spatial data needs to have clearly defined spatial relationships to be used successfully in the kinds of spatial analysis undertaken by strategic planners. Given these different data requirements to meet the decision-making characteristics of different managers, we can expect that the technology and information systems required to deliver such different systems might be different.

The organisational support required will vary for different types of decisions. Bringing IT into an organisation to support decision making will serve to threaten existing power bases and build new power bases for others. Technology can serve the power interests (Child 1985) of users and anlaysts in their role of implementing change. Chapter 7 will discuss the implementation issues further. Chapter 2 provided some discussion about the organisational issues relating to the *timescale* dimension of the taxonomy of information systems.

Application of the information systems framework

How does all this discussion about decision making relate to types of information system? In Chapter 2 a taxonomy of information systems was introduced which was designed to further and assist the discussion of classifying information systems by proposing a three-dimensional framework. The task dimension is the one that essentially relates to the decision to be made. So the discussion so far in this chapter should serve to amplify your understanding of the task dimension. By way of example, the following classic types of information system (management information systems, decision support systems, expert systems and executive information systems) are discussed in relation to the taxonomy, decision making and GIS.

Management information systems (MIS)

This is one of the oldest terms in common usage within the subject area. There is generally no commonly agreed and universally adopted definition. The following quotations will give you an idea of the confusion surrounding MIS:

'. . . a prime example of a content-free expression. It means different things to different people.' (Keen and Scott-Morton 1978).

'A management information system has:
– an information focus aimed at middle managers;
– structured information flows;
– integrated data processing jobs by business function; and
– an inquiry and report generation facility means different things to different people.'
(Keen and Scott-Morton 1978).

Managers were promised MIS in the 1970s and generally they were oversold. The systems then failed to deliver the expected benefits. In conception the MIS was to be a comprehensive and integrated information system to provide managers with information covering the whole range of business functions. However, the technology of the time was not able to deliver such systems. Also, good operational systems need to be in place serving the day-to-day operational needs of the organisation before the managerial requirements can be met.

In terms of our taxonomy, the MIS is generally aimed at middle managers, with semi-structured decisions. The organisation needs some maturity in terms of the *time* dimension – probably somewhere at or beyond the 'linking' stage. However, the technology required to deliver such systems depends on the organisational structure, and it is likely to require computers with adequate communications to all departments and have good database management systems in place.

According to a well-known market analyst (Hale 1993) GIS may become embedded in existing applications and so be seen as simply part of the MIS. Such a view was echoed by Maguire *et al.* (1991) (see Chapter 1). Progression to this state of affairs is likely when data is regarded as a corporate resource and its utility for solving real business needs is embodied in the information strategy and clearly related to the business strategy.

Decision support systems (DSS)

'A decision support system (DSS) is a computer based system that helps the decision maker utilise data and models to solve unstructured problems.' (Sprague and Carlson 1982). The key characteristics of DSS are:

1. Incorporate both data and models;
2. Designed to assist managers in semi-structured or unstructured tasks;
3. Support rather than replace management judgement;
4. The objective of a DSS is to improve the efficiency with which decisions are made.

In terms of the taxonomy a DSS is aimed at senior managers with unstructured, strategic decisions. The organisation may either be very mature and, for example, rely on extracting data from a number of operational systems, or it may be at the *ad hoc* stage where DSS are developed by end users without recourse to the information systems strategy.

In so far as many GIS have been designed as DSS they often fail for two reasons according to Densham (1989). Insufficient attention is given to the process and context in which decisions are made, and secondly many GIS do not support the analytical and statistical modelling required by many decision makers. Many of the modelling approaches are complex (see the Further Study section at the end of the chapter) and, like statistical techniques, offer the user ample scope for misapplication. According to Densham (1991) the embodiment of knowledge about the selection of appropriate models is an area of application of expert systems to the GIS world.

Expert systems

A definition of an expert system was given in Chapter 1. The key characteristics of an expert system are:

1. The capture of expertise from one or more experts;
2. To give an explanation of how solutions are arrived at;
3. Solve problems by providing answers rather than data;
4. Use expertise to solve complex problems by inference.

Example of an expert system

Recently a well-respected professor from Warwick Business School had just finished an arduous lecture course in Lisbon. He had a couple of hours to spare before the flight back and happened to find a rare manuscript in a bookshop in the old town. Fortunately, the shop accepted his American Express card. The point-of-sale terminal read the transaction into the European computer centre in Brighton, England. However, the transaction was exceptionally large for the normally cautious professor to spend, therefore, it was referred to the human authoriser at Fort Lauderdale in the USA.

The authoriser has 70 seconds in which to make a 'creditworthy' decision. Information that would help in this decision was traditionally kept in 13 different databases and the 'rules' were in a manual of 4 inches thickness. American Express decided that these rules, derived from statistics about purchases and purchasers, could be coded into an expert system.

The 'authoriser's assistant' is an expert system which is used by the human authorisers to give them advice, for example, 'credit on this transaction is recommended'. Explanations of the expert system reasoning are available to the authorisers if they wish.

In terms of the taxonomy an expert system is aimed at supporting decision making by experts. These experts do not necessarily have to be senior managers. The organisation is likely to be a fairly mature one in terms of the use of IT because expert systems are quite difficult to develop and require access to much existing information probably contained in company databases. The technology required involves powerful computers, systems development tools and access to databases.

How are expert systems used in GIS? Essentially expert systems provide a way of embodying knowledge in the system. In traditional expert systems the domain of knowledge has related to an area of expertise in relatively short supply, such as medical diagnostics. In relation to GIS, Smith and Je Yiang (1991) argue that a knowledge-based approach can be applied to acquisition, storage, access, analysis and processing, and user interfaces.

Executive information systems (EIS)

A definition of an EIS was given in Chapter 1. The key characteristics of an EIS are:

1. Easy access to external information;
2. Deal with unstructured strategic decisions;
3. Linked to the key variables identified as critical success factors by the business mission.

Example of an executive information system

Boots the Chemists PLC are the largest EIS user in the UK. As a major user of electronic point of sale (EPOS) Boots needed some way of analysing and reporting on the vast amount of data. Within Boots the Chemists there are seven business centres, and they need to monitor merchandise in terms of sales, stocks, returns and profit margins. The reporting systems available on the mainframe computers became slow because of the heavy demand on Monday mornings for access to last week's figures.

A review of the IT strategy in 1989 led to a decision to move towards distributed computing. A simpler reporting system for the business centres was required because one of the managers had observed that, 'I pay my staff to make decisions, not to analyse data.'

A performance reporting system (PRS) was developed so that users could 'drill down' from a business centre performance to individual products and generate graphs which highlight anything unusual. For example, following a period of sunny weather the increase in sun product sales can be quantified. Further information might then reveal that the profit margins are reducing because people are buying cheap sun oil products for home use and luxury lines to take on holiday. The managing director and the merchandise director both have the PRS on their desks. Summarised data is downloaded on a Sunday night to the local area network supporting the executive workstation.

In terms of the taxonomy the EIS is aimed at the most senior managers – the executives. The tasks are essentially strategic and unstructured. The organisation needs to be very mature in order to develop EIS successfully. There should be a good infrastructure of existing information systems. The technology is likely to be a sophisticated, powerful workstation providing speedy access to information with a graphical user interface.

Many EIS products on the market use maps as a form of display output. This represents a limited use of GIS, maps are being used much as any other business graphic might be used. The real power of GIS for executives is likely to be unleashed when the user-friendly interfaces, common on EIS, are used to access GIS.

Application of GIS to decision making

Geographical information systems (GIS) have traditionally been applied in the public sector and the utilities. These 'first-wave' applications supported operational requirements. Development of applications in the private sector to support decision makers has been held up by a number of factors like the lack of tradable data from government sources. In the short run the gap in the market has been filled by data service agencies offering geodemographic data analysis (see Chapter 3). Within the marketing function of organisations operating in the private sector, however, substantial amounts of data with a geographical dimension are captured and are being generated. Taking retail store location planning as one application in marketing decision making, the next section argues that the time is now ripe for 'second-wave' GIS to become a practical reality. The main characteristic of these DSS is their integrative nature. The marketing decision maker can enhance existing internal marketing information by integrating external data sources, utilising geodemographic data and by displaying the outcome via a GIS environment. The chapter concludes by suggesting that marketing managers might be asking for a marriage between DSS (or even EIS) and GIS as we know it. Information systems managers would do well to ensure that any such marriage is consummated with the blessing of an information management strategy as outlined in the previous chapter.

GIS as decision support: the case of support for marketing

The applications of information systems in the marketing field has been changing rapidly due to GIS's suitability to support marketing decision making (Grimshaw and Maier 1991). Despite recent activity in this area, most of the examples of applications come from the consumer market rather than the area of business-to-business marketing (Grimshaw 1993).

Marketing decisions and their outcomes very often have a geographical dimension. For example, sales performance is measured by geographic region, the design of sales territories and the subsequent allocation of salespeople is often based on geographical grounds, retail store location planning is fundamentally linked to geography.

In the light of advances in technology it is no surprise that researchers in information systems conclude that not since the heady days of the search for comprehensive management information systems had there been such optimism that there might be an 'information systems' solution to a range of management problems. As with other areas of decision support, much of the early focus was on the technology. It is now time for researchers in marketing to shift that focus to the organisational issues in the application areas of GIS.

As we move forward, in the 1990s, we would do well to remember that most application areas of information systems have had their 'time'. For example, in the 1960s and 1970s there was a ground swell of interest in the idea of 'management information systems' (Head 1967). Many of the organisational issues that emerged in the 1970s and 1980s are relevant for GIS in the 1990s; particularly the need to ensure accurate data, monitoring the use made of data, and building a strong central support team (Grimshaw 1988a). In particular the evolving role of GIS has to be seen in the light of the evolving developments from transaction processing via MIS and DSS to executive support systems and from there to work group support systems and expert support systems (Senn 1990).

Table 5.1   A comparison of MIS, DSS and EIS

	MIS	DSS	EIS
Focus	Standard reports Functionally based	Analysis, decision support Modelling	Status access Integration from functions
Decision support capability	Direct/indirect support for structured routine problems	*Ad hoc*, semi-structured or unstructured decisions	Indirect support for high-level and unstructured decisions
Treatment of information	Provided to a diverse group of users who abstract information	Input from MIS What if?	Filters and compresses information, tracks critical data and information
Use	Tactical planning and control	Planning, organising, staffing, control	Strategic planning
Source of data	Internal, company data from operational systems Some historical data	Increasing % of external data	Many sources
Justification	Efficiency	Effectiveness	Transformation

Source: Grimshaw and Maier (1991), adapted from Turban and Schaeffer (1989).

Table 5.1 illustrates the development from MIS to EIS. For EIS it is apparent that the emphasis has been moved from an operational level to a more strategic application of the 'system'. This is also reflected in the level of user involved. In this chapter we are arguing that the developments related to GIS are following a similar pattern.

Table 5.2 Developments of GIS

	GIS 1st wave	MGIS 2nd wave	? 3rd wave
Focus	Geographical information Technology	Analysis, decision support Modelling	??
Decision support capability	Direct or indirect support for structured routine problems	Direct or indirect support for semi- and un- structured decisions	
Treatment of information	Provided to diverse group of users who abstract information	From MIS and EIS related to GIS What if?	
Use	Operational tracking, control	Planning, staffing, organising, control	
Source of data	Internal MIS Ordnance Survey	Market research data MIS Ordnance Survey	

Source: Grimshaw and Maier (1991), adapted from Turban and Schaeffer (1989).

Typically the 'first-wave' GIS (Table 5.2) is characterised by being an operational support system. For example, British Gas have a GIS which documents their pipelines (location, depth, size, maintenance record, etc.) in order to improve the operational performance of the organisation (see Chapter 9 for a discussion of this case). In the USA reported applications of GIS have included the planning of hazardous waste sites (Foresman 1986; Jensen and Christensen 1986) and other municipal applications (Star and Estes 1990).

Most systems of this type would be justified on the basis of helping to improve productivity. Generally, the information held on these systems will come from the operations themselves, that is, information internal to the organisation (Grimshaw 1989). Thus this stage of the development would be similar to the stage MIS identified at the IS development stage (cf. Table 5.1).

Higher levels of managers are unlikely to benefit from such information systems. Studies of the stages of growth (see Chapter 3) have shown that the characteristics of later information systems differ from those first developed. Information systems become important for the strategic decision makers in the organisation. Justification of such systems tend to be couched in terms of improving the competitive advantage or transforming the business rather than simply being concerned with efficiency and effectiveness.

The 'second-wave' applications of GIS will differ from those of the 'first wave' by being integrated into the corporate information plan. The emphasis moves away from a fascination with the 'new' technology towards the organisational issues that arise when a new information system is being designed and implemented. More importantly, as the example has illustrated, very effective use can be made of internal data in conjunction with commercially available external data (Healey 1988).

The focus of these 'second-wave' GIS will be much more on decision support, lifting the level of application one step up from the operational applications seen in the 'first wave' (Angehrn and Luethi 1990).

Marketing as a business function seems to be a very strong candidate for early implementations of GIS due to the manager's experience in analysing business problems along geographic dimensions. Moreover, managers working in this function are used to spending money on market research information. This makes them less dependable on utilising publicly available data (Davies 1985). On the other hand, a GIS offers opportunities to utilise external and internal data more effectively by adding display facilities on a geographical basis.

Many activities within the marketing function have a geographic dimension, for example the geographical spread of sales, the location of potential customers, and the question of how the company can organise itself to cater for the geographically dispersed demand. Consequently, marketing managers tend to be very interested in analysing marketing information along a geographical dimension (Beaumont 1989).

Those applications that have been documented are *ad hoc* type systems (DoE 1987). The Chorley Report documents a case of a retail store location study in the Oxford area where a microcomputer-based model was developed to provide retail management with 'what if' simulations of store location. The basic input to the model was a survey of household shopping patterns, weighted by social class and summarised at postal district level. On the supply side, existing supermarkets were referenced by postcode and national grid reference. The net floorspace of each supermarket and its distance to the centre of each postal district was also fed into the model. For a more detailed discussion of some specific case studies in the retail sector see Chapters 9 and 10.

The above examples of the use of geographical information in the private sector rely on a mix of internally generated information like customer records and externally held data like the Census of Population. Use of some amounts of data held by public bodies is likely to be always a feature of GIS applied to the private sector. Where is this data held and how can companies gain access to it?

National statistics in the UK have been subject to a number of cutbacks in recent years; for example, the Census of Distribution is no longer published. Despite this, a considerable amount of information is still available from a variety of private and public sources and the problem, as yet, is more one of data compatibility, rather than availability.

In response to government cutbacks and the problems of data acquisition and compatibility, several commercial agencies have computer-based census data which has then been linked to other market research statistics, in order to produce new and quite powerful GIS. This has allowed marketers to utilise much more proactively geodemographic data (see for example, Market Research Society, 1989, Special Issue on Geodemographics).

Geographic information has been an important part of marketing DSS as the above examples show. However, the supply of geographic information is a necessary but not a sufficient condition for the successful development of a GIS.

From the point of view of a marketing manager, there are currently three options available for making use of geographic information:

1. *Geographic output from models.* In this option the current models used, for example, for retail store location planning (Johnson 1989), have a facility attached to enable output in map form. Here the map is rather like a pie chart or histogram: a method of displaying results from modelling. This is a one-way process, in the sense that 'what if?' questions cannot be asked from the map and fed back to the modelling process.

2. *Use data agencies.* There are three leading agencies in the UK: CACI Market Analysis, CCN Systems and Pinpoint Analysis (Ardill 1988). These agencies offer a range of data services. The major GIS offered are ACORN, MOSAIC and PIN. ACORN (Humby 1989) is a classification of residential neighbourhoods using 11 housing groups and 38 socio-demographic types. According to a recent MORI survey of marketing directors in blue chip companies it is the most widely used of the systems currently available. MOSAIC (Webber 1989) is a database containing demographic, housing, financial and census data. The Pinpoint system (Sleight and Leventhal 1989) is based on a digitised postal district system; profiles of census, wealth and financial data are available.

3. *Integrated GIS.* On the basis that information is a corporate resource, there is an argument for investigating the information requirements of the organisation as a whole. This would mean developing an information management strategy. The process of developing such a strategy would be firmly linked to the corporate strategy of the organisation. Many methodologies exist for helping with this process (see Chapter 3 for a discussion of this topic).

A framework for an MGIS

A framework for a marketing geographical information system (MGIS) is displayed in Figure 5.4. This framework demonstrates how the MGIS is receiving data input from two internal and three external sources. The internal sources

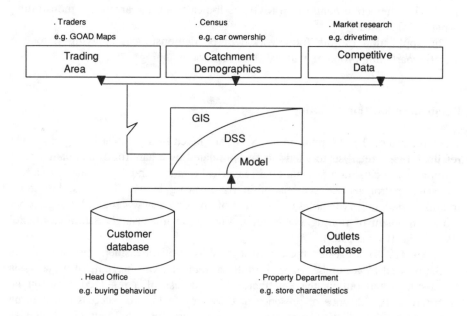

. Traders
e.g. GOAD Maps

. Census
e.g. car ownership

. Market research
e.g. drivetime

Trading Area

Catchment Demographics

Competitive Data

GIS

DSS

Model

Customer database

Outlets database

. Head Office
e.g. buying behaviour

. Property Department
e.g. store characteristics

Figure 5.4 A framework for a MGIS (*Source*: adapted from Grimshaw and Maier 1991)

consist of data on current customers such as addresses and data on their buying behaviour. The internal sources also supply data on the company's operations such as number of employees in a region/outlet, sales turnover, etc.

The external data sources supply data on the market environment, potential customers and the competition. The data on the environment covers aspects such as the trading environment in which the company chooses to operate. For example, data on the composition of industry structures (Standard Industrial Classification (SIC) codes) in the region. Data on potential customers in turn can contain data on the catchment demographic which include data on demographic profiles such as social class, car ownership, etc. Competitive data provides information on competitors' performance as well as on their organisation. Quite often the data held on competitors is very patchy and often widely dispersed. The inclusion of competitive data as an external source reflects the often substantial efforts required in compiling publicly available data on competitors and to join those to the data internally available.

At the heart of the MGIS one will find elements traditionally included in a marketing DSS (Little 1979). However, of crucial importance here are models utilising the data to identify structures and patterns in the data allowing improved decision making.

Important in the context of a MGIS are the facilities associated with a GIS, namely the ability to display the information geographically, utilising digitised maps. The interactive nature of a MGIS is indicated by the arrows, demonstrating 'what if?' facilities.

The application of this framework will be demonstrated, applying it to one specific marketing problem, namely store location planning.

Retail store location planning

The structure of the UK retail industry is very much biased towards large multiple retailers. Many retail sectors tend to be dominated by a handful of companies each owning or franchising a few hundred (electrical retailers and dry cleaners) to a few thousand (petrol service stations or in the brewing industry) outlets. For those multiple retailers it is thus less a question of entering a new geographic region but more a problem of finding viable retail sites in an increasingly saturated market (Penny and Broom 1989).

Simkin (1989) suggested the use of a store location assessment model which is currently used by a number of such multiple retailers. On the basis of an analysis of existing retail outlets the key factors for success of a retail concept can be determined. The absence or presence of these key factors for success can then be in turn used for predictive purposes when assessing a potential new site. Likewise the outlet's performance can be gauged against the predictions of the model, allowing the detection of reasons for a particular performance (Simkin 1990).

Simkin's model, however, presents its findings mainly in numerical form although the implementation on a spreadsheet allows for some 'what if' analyses. However, the application of that model within the framework of a GIS offers interesting insights into how the model's utility to marketing managers can be enhanced significantly. The framework provided by his work is providing an important insight into what data is required in the context of marketing strategy. Thus, this approach assures that the application is driving the design of the MGIS and not the other way round.

The components of a GIS for store location planning

Following Simkin's model the components of the GIS comprise mapping facilities, catchment demographics, outlet accessibility, competition, trading area composition and outlet characteristics. Each of these components will be discussed in turn.

Mapping facilities

The backbone of a GIS is obviously its ability to display the relevant maps to the case under examination. The geographical information should be significantly enhanced by overlaying the structure of the road network. In today's retail environment accessibility by car seems to be an integral part of a company's success.

Catchment demographics

Depending on the outlet's target segment, the absence or presence of individuals fulfilling the required criteria is an important factor when assessing potential turnover in a particular location. External databases such as ACORN or MOSAIC provide very detailed profiles on individuals living within certain postal districts. Enhanced by the UK's postcode system, which allows as the smallest unit for a population of no more than 20 households, this demographic information seems to be very accurate indeed.

Store accessibility

The demographic information can be significantly enhanced when taking into account not only the distance from a particular location to the target segments but also, more importantly, the drive times. Data on drive times is now commercially available between any two postcodes in the UK. The algorithms take into account the various average speeds feasible on the various types of roads. Even the snail's pace speed on the M25, London's orbital motorway, has been considered appropriately!

Other data considered under this heading includes information on pedestrianisation, pedestrian traffic passing the store, as well as accessibility by rail and other means of public transport.

Competition

Information on the competition is vital when assessing the potential of a site. Obviously, a competitor can have a negative effect on the business available to the company. However, quite often a positive effect can be observed when a competitor acts as a benchmark for customer comparison or offers the critical mass desired by customers. The latter can often be observed for antique shops, for which only the presence of a number of competitors creates the necessary weight to 'pull' customers into the area. Consequently aspects such as the kind of competition, their number, distances to them, size of outlet and number of personnel employed need to be considered.

Trading area composition

The general trend towards shopping centres needs to be considered in this section. What are the specific features which attract customers to the trading area, i.e. key traders such as large department stores, post offices, amenities such as cinemas, theatres, etc.? These aspects require attention when assessing the 'pull' capability of a trading area.

Outlet characteristics

The physical attributes of the outlet need to be included, such as the number of employees, the size of the store, its frontage, time lapsed since last refurbishment, etc.

On the basis of the data taken into account it is then comprehensively possible to statistically determine the key factors for success for a particular retail concept. Based on the key factors for success, the model can then be used for predictive purposes or performance assessment. The major benefit added within the context of GIS is the ability to display information related to maps rather than just allowing for numerical 'what if' applications of data in the context of a spreadsheet. The benefits of utilising the model within the context of a GIS are significant.

Graphical display of results will offer benefits in terms of comprehending the model's predictions (Jarvenpaa and Dickson 1988). However, it is worth arguing that a number of additional benefits can be observed. By going through the process described above it is possible to establish a very powerful database for the company. The GIS then offers the facilities to display the locations of not only the company's outlets but also those of the competition. More often than not this type of analysis will have been done for the first time by a company. The quality of analysis and subsequent decision making can also be enhanced when the demographic information on customers is related to this competitive situation in a geographical context.

It is worth noting, however, that the maps within the context of an MGIS do not have to be very detailed. Information on the region's topography can remain very limited; much more important is the opportunity to include the road network allowing an assessment of store accessibility. This is an interesting contrast to the desires of geographers who focus much of their attention to improving the mapping facilities within a GIS. Making maps more accurate will not offer any substantial incremental benefits to the marketing decision maker.

The benefits to marketing managers are so obvious that the authors observed a strong tendency in a number of companies for marketing managers to develop GIS-based systems themselves, often leaving traditional systems departments with very little involvement. This observation might function as a warning to systems oriented individuals that the 'second-wave' GIS movement has already begun, but driven by an application orientation.

The case of marketing has illustrated that the time of 'first-wave' GIS applications is over and that the 'second- wave' GIS will have to be driven much more by applications than technology. In particular for business applications this change in focus is essential. Marketing is used as an example for an important area of GIS applications. Sales force planning and retail outlet location planning are prime examples for the utilisation of GIS.

The example of retail location planning is used to illustrate the enormous potential for utilising internal and external data. Since marketing oriented companies are used to spending significant sums on market research data the availability of government-based data is not crucial. Moreover, a GIS is offering an environment allowing better utilisation of data which in most cases would have been bought in any case.

On the other hand it can be expected that not only better use of existing data will be made but by allowing the analysis of 'what if?' scenarios the decision maker will require additional data. In particular it is expected that more data on the competition will be required due to the ability of MGIS to display the geographical presence of competitors. Thus, the decision makers are expected to improve the data on important marketing-related issues and will be in a position to utilise this data comprehensively. Thus, decision makers are expected to gain a better understanding of their competitive position in the market place and to subsequently to improve their ability to develop competitive marketing strategies.

This development towards an integrated GIS, however, should not be seen in isolation from other developments in the information systems area. Numerous companies these days have joined the bandwagon in developing EIS. The 'third wave' of GIS may, we can speculate, follow the characteristics of the EIS (as demonstrated in Tables 5.1 and 5.2). In particular, in terms of marketing decision making, multiple dimensional analysis is an important feature here. These EIS offer managers opportunities to aggregate and disaggregate data along a number of dimensions such as by product, by customer type and by geographical region. Usually EIS are unable to display the information on the basis of maps. Users such as marketing managers might be asking exactly for that: a marriage between EIS and GIS as we know it. Information systems managers would do well to ensure that any such marriage is consummated within the 'church' of an information management strategy.

Summary

A useful way of summarising many of the points made in this chapter is to start by considering the factors leading to successful GIS. It was stressed, early in the chapter, that generally information systems fail for organisational rather than technical reasons; GIS are no exception to this. As with all information systems, GIS must be founded upon justifiable business reasons expressed in the information management strategy (see Chapter 3). Even more fundamentally the organisation must give a great deal of thought to exploring the kinds of decision-making activities where GIS can be of help.

Making business decisions is at the heart of any business. Choosing which decisions can be helped by geographic information is a fundamental step. Clearly this varies with the kind of business and the business environment that is being operated in. All firms will differ in their answers to these questions. In all organisations, to be successful, the GIS must be part of the organisation or as Wellar (1993a) put it, 'to be fully effective a GIS is *of* the corporation, not just *in* it'.

Figure 5.5 shows an approach to relating GIS to decision-making activities. Wellar (1989) used a similar diagram to suggest that about 90% of 'informational

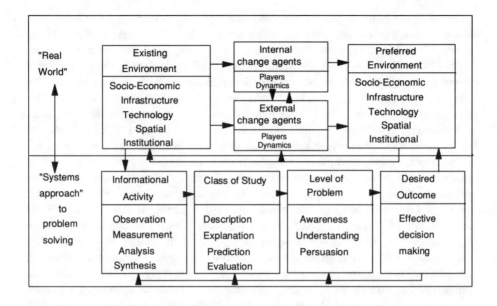

Figure 5.5 GIS as DSS (*Source*: adapted from Wellar 1993b)

activity' has been at the observational, measurement, classification level and only about 9% has been analysis. In terms of class of study Wellar is even more pessimistic in commenting that 99% of the research effort has been allocated to description.

The first step to understanding the role that GIS can play in your business is to understand the decision-making activity that goes on in the business. From that analysis, the information requirements are derived. This process must not be seen simply as a way of using the computer to assist in the choice part of the decision process, rather it should become an iterative and integrated part of the organisation as a whole.

Making such aims achievable depends not only on understanding the decision-making activities (this chapter) but also understanding the role that geographic information can play in the wider information management strategy (Chapter 3) and being able to combine these understandings in a sound business case for investment (Chapter 6).

The traditional assumption that more information leads to better decision making was questioned at the start of this chapter. Without knowing the business strategy, the policy objectives and the decision model, information is likely to lead to overload. Asking a manager what information is required to make a given decision is fraught with difficulties. Either the manager will turn the question round and tell the analyst that he is supposed to be the expert on information, or the manager will simply overestimate requirements and give the analyst a 'wish list'.

Bringing GIS into the organisation requires an understanding of business requirements and the development of an information management strategy process as discussed in Chapter 3. Only then can GIS hope to become part of the organisation addressing real business problems, not simply a toy of a particular enthusiast.

Further study

The subject of spatial DSS is itself the subject of many complete volumes. For those readers who wish to study this subject further the following sources can be recommended:

Densham P J, Gould M D 1991 *Spatial Decision Support Systems: A Bibliography* Technical Paper 91–9, National Center for Geographic Information and Analysis, State University of New York at Buffalo, Buffalo, NY

Sprague R H, Watson H J 1986 *Decision Support Systems: Putting Theory into Practice* Prentice-Hall, Englewood Cliffs, NJ

Wrigley N (ed) 1988 *Store Choice, Store Location and Market Analysis* Routledge, London

References

Ackoff R L 1967 Management misinformation systems. *Management Science* **14**(4) B147–56

Angehrn A A, Luethi H-J 1990 Visual interactive modelling and intelligent DSS: putting theory into practice. *ETH Working Paper*, Swiss Federal Institute of Technology, Zurich, Switzerland, pp 1–12

Anthony R N 1965 *Planning and Control Systems: A Framework for Analysis* Harvard Business School Press, Boston, Mass

Ardill R J 1988 Towards a store location decision support system. Unpublished MSc thesis, University of Warwick, Coventry, UK

Bardon K S, Grimshaw D J, Mason G M, Stothers N 1986 *Computers in Planning* Royal Town Planning Institute and Birmingham Polytechnic, UK

Beaumont J R 1989 An overview of market analysis: Who?, What?, Where? and Why? *International Journal of Information Management* **9** (Jan 1989): 51–62

Calkins H W 1989 Position paper on the use and value of geographic information in decision making. In Calkins H W, Osrud H J, Obermeyer N J (eds) *Use and Value of Geographic Information: Initiative 4 Specialist Meeting Summary Report and Proceedings* Technical Paper 89–7, National Center for Geographic Information and Analysis, State University of New York at Buffalo, NY, pp 14–16

Child J 1985 Managerial strategies, new technology and the labour process. In Knights D, Willmott H, Collinson D (eds) *Job Redesign: Critical Perspectives on the Labour Process* Gower, Aldershot, UK, pp 107–41

Davies J 1985 *Tradable Information in the Department of Trade and Industry* Department of Trade and Industry, London

Densham P J 1989 GIS as a decision support system. In Calkins H W, Osrud H J, Obermeyer N J (eds) *Use and Value of Geographic Information: Initiative 4 Specialist Meeting Summary Report and Proceedings* Technical Paper 89–7, National Center for Geographic Information and Analysis, State University of New York at Buffalo, NY, pp 17–19

Densham P J 1991 Spatial decision support systems. In Maguire D J, Goodchild M F, Rhind D W (eds) *Geographical Information Systems* Vol 1 *Principles* Longman Scientific & Technical, Harlow, pp 403–12

DoE (Department of the Environment) 1987 *Handling Geographic Information, Report to the Secretary of State for the Environment of the Committee of Enquiry into the Handling of Geographic Information* chaired by Lord Chorley, DoE, HMSO, London

Friend J K, Jessop N 1969 *Local Government and Strategic Choice* Tavistock, London

Foresman T W 1986 Mapping, monitoring and modelling of hazardous waste sites. *The Science of the Total Environment* **56**: 255–64

Grimshaw D J 1988a A review of land and property information systems practice. *International Journal of Information Management* **8** (June): 81–92

Grimshaw D J 1988b The use of land and property information systems. *International Journal of Geographical Information Systems* **2**(1): 57–66

Grimshaw D J 1989 Geographical information systems: a tool for business and industry? *International Journal of Information Management* **9** (June 1989): 119–26

Grimshaw D J 1993 Information systems for industrial marketing *Proceedings of the Canadian International Conference on GIS* 23–25 March, Ottawa, 39–49

Grimshaw D J, Maier J R 1991 *The Integration of GIS into a Marketing* DSS Research Paper No 33 Warwick Business School, University of Warwick, Coventry, UK

Grindley K 1991 *Managing IT at Board Level* Pitman, London

Hale K 1993 *GIS in business: market trends.* Paper presented at the GIS in Business '93 Conference, 7–10 March, Boston, Mass

Head R V 1967 Management information systems: a critical appraisal. *Datamation* May: 23

Healey R 1988 Interfacing software systems for geographical information systems applications, working with geographical information systems. *Economic and Social Research Council, Newsletter* **63** October

Humby C R 1989 New developments in demographic targeting – the implications of 1991. *Journal of the Market Research Society.* **31**(1): 53–73

Jarvenpaa S L, Dickson G W 1988 Graphics and managerial decision making: research guidelines. *Communications of the ACM* **31**(6): 764–74

Jensen J R, Christensen E J 1986 Solid and hazardous waste disposal site selection using digital geographic information system techniques. *The Science of the Total Environment* **56**: 265–276

Johnson M 1989 The application of geodemographics to retailing – meeting the needs of the catchment. *Journal of the Market Research Society* **31**(1): 7–36

Keen P G W 1977 The evolving concept of optimality. In Starr M K, Zeleny M (eds) *Multiple Criteria Decision Making* North-Holland, New York

Keen P G W, Scott-Morton M S 1978 *Decision Support Systems: An Organisational Perspective* Addison-Wesley, Reading, Mass

Little J D C 1979 Decision support systems for marketing management. *Journal of Marketing* **43**(3): 9–27

Maguire D J, Goodchild M F, Rhind D W 1991 Epilogue. In Maguire D J, Goodchild M F, Rhind D W (eds) *Geographical Information Systems* Vol 1 *Principles* Longman Scientific & Technical, Harlow, pp 313–27

Market Research Society 1989 *Journal of the Market Research Society* **31**(1), Special
Issue on Geodemographics

Newell A, Simon H A 1972 *Human Problem-Solving*, Prentice-Hall, Englewood Cliffs, NJ

Nichols G E 1987 On the nature of management information. In Galliers R D (ed)
Information Analysis Addison-Wesley, Sydney, pp 7–17.

Penny N J, Broom D 1989 The Tesco approach to store location planning. In Ridley N
(ed) *Store Locations and Market Analysis* Routledge, London, pp 106–11

Pile S 1988 *The Return of Heroic Failures* Guild Publishing, London, pp 94–5

Senn J A 1990 *Information Systems in Management* 4th edn. Wadsworth, Belmont, Calif

Simkin, L P 1989 SLAM: store location assessment model – theory and practice. *OMEGA
International Journal of Management Science* **17**(1): 53–8

Simkin L P 1990 Evaluating a store location *International Journal of Retail and
Distribution Management* **18**(4): 33–8

Simon H A 1972 Theories of bounded rationality. In McGuire C B, Radner R (eds)
Decisions and Organisation 2nd edn, North Holland, Amsterdam, pp 161–76

Smith T R, Je Yiang 1991 Knowledge-based approaches in GIS. In Maguire D J,
Goodchild M F, Rhind D W (eds) *Geographical Information Systems* Vol 1 *Principles*
Longman Scientific & Technical, Harlow, pp 413–25

Sleight P, Leventhal B 1989 Applications of geodemographics to research and marketing.
Journal of the Market Research Society **31**(1): 75–101

Sprague R H, Carlson E D 1982 *Building Effective Decision Support Systems*,
Prentice-Hall, Englewood Cliffs, NJ

Star J, Estes J 1990 *Geographic Information Systems* Prentice-Hall, Englewood Cliffs, NJ

Turban E, Schaeffer D M 1989 A comparison of executive information systems, DSS,
and management information systems. In Sprague R H Jr, Watson H J (eds) *Decision
Support Systems: Putting Theory into Practice* 2nd edn. Prentice-Hall, Englewood Cliffs,
NJ

Webber R 1989 Using multiple data sources to build an area classification system:
operational problems encountered by MOSAIC. *Journal of the Market Research Society*
31(1): 103–9

Wellar B 1989 Emerging trends in structuring and directing GIS research. *Proceedings,
Challenge for the 1990's: Geographic Information Systems* Canadian Institute of
Surveying and Mapping, Ottawa, pp 601–8

Wellar B 1990 Politicians and information technology. *Computing, Environment and
Urban Systems* **14**: 1–4

Wellar B 1993a Key institutional and organisational factors affecting GIS/LIS strategies
and applications. *Computing, Environment and Urban Systems* **17** (June): 1–12

Wellar B 1993b GIS fundamentals. In Castle G H (ed) *Profiting from a Geographic
Information System* GIS World Books, Fort Collins, Colo, pp 3–21

6

Making the business case for investment in GIS

'Engineering managers proposing the introduction of CAD systems were forced to play the game and engage in return on investment and discounted cash flow rituals in order to justify the technology to top management.'

Currie (1989)

Preamble

Investment in IT is often overlooked and this chapter sets a framework for considering the benefits, and costs of any investment decision. The relationship between the investment decision and the business strategy is emphasised, with strong links to Chapter 3.

The concept of managing benefits is introduced as a link to Chapter 7. Benefits must be identified at an early stage in the project and a means of tracing them through to implementation is considered.

Gaining top management support for IT projects has been found to be essential for success. The role of the project sponsor and project manager is discussed.

The case for investment in GIS

Making the business case for investment in GIS should be seen as part of a wider question of making a case for investment in IT. The basis for any investment in information systems is to support decision making. In Chapter 5 some of the problems of the traditional assumptions associated with this approach were explored.

The quotation at the head of this chapter makes the point that many managers have to engage in a 'game' of using simple cost accounting techniques such as return on investment (ROI) in order to justify technology to top management. Figures to quantify cost savings are sometimes put before top management as a way of getting round the system. And some costs can be creatively accounted for by putting them on to other budgets (Walsham 1993). Such games, often played out in practice, serve to mislead management by placing undue emphasis on quantifiable cost reduction at the expense of neglecting the qualitative benefits to do with the human and organisational issues.

The making of the business case sets the expectations that senior management have about the delivery of a new system. Over-optimistic expectations are an often cited reason for systems failure. The fact that the business case should be sound is underlined by the story of the Performing Rights On-Line Membership Services. The Performing Rights Society collects performance royalties for about 26 000 people in the UK. A computer project was meant to speed up registration of works and prevent backlogs. However, Jury (1993) reveals that an independent report suggested that the 11m. project was fundamentally flawed when it was recommended to managers.

From the above example it can be argued that no matter how good the technical development of the system was, if the business case and information requirements were flawed to start with there was little prospect of success. The evidence is far from clear-cut. A seemingly contradictory view, on the basis of survey evidence, is put forward by Earl and Runge (1987) who say that 80% of successful 'competitive edge' applications bypassed the normal approval process. They were given the go-ahead on the basis of 'hunch'. The reasons given for proceeding in this way were that it was difficult to predict the costs and benefits and that it was a matter of urgency to realise the benefits quickly.

Studies by Strassman (1985) found that information systems reduced both direct and indirect costs, but their contribution to overall profitability was marginal. One of the key reasons for this was reported as a preoccupation with cost reduction rather than a focus on employing technology within the organisation. The overriding message from both academic studies and practical case studies is that the justification and evaluation of information systems need to be transformed from a cost focus to measures that account for the impact on the business and organisation as a whole.

Making the business case for investment in GIS has traditionally been viewed as making a cost–benefit case, largely based on cost reduction arguments. A more radical view is needed to gain the maximum benefits from GIS. Changing the focus from cost to value added is the first part of this view. The second part involves understanding evaluation of GIS before the implementation of the project rather than something which takes place after the system is up and running.

The traditional approach to systems development needs to be widened to become more people centred and to take account of stakeholders and power in the organisation. Accepting such arguments means that much of the traditional literature (see for example Clarke 1991) needs to be examined critically. In this chapter a wide view of the business case is taken so that an appropriate GIS may be developed to serve the business needs and be used effectively within the organisation. The first step in this process is to re-examine the role that IT can take in the business.

In Part One it was argued that to be successful IT has to be identified as part of the business planning process so that the contribution to the business is clear from the start. Figure 1.2 introduced a general framework, that has again been referred to in subsequent chapters, to help understand the overall place and role of IT in the business. The process of introducing technology to the organisation is complex. This diagram is an oversimplification of this complex process. Rather

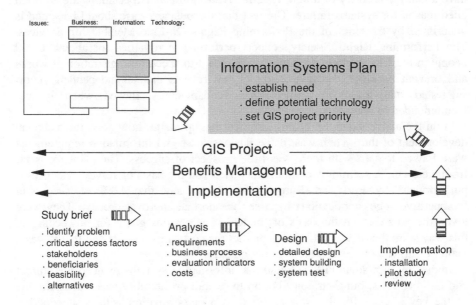

Issues: Business: Information: Technology:

Information Systems Plan

. establish need
. define potential technology
. set GIS project priority

GIS Project

Benefits Management

Implementation

Study brief

. identify problem
. critical success factors
. stakeholders
. beneficiaries
. feasibility
. alternatives

Analysis

. requirements
. business process
. evaluation indicators
. costs

Design

. detailed design
. system building
. system test

Implementation

. installation
. pilot study
. review

Figure 6.1 The case for investing in GIS

like a road map, it serves to show where the junctions occur, where the major and minor roads are and provides a way of plotting a route from A to B.

Where does the process of making the business case for the investment in GIS come in the overall process? Taking the shaded area of Figure 1.2, labelled GIS applications, Figure 6.1 shows in more detail some of the considerations that are required for the duration of the GIS project. The starting assumption here is that a need for GIS has been established, the potential technology has been identified and the GIS project has been allocated a priority within the overall information systems plan of the business. The GIS project can then begin.

Two aspects of the GIS project are examined and discussed in this chapter: making the business case and benefits management. In simple terms the business case for investment in GIS must be made before there can be a GIS project. The case is made as part of the rationale contained in the information systems plan. At this early stage – the pre-project stage – broad benefit expectations will be considered. This should not be the end of benefit considerations. It is argued in the rest of this chapter that benefit management must be a process which continues for the whole of the GIS project.

In the next chapter the overall implementation of the GIS project will be discussed. Note here that Figure 6.1 indicates that implementation is a process covering the full lifetime of the GIS project. It is considerably more than the installation and review of hardware; therefore, implementation warrants a full chapter.

The question of making the business case for investment in GIS essentially falls into two parts. The first question is concerned with how to justify investment in GIS specifically, in other words what added value is GIS over and above the general level of investment in IT. The second question is concerned with establishing justifiable reasons, costs and benefits of investing in IT generally.

An often heard remark from the business community (and from some fellow academics) about the use of GIS is 'Very interesting and attractive, but I don't understand how it will be useful to me.' In fact, GIS represents a way of taking data from the real world and encoding that data with spatial references. Via some kind of spatial analysis the raw data is transformed into information for the decision makers in the organisation. The usability of this information is dependent on the manager being able to decode, or interpret, the information. Geographic information requires some skill to interpret, some people find this easier than others. If GIS is to succeed in leveraging its potential it has to become a well-accepted currency and medium of exchange of information (Maffini 1993).

Maffini (1993) goes on to suggest ways in which GIS might specifically contribute to the business:

1. Change the collection and processing of information by substituting GIS rather than adding GIS to existing systems.
2. Use GIS to facilitate spatial analysis rather than simply a reporting (map output) tool.
3. GIS can help to restructure the business by promoting decentralised units.

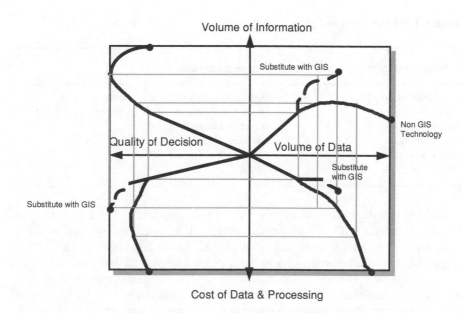

Figure 6.2 The value of GIS to business (INTER TYDAC) (*Source*: Maffini 1993)

The thrust of the ideas expressed by Maffini (1993) is that greater benefits will come from using GIS as a substitute for some existing IT (scenario B). At the moment, however, most of the investment in GIS is simply added to existing IT – producing more data and increasing the overall level of cost of data processing (scenario A). Figure 6.2 expresses this relationship in terms of a graph showing the impact of the two scenarios. The impact of scenario B, where GIS is introduced as a replacement for some of the other data management and processing tools, is much more beneficial than scenario A. The strategy will lead to reduced costs of collection and processing of data together with an increase in the volume of information and better-quality decision making. However, according to Maffini (1993) scenario A is more acceptable to business institutions.

Identification of costs

Given the procedural hurdles in existence in most organisations the business case will, to some extent, depend on the ability to identify the costs of the proposal. Parker *et al.* (1988) suggests there are a range of costs that can broadly be classified into development costs and ongoing expenses. Table 6.1 gives the main categories of these costs. The proportion of cost incurred by each category will differ according to the application and the characteristics of the organisation. A study by Smith and Tomlinson (1992) analyses the costs of a GIS in Ottawa, Canada, between 1990 and 1996 to reflect the lifetime of the system. Figure 6.3 shows the proportion of total costs divided into the categories used.

Table 6.1 Main categories of cost

Development costs	Ongoing expenses
Development effort	Application software maintenance
Hardware	Incremental data storage expenses
Software	Incremental communications
User training	Software licences
Data conversion	Consumable supplies
Other costs	Other

The time period chosen to collect and analyse the cost and benefit data is an important decision. Should the clock start to tick when the system was first suggested, when management commitment was obtained, or when work was first started? The period chosen can make a big difference to the outcome when using techniques like discounted cash flow (DCF). Sometimes it might be important to undertake some sensitivity analysis. In any event it is important to make sure that there is some consensus amongst managers that a certain time-scale will be used.

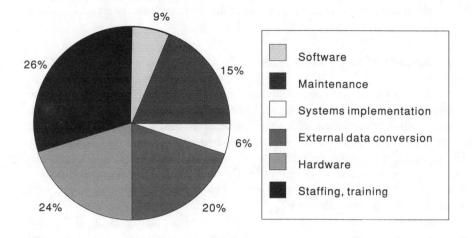

Figure 6.3 Costs of GIS in the city of Ottawa

Traditional calculations of costs have been limited to internal costs, in other words the costs to be borne by the organisation proposing a GIS. However, there may be external costs involved. The calculation of cost could be limited to direct costs or could include overheads. This issue is at the heart of the debate about choosing a marginal cost or an average cost approach. It is sometimes argued that if there is excess capacity in the computer system, a new application only needs to justify the marginal cost incurred. The main difficulty with this view becomes apparent if you imagine the consequences of applying the argument to a number of potential applications. Eventually a situation is reached when a hardware upgrade is required to maintain performance. Should the marginal application pay for the whole cost of this upgrade? The average cost method treats all applications on an equal basis no matter when (in the life of the computer) they are being considered.

A useful distinction can be made between reduced costs and avoided costs, and at least one major computer supplier considers that both are legitimate (IBM 1988). Reduced costs are actual savings as measured against the current level, for example the cost of saving two staff posts. Avoided costs are those that would have been incurred (due to expanding business levels) at some time in the future if the system had not been implemented. It could be very tempting to construct an alluring case for investment based on the cost avoidance argument. Be prepared for a sceptical response, unless the quality of the business plan, upon which the figures for the future are based, is one that has general agreement and is of the highest quality.

As a final note on cost, it is worth considering that price is often used in an organisation in an effort to bring the supply and demand for computer-based information systems into equilibrium. Large centralised organisations often have a system of 'charge-out' for computer services. In other words the buying power is given to the users. This may not always serve the best corporate interests.

From cost reduction to value added

The traditional focus on cost reduction when making a business case for investment is a natural one given a starting point which views information technology like other forms of capital. The economist's approach is then to sanction investment up to the level where the benefits outweigh the costs. Where there are multiple projects competing for limited funds (the most usual case) then projects may be placed in a priority order by simply ranking the payback period. Those with the shortest payback will attract resources first. What is wrong with this simple and well-tried approach?

One of the key issues facing information systems managers in the major corporations of the UK, according to a survey by Grindley (1992), is how to get better value from investment in IT. In part this is a topical issue because of the effects of economic recession. The main reasons, though, go beyond that simple explanation to question the rationale for investment in IT. Research by Hochstrasser and Griffiths (1990) has claimed that over 40% of companies surveyed either did not know or believed that the return on capital of their IT investment was actually worse than other capital investments. There is often an absence of agreement about what business gains IT investments are meant to achieve. The conclusion sounds self-evident when spelt out, yet the evidence from surveys is that many organisations are ignoring the basic starting point. The essential starting point for making the business case is to identify the business objectives.

Many observers, for example Meyer and Boone (1987), have argued that IT can add value to the business. Such thinking represents a change in focus from a cost reduction to a value added approach. Generally, a number of barriers to the widespread adoption of a new approach can be identified as follows:

1. Decision making is dominated by financial measures, for example, ROI, DCF.
2. Factors that create value, for example time, are not generally measured.
3. The intangible assets created by knowledge workers are difficult to quantify.
4. Long-term behaviour is not motivated by the annual budget round.

Moving towards new performance measures needs to take account of the long term. Intangible benefits should be accounted for, even if this is more difficult. Measuring time saved is just the start, more important is to measure how that time is then used – what does this time contribute to the business?

By changing the emphasis away from the strictly financial measures, by starting with the business needs and requirements, the full potential of GIS can be harnessed. This represents a move away from cost reduction towards value added. In terms of the shared values of the stages of growth model (discussed in Chapter

3) cost control is a feature of the 'opt-out' stage whilst adding value is a feature of the 'opportunistic' and 'corporate' stages. Information systems are evolving from their initial role in cost reduction to the more mature role of improvement to the organisational effectiveness and competitiveness.

The idea of value added is being taken seriously by those propounding the economics of information. Parker *et al.* (1988) suggest six classes of value:

1. *Return on investment.* The traditional approach is based on quantifiable costs and benefits leading to a return on investment (ROI) figure.
2. *Strategic match.* Value to the business is very strongly related to the extent to which GIS supports the business strategy. A strong alignment is more likely in an organisation that has included GIS within its information management strategy (as discussed in Chapter 3).
3. *Competitive advantage.* Value to the business may come from product differentiation, market focus or cost leadership in the market. In some cases GIS may help in these areas to give a competitive advantage. The ways in which GIS may specifically lead to competitive advantage were discussed in Chapter 3.
4. *Competitive response.* Often investment in IT is done because organisations observe their competitors' investments. Studies of particular industrial sectors have shown that each organisation within the sector will spend about the same proportion of turnover on IT and will broadly have the same kind of information systems. There is a risk associated in not investing in GIS if all your competitors are doing so. By investing in GIS, competitors may gain a competitive advantage. The value from competitive response is an attempt to measure the cost of not investing in GIS.
5. *Strategic IS-architecture.* The information management strategy talked about in Chapter 4 sets out the priorities for information systems development. Value is created when there is a strong fit or alignment of proposed investments in GIS and the information management strategy. The degree of fit can be examined in terms of the data, applications, computing and communications architectures (see Chapters 3 and 4).
6. *Management information.* As was emphasised in the last chapter, the main benefit and purpose of an information system are to deliver information to decision makers. Value is added as a result of this process. Difficulties arise in measuring this kind of value. However, strong indications are given by looking at the critical success factors of the business and relating the information requirements to these key business decision areas.

The concept of value added can best be summarised in the words of Lodahl (1980:173) who suggested that the key question to ask is: 'What new things does it allow a person to do, or how much more work, or what does it add to the person's capacity or worth to the organisation?'

The role of IT in the business

The traditional role of IT in the business has been to support the operations and key functional areas of activity. Using this perspective of IT leads to the view that managers are concerned with efficient use of resources. However, recently managers have realised that IT can be used to redefine markets and launch new products. The specifics of how GIS can be used in this way were discussed in Chapter 3. Some examples of organisations using GIS to support strategic decisions are given in Chapter 11.

Putting this another way, we could say that IT has traditionally been seen as a way of implementing business strategy. This view sees IT as a business expense rather than an investment. However, IT can be seen as an input to strategy where there is two-way traffic on the bridge between IT and the business strategy. Opportunities for IT can influence the strategy and the business strategy influences the IT infrastructure.

One set of influential ideas about how to align IT with the business strategy emerged from a large and comprehensive research study undertaken at MIT and published in the book, *The Corporation of the 1990's: Information Technology and Organisational Transformation.* The fundamental notion in this thought provoking book is that management must 'reposition IT from its historic support function to where it can play a critical role in strategy formulation and implementation' (Venkatraman 1991:123). To use the jargon of the book, IT-enabled business reconfiguration is an evolutionary process of five stages. These stages are illustrated in Figure 6.4 and summarised in Figure 6.5.

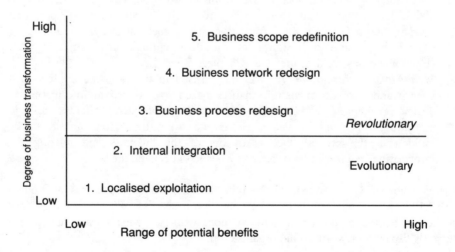

Figure 6.4   Five levels of IT-induced reconfiguration (*Source*: Venkatraman 1991)

Level	Theme	Potential impact	Major objective	Implications
1	Localised exploitation	Potential high savings in narrow areas of business	Reduced costs and/ or improved service	Identify firm specific areas
2	Internal integration	Integration offers both efficiency & effectiveness	Elevate IT as a strategic resource	Articulate the logic for integration
3	Business process redesign	Powerful in creating differential capabilities in the marketplace	Re-engineer the business with IT lever	Strategy - IT alignment
4	Business network redesign	Opportunities for creatively exploiting capabilities	Create a virtual organisation	Articulate the logic of network redesign
5	Business scope	Altering the business	Identifying new business	Identify new scope

Figure 6.5 Summary of the five levels of transformation (*Source*: Venkatraman 1991)

1. *Localised exploitation.* Here IT is exploited within a functional area, e.g. marketing. Essentially IT will be used here for efficiency benefits. Applications of IT in one area of the business do not influence related areas of activity.
2. *Internal integration.* Integration is conceived of as firstly, using a common IT infrastructure, and secondly organisational integration. The benefits of this stage are likely to be effectiveness as well as efficiency.
3. *Business process redesign.* The business processes that exist are not taken as a constraint on the development of an IT infrastructure. An optimum IT infrastructure is designed and used as a lever to redesign the business processes.
4. *Business network redesign.* The management challenge here is to use IT to redesign the whole business network. That includes tasks outside the formal boundary of the organisation.
5. *Business scope redefinition.* The possibility of using IT to redefine the mission of the business. This may be achieved through the launching of new products and services using IT.

The views so far expressed are summarised in Figure 6.6 which states clearly the emerging view that managers will need to adopt in their treatment of IT infrastructure.

Characteristic	Emerging view		
Focus	IT platform	NOT	Isolated systems
Investment vision	Business transformation		Technological sophistication
Investment criteria	Business criteria		Cost-benefit criteria
Scope of impact	Business domain		IT or IS domains
Executive responsibility	Strategic manager		IT manager
Guiding principle	Strategy-IT alignment		IT for implementation

Figure 6.6   The business view of IT infrastructure (*Source*: Venkatraman 1991)

When should managers look for payoff?

The traditional approach to making the business case has been typified as having an emphasis on cost. Another way of looking at this, put forward by Meyer and Boone (1987), is to suggest that traditionally the emphasis has been driven by the technology. This kind of 'technology-push' is typified by the wish to have the latest technology. Figure 6.7 contrasts the technology-driven approach with the value-added approach being advocated.

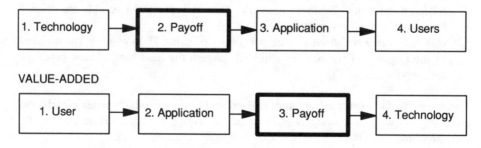

Figure 6.7   Looking for payoff (*Source*: Meyer and Boone 1987)

An approach to justifying the investment in GIS should start with the user. What are the information needs? How can the needs be met? From the analysis of user requirements (more on this in Chapter 7) comes the ideas for an application. The payoff of the application can then be determined, the technology selected and compared to the benefits. As Figure 6.7 shows, the value-added approach to defining payoff places the user and the business need at the forefront of the analyst's mind instead of being dominated by the lure and the cost of the technology.

There are three stages when payoff should be looked for. These stages are discussed in turn.

Initial project justification

At this initial stage it is most important that the business needs are identified. Some questions that could be asked at this stage might be a helpful way of focusing management attention (Lincoln and Shorrock 1990):

- Why not continue to invest in the current system?
- Will the system actually save money?
- Will the new system deliver tangible benefits?
- Do the users understand what they will get?
- Is the proposed system strategically right?
- Does the return exceed the cost?

Evaluation of alternatives

At the simplest level the alternatives may be different software packages, for example, ARC/INFO, SPANS or MapInfo. Alternatively a software package solution may be compared to developing a system in-house, or modifying a software package. In all these scenarios it will be useful to answer the following questions:

- Does the proposed solution fit into the IT architecture? (See Chapter 3 for a discussion of architectures.)
- Does the proposal fulfil the selection criteria in terms of availability, reliability, performance and flexibility?
- Does the technical solution deliver an answer to the organisational problem?

Post-implementation audit

After the implementation of a system many organisations simply regard the project as completed. However, given that the average life of an information system is 15 years, some monitoring of the performance of the system is essential to ensure that the expected benefits are gained. Additionally, if the expected benefits are not gained it is important for the organisation to learn why this has been the case. This organisational learning should then be fed back to the information management strategy.

A useful checklist of questions would be:

- Have expectations been met?
- Are users satisfied?
- Is there scope for further improvements?
- Why is my budget increasing when computers are getting cheaper?
- Is the system delivering the promised benefits?
- What has to be done to get more benefits?
- Are other organisations doing better?
- Is there a reasonable return on investment?
- Has the system been completely implemented?

Where should managers look for payoff?

Looking for the value added by a GIS is more problematic than simply calculating the costs saved (for example from reduced staff numbers). So where can a manager start to identify the possible areas of added value? Burn and Caldwell (1990) have identified a number of general areas that are worth thinking about.

1. *Piggybacking.* Some applications can be given a flying start to their justification because they can be introduced 'on the back of' another application. For example, in a utility company a GIS is initially justified on the basis on contributing to the operational management. The business case is made largely on the basis of a more efficient management of facilities and improved customer service on a day-to-day basis. Now, suppose the marketing department wishes to introduce a market analysis system, the basic hardware, software and data are already in place. Therefore, the potential benefits can be set against the marginal costs of the new application.

2. *Faster flow of information.* As an example of the benefits of a faster flow of information, take the case of GIS linked to a customer database. Response to customer queries is enhanced by faster access to the information about the local area. Much of the value added to the business is in terms of improved customer service.

3. *Easier access to information.* A well-designed information system with a good user interface will enable the manager to access the information more quickly than with previous methods. Easier access goes beyond the simply calculated time savings which reduce costs, towards the notion that more readily available information enhances the decision-making process. Therefore value is added to the business by adding to the effectiveness of decision-making.

4. *Opportunity hours.* A typical scenario might be a busy manager, working late one evening in order to complete a market research study needed by his boss for a meeting the next day. To complete the study the manager works at the GIS workstation blissfully unaware that the plane due to take his boss to tomorrow's meeting has been cancelled. If this piece of information had been to hand the manager would have had more time, or 'opportunity hours', available.

5. *Better control.* Managerial control over work flow and work programmes brings benefits of more proactive management.

Cost–benefit analysis

Having analysed the costs and the benefits arising from a potential GIS it may be appropriate to undertake a formal cost–benefit analysis. There has been much debate in the literature about how appropriate such an analysis is – see, for example, Dickinson and Calkins (1988), Wilcox (1990), Dickinson and Calkins (1990) and Smith and Tomlinson (1992). Some of this debate has centred around the issue of the applicability of cost–benefit analysis to GIS in the public sector. Since the applications domain of this book is largely centred in the private sector, where cost–benefit analysis has a long tradition, much of the criticism is irrelevant.

Dickinson and Calkins (1988) make the point that the type of evaluation used depends upon the purpose and use of the proposed GIS. In some circumstances the cost–benefit analysis may be too rigid. They argue for a more flexible approach to economic evaluation, yet in the end they favour reaching some 'dollar based values'. If this is interpreted as allowing for the notional allocation of numeric values to the concept of added value we are in agreement. However, their view could be interpreted as meaning the direct placing of monetary values on all benefits. In some cases, as suggested by Wilcox (1990), the use of ordinal scales of measurement may be more appropriate. A more serious criticism of the Dickinson and Calkins (1988) approach is that it appears to support the substitution paradigm. In other words they argue for the business case for investment to be based on the benefits of automating. This, as the thrust of the argument in this chapter indicates, is a rather narrow conception of what IT in general, and GIS in particular, can do for the business. There must be an open mind in terms of possible benefits of re-examining the business processes in terms of effectiveness measures, not simply the measures of efficiency implied by the author's approach.

Benefits management

After a great deal of consultancy experience Lincoln and Shorrock (1990) argue that benefits need managing much like any other project, therefore there should be a benefits management process. The function of benefits management is to:

1. Ensure that there is a corporate view of the opportunities offered by information systems.
2. Agree benefit measures and targets before implementation.
3. Give line managers the responsibility for realising benefits.
4. Set up a steering committee to set policy and review performance.

These procedural issues and ideas presume that benefits are well understood. However, this will frequently be far from the case. Benefits are simply the items that the organisation accepts may be used to outweigh the costs of the proposed investment, and later the actual system after implementation. There are three useful ways of subdividing benefits: efficiency, effectiveness, and transformation.

Efficiency measures the output given from a system for a quantity of input. Systems are said to be more efficient the fewer input resources are consumed to produce a given level of output. In colloquial terms this has been described as 'to do things right' (Drucker 1968).

Effectiveness measures the extent to which goals and objectives have been reached. In this way an effectiveness measure is able to demonstrate clear business benefits. In colloquial terms this has been described as 'to do the right thing' (Drucker 1968).

Transformation measures the extent to which the GIS enables the organisation to do new things. Benefits from transformation were described by Venkatraman (1991) as being revolutionary. Figure 6.4 showed these benefits to result from business process redesign, business network redesign or business scope redefinition. An example of an organisation that has achieved transformation by using GIS would be the Automobile Association in the UK. Traditional business was in the motor vehicle recovery sector. To carry out this business data about location of garages, hotels, and the road network was collected – GIS were brought in to help with this prime business. The opportunity arose to change the business direction by taking a market opportunity to sell electronic data derived, with added value, from the prime business.

Bringing GIS into business requires that benefits are identified from an organisational point of view (in other words the whole business). As it was stated earlier in the chapter, stakeholders and power groups need to be taken account of. A useful framework for helping to focus on beneficiaries as well as benefits is the one first introduced by Hammer (1985). Along the top of the matrix are the three beneficiaries: the individual, functional units like departments, and the organisation. Down the left of the matrix are the three levels of benefits identified by Hammer (1985): efficiency, effectiveness and transformation.

The matrix may be further divided into three domains (shown shaded in Figure 6.8. *Domain I* is the individual using a personal computer and at first being more efficient and later becoming more effective as decisions are improved as a result of (say) a catchment area analysis system. *Domain II* is where a department is sharing an GIS, initially installed to improve efficiency but again later on benefits come from improving effectiveness as a result of greater integration of systems. This would be the case in Arby's discussed further in Chapter 10. *Domain III* is achieved after some time has lapsed, the use of GIS makes it possible for the organisation to change its mission – the business is transformed.

The process of managing benefits must take account of the stakeholder interests as reflected in the three potential beneficiaries. It is a process which needs to be set up early on in the GIS project's life. So often in practice the measurement of benefits is left until the systems are implemented. A more fruitful time to consider benefits and to instigate a benefit management process is at the stage of making

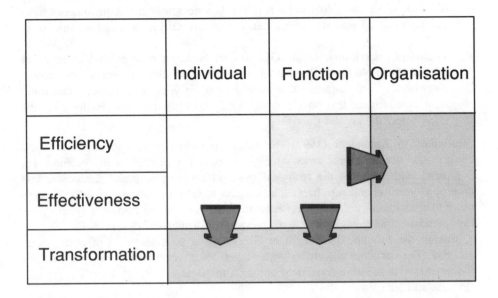

	Individual	Function	Organisation
Efficiency			
Effectiveness			
Transformation			

Figure 6.8   Benefits–beneficiaries matrix (*Source*: adapted from Hammer 1985)

the business case for investment. Then the benefits can be embodied in a statement of objectives with some criteria for measuring each of the benefits identified.

Assessment of risk

Every GIS project involves risk and uncertainty. Parker *et al.* (1988) define four useful classes of risk:

1. *Organisational risk.* Any project requires a mix of skills and organisational conditions present for it to be successful. With a GIS project in a business environment, because it will inevitably be a relatively new application, there may be particularly important skills unavailable. An important way of diagnosing this issue is to use the stages of growth model introduced in Chapter 4 as a way of identifying where the organisation is in terms of skills, structure, staff and style. The next step would be to identify where the organisation needs to get to. From this diagnosis, a plan of action to remedy any deficiencies can be made. These actions are part of the necessary requirements for bringing GIS into the organisation.
2. *IS infrastructure risk.* A GIS project, by definition, is introducing new technology into the business. Is the required level of technical support available? What is the level of risk involved?

3. *Definitional uncertainty.* Information requirements are almost notoriously difficult to define. How certain is the business that the requirements have been identified and the specifications of the GIS will suit the objectives set?

4. *Technical uncertainty.* Is the GIS project breaking new ground in terms of untried technologies? Remember that the fact that a technology works elsewhere is no guarantee that it will work in your organisation. The more new technologies, that have not previously been used in your business, in the GIS project the greater the risk.

According to Antenucci (1992) the risks associated with GIS are small and concern the organisational risks which are under the control of the business (as compared with some of the technical risks which may be under the power and control of vendors and suppliers). The success of GIS will depend on people much more than technology. It has been estimated that 20% of the cost of a system goes into personnel, yet this gives 97% of the success (Antenucci 1992).

Making the case for investment in GIS involves an assessment of costs, value and risk. The outcome will differ with each project, yet it will always be true that the process will create a consensus amongst management about what is important (Fredrix and Van Vugt 1993).

Summary

The process of making a business case for investment in GIS is unfortunately often seen as a necessary hurdle. However, fulfilling the bureaucratic hurdles is not a sufficient condition to ensure a successful GIS project. Taking the line of least resistance, by compliantly filling in the forms and adhering to the procedures will not lead to the best use of resources and is unlikely to maximise the potential benefits of a GIS.

A more proactive approach which views making the business case as a useful opportunity to gain managerial support, a time to look not only to cost reduction but also to value added and the instigation of a benefits management process will provide the building blocks of a sound system. Thinking needs to shift from a narrow focus on cost to a wider view of GIS adding value to the business. Following the philosophy outlined in Part One of this book, the need for GIS is established after a thorough analysis of the business requirements and the opportunities offered by GIS technology. Only after the identification of such requirements which will clearly spell out the contribution which GIS can make to the business will GIS be identified as a potential project.

Going from potential project to actual (approved) project has been the subject matter of this chapter. The approval process involves assessing cost, value and risk. An important part of this process is creating a managerial consensus about what is required. Commitment from all the stakeholders (beneficiaries), either individuals, functional departmental representatives or the business as a whole, is essential. A high-level sponsor is often a useful person to have give their backing to the project, especially to ensure that resources are allocated to the GIS project during the implementation phase.

Implementation is often seen as a narrow, rather technical phase of the information systems development cycle. However, as the next chapter will show, implementation is a process which starts from the very conception of the proposed system. It shares this characteristic with the making of the business case; both are essential to bring the GIS into the organisation.

Judgements have to be made, about the worth of the proposed GIS to the business, about the benefits to different people and about how to manage change. Value judgements will have to be made at the end of the day, despite attempts here to make explicit ways of categorising costs and benefits. A very appropriate guiding light comes from a Sioux Indian prayer: 'Great Spirit, help me never to judge another until I have walked two weeks in his moccasins' Alley (1990).

Further study

Evaluation as a topic has a long tradition, especially outside the field of GIS, and IT generally. Much of the work depends on economic theory. Further reading can be done on both the theoretical underpinnings and the application of evaluation to fields such as research, and social programmes, in addition to information systems.

Bennett C A, Lumsdaine A (eds) 1975 *Evaluation and Experiment: Some Critical Issues in Assessing Social Programs* Academic Press, New York

Bentkover J D, Covello V T, Mumpower J (eds) 1986 *Benefits Assessment, State of the Art* Reidel, Dordrecht

King J C, Schrems E L 1978 Cost benefit analysis in information systems development and operation. *Computing Surveys* **10**(1): 19–34

Schafer G (ed) 1988 *Functional Analysis of Office Requirements: A Multiperspective Approach* John Wiley & Sons, Chichester

Wortmann P M 1983 Evaluation research: a methodological perspective. *Annual Review of Psychology* **34**: 223–60

Zangemeister C 1975 Measurement of effectiveness of computerised information systems from a management point of view through utility analysis. In Frielink AB (ed) *Economics of Informatics* North-Holland, Amsterdam, The Netherlands, pp 440–51

References

Alley E (ed) 1990 *A Light to Walk By* Moorley's Publishing, Ilkeston, UK

Antenucci J C 1992 Management issues in implementing and utilizing GIS Technology. *Proceedings of the Third European Conference on Geographical Information Systems* Munich, pp 838–45

Burn J, Caldwell 1990 *The Management of Information Systems Technology* Alfred Waller, Henley-on-Thames, UK

Clarke A L 1991 GIS specification, evaluation, and implementation. In Maguire D J, Goodchild M F, Rhind D W (eds) *Geographical Information Systems* Vol 1 *Principles* Longman Scientific & Technical, Harlow pp 477–88

Currie W L 1989 The art of justifying new technology to top management. *Omega* **17**(5): 409–18

Dickinson H J, Calkins H W 1988 The economic evaluation of implementing a GIS. *International Journal of Geographical Information Systems* **2**(3): 307–27

Dickinson H J, Calkins H W 1990 Comment on 'Concerning ''The economic evaluation of implementing a GIS'' '. *International Journal of Geographical Information Systems* **4**(2): 211–12

Drucker P 1968 *The Age of Discontinuity: Guidelines to our Changing Society* Harper & Row, New York

Earl M J, Runge D A 1987 Using telecommunications-based information systems for competitive advantage. Research and Discussion Paper, RDP 87/1, Oxford Institute for Information Management, Templeton College, Oxford

Fredrix W M J, Van Vugt R 1993 The key factors to successful GIS-implementation: creating managerial awareness about what they are actually deciding on. *Proceedings of the Fourth European Conference on Geographical Information Systems* Genoa, Italy, pp 175–86

Grindley K 1992 *Information Technology Review 1992/93* Price Waterhouse, London

Hammer M 1985 A framework for applications. *Indications* **2**(2), Index Systems Inc, Cambridge, Mass

Hochstrasser B, Griffiths C 1990 *Evaluating IT Benefits: Strategy and Management* Chapman & Hall, London

IBM 1988 *A Business Case for DP Resources* G509–2214, IBM, Portsmouth, UK

Jury L 1993 11m performing rights computer fiasco 'always a flawed project'. *The Guardian* Thursday 3 June, London, p 2

Lincoln T J, Shorrock D 1990 Cost-justifying current use of information technology. In Lincoln T J (ed) *Managing Information Systems for Profit* John Wiley & Sons, Chichester

Lodahl T M 1980 Cost–benefit concepts and applications for office automation. *Proceedings of the Office Automation Conference* AFIPS Press, Atlanta, Ga, pp 171–5

Maffini G 1993 GIS in business: when it makes cents, *Proceedings of GIS in Business '93 Conference* GIS World Books Inc., Fort Collins, Colo, pp 17–20

Meyer N D, Boone M E 1987 *The Information Edge* McGraw-Hill, New York

Parker M M, Benson R J, Trainor H E 1988 *Information Economics: Linking Business Performance to Information Technology* Prentice-Hall, Englewood Cliffs, NJ

Smith D A, Tomlinson R F 1992 Assessing costs and benefits of geographical information systems: methodological and implementation issues. *International Journal of Geographical Information Systems* **6**(3): 247–56

Strassman P A 1985 *Information Payoff – the Transformation of Work in the Electronic Age* The Free Press, New York

Venkatraman 1991 IT induced business reconfiguration. In Scott Morton M S (ed) *The Corporation of the 1990's: Information Technology and Organisational Transformation* Oxford University Press, New York, pp 122–58

Walsham G 1993 *Interpreting Information Systems in Organisations* John Wiley & Sons, Chichester

Wilcox D L 1990 Concerning the economic evaluation of a GIS. *International Journal of Geographical Information Systems* **4**(3): 203–10

7

Implementation of the GIS project

'. . . implementation is a management problem not a technical solution'

Healy (1987)

Preamble

A broad concept of implementation will be introduced. Traditionally, in systems development literature, implementation has been seen as simply the final stage of development – during which the computer programs are tested out and the hardware and software are delivered to the users. However, it is more useful to consider implementation in a wider sense, to include consideration of all the human and organisational issues which can help make an information system successful.

The importance of post implementation reviews and the monitoring of technical and user perspectives to feed back the learning into future development is a central theme of this chapter.

A wider view of implementation

The traditional view of implementation, as the final 'technical' stage of systems development, is fraught with danger. The quotation at the head of this chapter focuses attention on the management problems, serving to deflect attention away from purely technical solutions. The essential truth is there; however, it might be more positive to think in terms of management solutions rather than management problems. The aim of this chapter is to widen your thinking about the critical issue of implementation. Thinking of implementation as a *process* rather than a *stage* is a prerequisite to begin tackling some of the critical human and organisational issues to do with successful information systems. Although the development phase is important, from a human and organisational perspective, the implementation process is the most critical (Eason 1988).

In the conclusion to his book Grindley (1991: 199) argues that during the early stages of using computers in business power and responsibility have been separated.

'Never give someone the responsibility for doing something if you haven't given them the power to achieve it. Even more important, never give anyone the power to do something if they are not held responsible for the results. The introduction of computers to organisations was accompanied by the biggest travesty of this law since the industrial revolution started. Because the users still had responsibility for achieving business results. But their power to achieve them was continually eroded, as they relied, more and more, on computer systems they had neither the time, nor the expertise, to control.'

The issue of power and responsibility is a recurring theme in the literature as researchers try to make sense out of the seemingly growing number of information system failures or abandonments, to use a more polite term. It is not just managers who need the power and responsibility to get systems right it is also the systems analysts. Whilst the ability of systems analysts may rarely be questioned in technical matters like analysis and design of hardware and software selection, such expertise and associated technical qualifications may form an insufficient *power* base for fulfilling the *responsibility* for seeing the project implemented (Willcocks and Mason 1987).

A useful way of thinking about implementation in the context of information systems more widely is to see it as an iterative part of the framework for developing an information strategy. Figure 7.1 illustrates this wider view of implementation.

The main critical issues in implementation to be discussed in this chapter are:

1. Why is implementation important?
2. How can implementation be successful?
3. What are the appropriate implementation strategies to use?

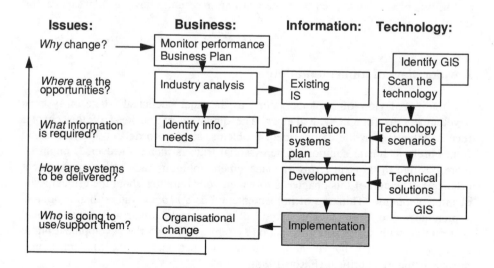

Figure 7.1 Implementation as part of the information strategy (*Source*: amended from Grimshaw 1991)

The starting point for our discussion of implementation is that the GIS project has been identified and given priority in the information strategy (see Chapter 3) and the case for investment in GIS has been made (see Chapter 6). What happens next? Who does what and how does the GIS project make progress?

The development of a GIS

The traditional approach, used over many years to develop information systems, is often referred to as the systems life-cycle. The stages used in this approach tend to be carried out in a linear fashion which Figure 7.2 illustrates as a 'waterfall model'. Underlying the use of this model are a number of organisational features that it would be worth reminding ourselves of. The traditional data processing department where this model is used would be responsible for information systems development in the organisation. It would typically employ systems analysts and programmers. Involvement of the end users of systems would be minimal – consultative rather than participative by nature.

Feasibility study

The purpose of the feasibility study is to determine whether the existing system can be improved. If it can, the following questions are addressed:

1. How much will it cost?

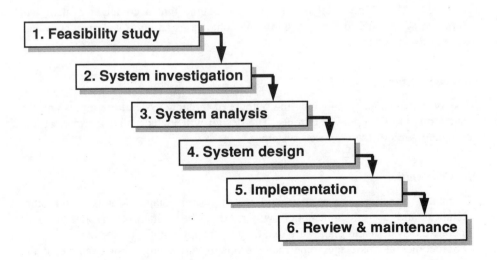

Figure 7.2 Traditional 'waterfall model' of systems development

2. What are the benefits?
3. What are the alternative solutions?
4. What is the recommended solution?

The feasibility study concentrates its attention on issues of efficiency and effectiveness. Generally the wider business issues of fundamentally questioning the underlying business process under study will not be part of the brief.

Systems investigation

A detailed investigation and fact-finding mission of the current system are undertaken. Personnel are interviewed, either in person, by questionnaire, or both. The existing (manual) records are examined. The data that is collected is documented by type and volume. Part of this systems investigation may involve using documentation aids such as flowcharts as recommended by the National Computer Centre.

The main problem at this stage is that because the 'system' has been defined in terms of the existing system the focus of the investigation may well be too narrowly defined. This is a particular problem in relation to GIS because existing processes are often not using map-related or spatial analysis. So a focus on existing 'systems' could overlook a real business opportunity to use GIS.

Systems analysis

Following the fact collection undertaken previously as part of the systems investigation phase, the systems analyst now reflects on why problems exist, why the methods of work were adopted, and what alternative methods exist.

Unfortunately, in practice, the alternative approaches considered tend to be restricted. Also, a potential trap here is to assume that a computer system will form part of the solution. It may be that in some cases an improved manual system would provide good results.

Systems design

The systems design will include the outputs of the new system, the inputs and the transformation of inputs to outputs. The design will include both the clerical and computer parts of the proposed system.

Implementation

Computer programs are written and tested at this stage. Manuals and other technical and user documentation will need to be written. User staff need to operate the system and make sure that they are happy with it in practice.

Sometimes at this stage some major problem will emerge. For example, if the analyst misunderstood the user requirements or failed to communicate the requirements to the programmer the system will not achieve the needs.

Review and maintenance

The final stage is post-operational. It is inevitable that there will be a need for some minor changes and enhancements to the system to meet changing business requirements.

The traditional approach to review was extremely limited. It is unlikely that any review against the objectives of the system would take place. Sometimes even minor enhancements would take a long time to implement and consume many scarce programmer resources because the system had not been written in a flexible way.

Problems associated with particular stages of the development process have been discussed above. Here we turn to the wider problems of the systems development life cycle.

The traditional systems development life-cycle model (Daniels and Yeats 1971) has served as basic guidance for information systems development over many years. During the 1960s and 1970s when most business information systems were run on highly centralised computers the waterfall model of development was criticised for, amongst other things, neglecting the needs and real requirements of the users (Avison and Fitzgerald 1988). Many methodologies that came to the fore in the late 1970s and 1980s tried to remedy this and other deficiencies. However, there are still enormous problems with the currently used methodologies.

A student at Warwick recently observed during a seminar that all the so-called new methodologies are really based around a similar process to that advocated by the waterfall model. This observation leads us to question the applicability of a model formulated in a time of centralised business information systems to a time of increasingly decentralised organisations. Support for this view is also given by Hirschheim and Klein (1992) who say that information systems development methodologies are primarily influenced by functionalist paradigms. Such a paradigm is essentially concerned with explaining the status quo. Yet, almost by definition, when information systems are introduced into the organisation there is change. Where is the scope for including change in our information systems development methodologies?

The idea of iteration is not new; most of the participative and structured methodologies embody the idea that to 'get it right' will require several passes through a given procedure. This kind of iteration is, however, rather limited and the end result is typically an agreement between developer and user. What is required is a method for including organisational change in the systems develop-ment process. It is fundamental to the argument of this chapter that this requires an underlying model of organisational change.

The debate so far has been well characterised by Grunden (1986) as representing a shift from the conventional view to a human-oriented view. The discipline of information systems has been infused with ideas from many contributing traditional disciplines. This includes computer science, economics and other social sciences, ergonomics and the human sciences. However, in terms of organisational theory and technology the life-cycle model is grounded in hierarchical organisations and centralised technology. Neither of these features are currently prevalent. What can we learn from an analysis of the paradigm shift of technology? What lessons are there from an analysis of organisational change?

A recently published study (Tapscott and Caston 1993) argues that a fundamental paradigm shift has occurred in the application of IT to organisations. This shift represents a move from a centralised technology under the remit of a specialised group of people to a decentralised technology where there is much greater involvement of users.

The taxonomy of GIS introduced in Chapter 2 based on tasks, technology and time frame can be used to understand what is happening with information systems development methodologies. If we view the taxonomy from the viewpoint of the information systems developer, then the tasks part of the taxonomy could be seen as the traditional model. The argument then widens to a suggestion that two additional components need to be included in our model of information systems development. We should include technology (infrastructure) and time frame in our model.

An analysis of the role of infrastructure in the development of effective information systems by Kling (1992) suggests that analysts should take account of infrastructure issues early on in systems design. Taking into account the changes that inevitably happen in all organisations over time has been one of the recurring themes in information systems literature. The earliest theories of the subject, the stages of growth model (Gibson and Nolan 1974), and the latest incarnation of that theory (Sutherland and Galliers 1991) all testify to the importance of learning as an aspect of organisational success.

The identification of problem areas within the business that are to form the focus of systems development is often rather *ad hoc* in practice. From Chapter 3 we know that it is important to plan information systems development in line with the business plan. The problems tackled may not be 'real' problems. The traditional approach does not question whether the business is doing the right thing, merely whether it is doing the thing right. The systems are frequently inflexible, difficult or costly to maintain, incomplete, have problems with documentation, and lead to a high maintenance workload.

Factors influencing a changing environment

Since the advent of the systems development life-cycle model and in the light of the problems with that model it is important to consider relatively recent changes.

More software packages available

Over a third of all software is now purchased as a package (Grindley 1991). In the GIS market-place there are some very sophisticated packages available. Some are generic GIS which may require tailoring to fit the organisational requirements, whilst others are more specific packages (for example to analyse retail catchment areas).

More contract programming staff available

By the year 2000 Grindley (1991) predicts that the proportion of systems development done by contract programming staff will have doubled. The implication of this is that the technical work of program writing will be moved further away from the control of the user community. This is a particular concern given the already strained communications between these two groups.

Software is increasingly easy to use

Since the mid 1980s systems development has moved from using traditional development tools to using fourth-generation and computer-assisted software engineering (CASE) tools. Many GIS software packages contain a systems development capability (language) so that experienced users or specialists can tailor the system to run more specific applications. There are many consultancies and data agencies in the market who will offer such software development services using the development tools that come with GIS packages.

Greater involvement of end users in systems development

Following on from the last point, there are many more users who simply develop their own systems by tailoring an application package. This provides an opportunity to get things right but also a challenge for managers to provide a supportive environment whilst exercising some control on their activities.

Automated tools for software development

There are three sets of tools to consider here.

CASE (computer-assisted software engineering)
The attraction of CASE is easy to understand. However, in practice its use to date has been limited. Yet the IT directors believe that in the future CASE will play a much more significant role in systems development.

Two key arguments in favour of the CASE approach are the ease of documentation (often automatically produced) and a consistent set of data definitions. There is currently a lack of available CASE tools specific to GIS application development. This has been perceived to be due to GIS purchasers failing to understand the importance of formal software engineering tools to the development of GIS (Paschoud and Bell 1993).

IPSE (integrated project support environment)
Software development projects are often very large. For example, some real-time applications in the defence industry take around five years to develop. The idea of an IPSE is that it provides support for project management and automated programming and documentation all in the one package.

Much research and development effort has been put into the development of IPSE. It is a relatively new technology that management need to be aware of in their planning.

4GL (fourth-generation language)

Fourth-generation languages have been made possible because of the rapidly improving price/performance ratio of computer hardware. There is always a trade-off between the time it takes to develop an application and the amount of processing power needed to run the application. Broadly, an application written using a 4GL is developed relatively quickly but it will require more processing power to run. So the tool chosen will depend on business judgement. For example, large transaction systems like bank clearing have to cope with huge volumes of transactions per day so the speed of each transaction is critical. A DSS that is used by a small work group, however, needs to be frequently rewritten because of changes in the business environment, yet the speed of running is not critical – an ideal candidate for development using a 4GL.

Because of the reduced speed of applications development made possible by using a 4GL they are often used to develop a prototype system. Users may then get the 'look and feel' of the system. This will often help users to define their needs more precisely.

Many of the changes outlined here are of a rapidly improving technology. The consequences of this changing technology present managers with considerable challenges. It is to these challenges that we now turn.

Systems development methodologies

As an effort to overcome either all or some of the problems associated with the traditional systems development life cycle a number of alternative methodologies are available. Although it has been estimated that there are around 300 different methodologies on the market to choose from, in practice the choice is somewhat more limited.

Essentially methodologies can be grouped into the following categories (Avison and Fitzgerald 1988):

1. Structured systems, e.g. SSADM, LBMS;
2. Data analysis;
3. Soft systems, e.g. SSM;
4. Participative, e.g. ETHICS;
5. Hybrid, e.g. MULTIVIEW.

The choice of appropriate methodology will depend on a number of technical and business factors, for example level of documentation required, complexity of system, and level of involvement by end users. There are a number of important questions to have in mind. What methodology is appropriate to use for any given

GIS? What methodologies, if any, are used in practice to develop GIS? Are GIS different from other information systems in their needs and demands for systems development methodologies?

Hobson (1991) tried to answer these questions by undertaking some empirical research. The survey was undertaken specifically in the utilities sector, where it could be expected to find a large number of corporate GIS. The importance of looking for corporate GIS organisations was that they are the ones that could be expected to be using systems development methodologies. Firm generalisations from the survey are difficult to make because of the relatively small response, however the findings are likely to be indicative. About 60% of respondents said that their strategy was to integrate GIS with other systems. Of those organisations that used a systems methodology, their adoption was because it was a corporate standard. In other words, a particular methodology was adopted as part of the organisation-wide applications architecture. The methodologies used were generally structured rather than soft systems approaches. The two most widely adopted methodologies were SSADM and LBMS, with IE gradually being introduced in some organisations.

An interesting picture emerging here is the emphasis on technical design of systems. Findings from a survey by Medyckyj-Scott and Cornelius (1991) echo this concern by saying that fewer procedures were undertaken to evaluate and prepare for human and organisational implications compared to those used in deciding on the technical system. A staggering 27% of respondents to their survey said they did not engage in staff consultations, hold meetings on organisational implications, arrange awareness seminars, have meetings on job impacts or statements of human and organisational requirements.

A similar message is advanced by Le Duc (1992) in his arguments for the adoption of a systems approach to the design of GIS. The application of general systems theories and approaches is advocated in order to move the design of GIS away from technically predominated concerns towards the concern for solving problems. Following such an approach leads the analyst to focus on problem identification, moving to requirements specification and design. Involvement of users is essential in such approaches. There are many advocates here of using prototyping, a method for sustaining the dialogue with users in the later stages of systems design.

What is emerging here is a gulf between theory and practice. In theory everyone agrees that the organisational impact and the people-centred issues are very important components of systems implementation. In practice there is a predominantly technical approach as is evident by the adoption of traditional systems development methodologies and the lack of knowledge of softer systems approaches.

As far as the applications architecture is concerned it is important to consider which methodology is appropriate for which systems. Can the organisation adopt one methodology for all its systems development?

Systems acquisition policies e.g. make or buy

Many different sources of software are available:

1. *Development of in-house software.* This needs to be costed carefully and the time taken to develop the system must be estimated as accurately as possible. Expertise will be available on-site for amendments and updates to the system. But in practice there is often a reluctance to complete the last 20% of the system.
2. *Purchase of a standard software package.* The critical factors here are well summarised by Long (1989). The essential trade-off is between the reduced cost and instant availability of this option compared to the tailor-made solution.
3. *Purchase of a ready developed system from a third-party user.* Given that no two users or businesses do things in exactly the same way, the critical question here is how easy is it to amend the system to fit in with your precise requirements? It is important to remember that computer systems reflect the experiences and prejudices of their designers – can you live with another organisation's system?
4. *Employment of consultants specifically to write the software.* This is likely to be the most expensive option. Its success may well depend upon how well the system requirements can be identified and written down prior to inviting tenders. If changes are likely either as a result of experience with the system after installation or as a result of (say) changing legislation then updating the system may be an expensive and time-consuming task. Often such specifically written software is referred to as a 'turnkey' system. A case study of implementation, later in the chapter, explores the 'turnkey' option in more detail.

Quality control

The software development process may be approved by one of the standards bodies, for example BS 5750. Clearly a high-quality information system is a good objective to have, however a quality systems development process is no guarantee of a quality information system. Practical indicators of quality systems should include use and usability.

Systems use and usability

How do you know that a system has been successfully implemented? After all, not many people or organisations wish to admit to a failed system. Successful implementation will be examined in terms of lessons that can be learnt from a failed system and the *use* made of systems as indicators of success.

The literature about failed GIS is scant, in fact only one documented case has been found. Openshaw *et al.* (1990) report about the failure of the GIS at Northumbria police in the UK. This example comes from the public sector, where public accountability for mistakes means that organisations are more likely to declare problems. In the private sector there are many reasons, not least of which is commercial confidentiality, why declaration of failure is unlikely. What lessons are revealed by the Northumbria police case?

The possibility of using GIS as part of a police command and control system had been identified in the Chorley Report (DoE 1987). As part of the operational decisions made by the police, for example where to deploy patrol cars, a great deal of geographic data must be analysed. The Northumbria police decided to test out the potential of GIS in the area of crime pattern analysis – just one part of the business. Operational maps showing crime patterns with coloured map pins would be 'automated' using GIS. A GIS solution was purchased from a vendor to run on a personal computer using a relational database and Ordnance Survey 1 : 1250 digital maps. The GIS project was abandoned after 20 months – why?

The reasons for abandonment, given by the police, reported by Openshaw *et al.* (1990) were poor vendor support, unreliable systems, and inadequate usability and user friendliness. These could all be put under the banner of 'blaming the technology'. Yet the factors that led to abandonment, analysed by Openshaw *et al.* (1990), were much more to do with 'organisational' factors.

The use of GIS for crime pattern analysis was innovative which led to two problems. From the perspective of the vendor there was no ready-made solution to deliver. On the other hand the user did not have a clear idea of requirements. Before going any further, at this early stage the warning bells should have rung. This is a classic case of poor communications between user and analyst/vendor coupled with mismanagement of expectations. Also, when things start to go wrong management needs to be proactive to get the project back on track before irreparable damage is done to user expectations and user–vendor relationships. The training of the end user of the system, who was not a computer expert, was inadequate and the PC had to continue with normal duties – taking on board the GIS as additional work. Use and usability are key issues in this case.

Research into the implementation of computer systems has tended to stress the importance of the level of *use* of the system. The more traditional cost–benefit approach has been used but it is often difficult to assess the benefits of improved information processing to the organisation. Studies by Lucas (1975) suggest that where use of a system is voluntary high levels of use will be associated with a successful system. Many GIS will fall into this category, for example tactical applications.

Practical measures of the use of a system would include the following:

1. Frequency of inquiries;
2. Reported use;
3. Monitored frequency of use;
4. User satisfaction.

Research by Grimshaw (1988) studied the use made of land and property information systems – in many ways these systems were the forerunners of GIS – and reported that there were a number of generic lessons that could be learnt in order to promote more successful systems:

1. *Data must be accurate.* In a surprisingly large number of cases users say that they cannot rely on the data accuracy. Not surprisingly this leads to users deciding not to use the system. A frequent problem here is that the person responsible for data input is not the person who wants to get data out of the system. Generally it is a good idea to give someone who is inputting data something in return for their effort. In this way there is a personal incentive for greater accuracy.

2. *Systems should monitor the use made of data.* It seems obvious to suggest that information systems are monitored to see who uses them, why they are used, and what data is used for queries. However, in practice few information systems are monitored in this way. The feedback provided by monitoring is valuable for ensuring continued business benefits from the system and for providing pointers towards improving the system.

3. *There must be a strong support team.* A strong team of support and development staff with the necessary authority to develop and enhance the system is essential for the continued health of a system. Over time the role of such a team will change. Initially there will be high demands for training, but later the focus is likely to change towards maintenance and development. A key role at all times will be to ensure data accuracy, security and integrity.

Factors leading to successful implementation

Factor	Priority
Commitment from top management	1
Continuing support for users	2
Highly reliable systems	2
Involvement of users	4
Easy to use systems	5
Effective project management	6
Clear cost justification	7
Well proven systems	7
Full training	7
Precisely defined objectives	10
Facilities to meet specific needs	11
Use of pilots or prototypes	11
Organisational change	13

Figure 7.3 Factors leading to successful implementation (*Source*: Grimshaw and Kemp 1989)

A survey of local authorities by Grimshaw and Kemp (1989) reported on the factors significant in achieving a successful implementation of office automation. Figure 7.3 shows how the factors were rated by the IT manager respondents to the survey.

Often the lessons for the future arise from observing systems that have failed. The generic lessons from the research by Grimshaw (1988), reported earlier in the chapter, are an example of such an approach. Strassmann (1984) concluded that the main cause of failure was lack of managerial competence. In other words, systems rarely fail for technical reasons, rather for some reason attributable to management action or inaction. It might be tempting to think that this conclusion is, at least partly, due to the concentration of research studies in areas away from the leading edge of technology. However, Land *et al.* (1992) conducted research into the implementation of IPSE. Land *et al.* (1992) conclude that the failure of a merchant bank to introduce an IPSE was due to organisational factors. The introduction of an IPSE requires a great deal of organisational change. This is more easily accomplished within an organisational culture that is used to change.

The influence of systems *usability*

Earlier in the chapter, one of the measures of a successful system was the extent to which it was used. In essence this is what we mean by 'usability'. What factors influence the usability of an information system?

Eason (1988) argues that usability is a function of user expertise. The expertise of the user may be measured in two dimensions. Firstly, in terms of task expertise (where the professional is likely to have a high level of expertise). Secondly, in terms of systems expertise (where the computer specialist is likely to have a high level of expertise). Figure 7.4 shows how different users have varying levels of expertise.

		Task Expertise	
		Low	High
System Expertise	Low	The Public	Occasional Professional
	High	Computer Specialists	Application Specialists

Figure 7.4   Usability of information systems (*Source*: Eason 1988)

What does a system need to be usable?

The usability of the system is influenced by its design, particularly the part of the information systems design that the user first comes into contact with, namely (to use the jargon) the human–computer interface (HCI). The main attributes of a usable system, based on the research by Eason (1988), are:

1. *A match between how people give and receive information.* Most people are comfortable with verbal communications of information. A natural extension of this into the world of the computer would be voice recognition – the ultimate in a user-friendly computer.
2. *Ease of learning what the system is doing.* For example, an expert system that gives advice and then displays the rules and logic which led it to give that advice.
3. *The system should conform to the user's model.* Take, for example, an accounting system – the user of which would expect the program to conform to the standard 'rules' of accounting appropriate to the institutional framework of the country. If the program does indeed conform to these expectations then it can be said to conform to the user's model.

The idea of a cognitive match is taken further by Eason (1988) and can be illustrated in Figure 7.5.

Criteria	Potential Provision
1. Expectations	Match "user model" of system e.g. common vocabulary, syntax and inference.
2. Task compatability	Match "user model" of application; Dialogue flexibility
3. Navigability	Status, direction, "road maps" Indication of options
4. Transparency	Protection from "housekeeping"

Figure 7.5 The user cognitive match (*Source*: Eason 1988)

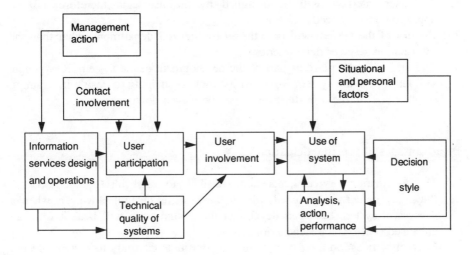

Figure 7.6 Influences on the implementation of information systems (*Source*: adapted from Lucas 1990)

This chapter has discussed the forces that shape a successful information system. There are many influences at work. The model shown in Figure 7.6 is a descriptive model of information systems in the organisational context, adapted from Lucas (1990). The original model showed the user attitudes and perceptions (behavioural factors grouped together as 'user participation') as the dominating influences. The model has been adapted in the light of research by Kappelman and McLean (1991) which suggests that 'user involvement' (psychological factors), as distinct from user participation, is a more important determinant of a successful information system.

Implementation strategies

If change is forced on potential users this is likely to create an unfavourable attitude as people perceive the change as threatening. To follow this scenario would probably lead to a poor system because the user staff would fail to cooperate with the technical design staff. The consequent poor technical system would in turn lead to a low rate of use of the new system.

How can this scenario be avoided? A number of possible implementation strategies will be discussed. Whichever implementation strategy is adopted, user participation is crucial.

Advantages of user participation

1. The user interface will be designed by the user and therefore will be appropriate to his needs.
2. Control of the system will be retained by the user department rather than the information services department.
3. Training will take place as part of the development of the system. Key people will learn how the system works whilst they are helping to design it. Training of other staff in the user department can be passed down.

Disadvantages of user participation

1. The information services department are likely to resist this approach because they may perceive a reduced role in the systems design. However, when a successful system has been developed the design team will benefit from an enhanced sense of job satisfaction.
2. Users may question their own ability to contribute centrally to systems design and development. Management support will be crucial at the initial stages until the users are stirred by the excitement of designing their system.

Alternative implementation strategies

The selection of an implementation strategy will always depend on the type of organisation and the particular application. Eason (1988) has identified five alternative strategies which illustrate the main approaches. These alternatives may, in practice, be mixed.

The 'big bang'

This is the most revolutionary approach and therefore presents the users with the greatest potential difficulty in adapting to the new system. A recent example of this approach is the overnight transfer of the London Stock Market to electronic trading in 1986. The risks entailed with such an approach do not need emphasis here. History can tell its own story as the Taurus stock exchange system has now been very publicly scrapped at an estimated cost of 75m.

Parallel running

Sometimes, in order to minimise the risks to the business of a failure in a new system, an organisation chooses to have old and new systems running together for a short period. Recognition that this approach inevitably means extra demands on existing staff should always be made. If existing staff are expected to handle both systems then it may well lead to negative reactions.

Phased introduction

Commonly, this approach is used to introduce a new system to a single functional group. If users can use the same system in different functional areas, the approach may work well. However, it is common for there to be exchange of information between groups. This may lead to only partial use of a system until fully phased.

Pilot projects

Pilot projects were commonly used in a number of office systems implementations. Where a large critical mass of users is essential for success the approach is doomed to failure. Choice of pilot project group and the speed of transfer to full working systems are the critical factors here.

The UK government, as part of its Information Technology Year in 1982, announced that it was to sponsor a number of pilot projects concerned with the office of the future. These projects involved partnerships between public sector users and computer suppliers and grants were available up to 250 000.

The major benefits of a pilot study approach, reported by Pye *et al.* (1986), were:

- hands-on experience can be gained;
- 'dead ending' can be avoided by trying out several vendors and avoiding making a firm commitment to one supplier too soon;
- basic assumptions can be tested, for example whether the system can be cost justified;
- the effects of the system on traffic flows and activity analysis schedules can be established;
- any organisational restructuring can be identified;
- redeployment and training requirements can be identified;
- hardware/software/user interface problems that have to be overcome before the system can go into full operational service within the organisation can be identified;
- the reliability of the system can be determined;
- the awareness of the staff can be raised without imposing an immediate and irreversible change.

Incremental applications

This is the most evolutionary approach. An example would be the *ad hoc* development of end-user applications. The balance between control and support is the critical issue here.

Choosing an implementation approach

The choice of implementation strategy is an important decision. The most appropriate approach will vary according to factors like the size and culture of the

Table 7.1 Variables associated with successful information systems

Information systems department	Technical quality	Management	User participation	User involvement	Use of system	Situational and personal factors	Decision style
Systems design methodology	Quality of interface	Policies	Expectations	Origination of system	Reported use	Personality type	Cognitive style
Operational policies	System flexibility	Culture	Interpersonal relations	Influence	Frequency of use	Business history	Shared values
Technology choices	Responsiveness	Support	Team building	Appreciation	User satisfaction	Past experience	

Source: Adapted from Lucas (1990).

organisation, the criticality of the information system, the number of users, and the newness of the technology.

A number of questions to ask, when considering which approach to use, are as follows:

1. *Does the system need a large critical mass?* If so, the 'big bang' or 'parallel running' approach would be the most appropriate.
2. *Is normal business at risk?* If so, the 'parallel running' or 'phased introduction' approach would be the most appropriate.
3. *How fast are users willing to change and learn?* Essentially the approaches range from the revolutionary 'big bang' to the evolutionary 'incremental applications'. The choice depends on how quickly it is possible and/or desirable to change.
4. *Are local needs important?* Sometimes the needs of groups of users will differ. One department, say marketing, may have different needs from the finance department. If this is the case, it may be most appropriate to test out the variations via 'pilot projects'.

Essentially, the outcome of the various research studies discussed is that there are a number of independent variables associated with successful implementation as shown in Table 7.1. Users who develop negative attitudes, afraid to participate in the systems design process, will adversely affect the technical quality of the system. The management strategy should recognise that the systems development process is about change. Users should then be supported in making that change in attitude that will lead to user involvement. What can we learn from a case study of a successful GIS implementation?

Case study of Hong Kong airport project

If it can be done, then it can be done in Hong Kong faster than anywhere else. There is a bustle and excitement about the place that is infectious – truly a place that never appears to sleep. What better place to choose for a case study of the implementation of a GIS project? The Hong Kong territory is set to revert to governance from mainland China in 1997. The time-scales have been set, there is uncertainty about the future and the Hong Kong government is trying to provide improvements to the infrastructure to ensure that Hong Kong remains the major gateway to southern China. A major part of these plans is to develop a new airport and extend the port facilities.

Anyone who has visited Hong Kong will realise that land is in short supply, the steep mountains shelving directly into the sea. Buildings have a short economic life as it becomes financially attractive to pull them down and build ever taller ones in their place. Land for expansion has to be created by reclamation using marine filling. Recognising the importance to the economy of these marine filling projects, the Hong Kong government set up a Fill Management Committee (FMC) as a high-level coordinating body. Given the short time-scales, and the strategic importance of the task, the FMC searched for an appropriate form of IT to help them.

The FMC did not have the required skills to develop any information systems themselves, and as has already been pointed out, the time-scales for the project were critically short. Therefore, the decision was taken to search for consultants who could advise on what IT was available to assist. A consultancy from the USA was commissioned to search for available technologies and advise accordingly. The Hong Kong government has a tradition of appointing engineering consultancies to carry out major infrastructural projects like the harbour tunnel. Following this well-established cultural tradition of the organisation, a firm of engineering consultants was appointed to provide a turnkey GIS.

The task set for the appointed consultants, Posford Duvvier, was reported by Giddings (1991) as being to place in the hands of the FMC managers, in their offices, nine months after appointment, a system fully tailored to meet their specific needs. Quite a challenge. Like any project, the first task was to identify the critical activities, the milestones and the key people from within the organisation and from the consultants.

The GIS project was a key feature in the business plan of the FMC, assuring the project of high-level commitment. There was also a sense of importance and urgency about the project. Managing the key resource – sand below the sea bed – in terms of allocation to development projects, bearing in mind the constraints of cables, pipelines and navigational channels, was the challenge. The FMC has to control the allocation of fill material to the most suitable development projects. The urgency stemmed essentially from the time-scales on major projects such as the airport development with the political commitment to complete by 1997.

Most GIS projects will have an agreed systems specification early in the process. However, FMC agreed to the project and employed the engineering consultants without a detailed systems specification. What were the critical success factors? High-level commitment coupled with an urgent need for the project have already been mentioned. Effective communications between the consultants and the users was enabled by a common technical language. In other words, both groups of people knew about geology, marine environments and civil engineering projects. High priority was given to training and documentation, with one full-time member of the project team allocated for the last five months of the project. Data collection and data entry formed an integral part of the system implementation. All existing maps of marine resources and constraints were digitised and data from 400 boreholes was entered as part of the project set-up.

Tried and tested hardware and software were selected for the project. This gave the system designers flexibility to change the system as user requirements became clearer. The GIS software package chosen was ARC/INFO running on a workstation under the UNIX operating system. Links were made to a database using dBase IV running on personal computers. By selecting such a combination of software it was possible to test out modules, feedback problems or amendments from the users, and then change the system design relatively quickly.

The Hong Kong case study shows that it is possible to complete a complex GIS project in a short period of time (nine months). Some of the critical success factors may be unique to the Hong Kong culture and organisation, yet there are lessons here for all of us.

Summary

Tell me I forget, show me I remember, *involve* me, I understand (Chinese proverb, author's italics).

After a case study based in Hong Kong it seemed appropriate to insert an apposite Chinese proverb. *Involvement* is the key word when considering implementation. This is true of users, managers, technical computer staff and vendors.

The fundamental assumption, stated early in the chapter, is that more use of an information system is an indicator of a successful system. This chapter has focused on the question of the influences at work in implementing information systems successfully. Implementation is seen in a wider context than the traditional view as a stage in the information systems development life cycle. The following points provide a summary:

1. The traditional approach to implementation is a narrowly defined stage in the systems development life cycle. This leads to an undue emphasis on the technical aspects of testing the code, documentation, etc. An emphasis on problem identification and use of softer systems approaches are likely to provide the way forward.
2. It has been found that GIS fail because of managerial problems rather than technical problems.
3. At the heart of the managerial problem is the split between power and responsibility. The technical experts often have the power whilst the business manager has the responsibility.
4. Successful information systems must contain accurate data, the use of that data should be monitored, and there should be a strong support team.
5. There are five possible generic implementation strategies: big bang, parallel running, phased introduction, pilot projects and incremental applications.
6. The choice of an appropriate implementation strategy depends upon the size and culture of the organisation, the criticality of the information system, the number of users, and the newness of the technology.
7. Empirical research studies have suggested a number of factors that lead to successful implementation; first among these is *commitment* from top management.
8. The *usability* of a system will be influenced by the human–computer interface which should conform to a number of guidelines.
9. Both user participation and user *involvement* are important ingredients in a successful implementation.

The implementation of GIS involves the management of change. This has for many years been recognised as a challenge. The role of the person championing that change was aptly discussed by Machiavelli (1968: 51):

'It ought to be remembered that there is nothing more difficult to take in hand, more perilous to conduct, or more uncertain in success, than to take the lead in the introduction of a new order of things. Because the innovator has for enemies all those who have done well under the old conditions and lukewarm defenders among those who may do well under the new.'

Further study

There are many papers and books on systems development that make reference to implementation; however, their interpretation is somewhat restricted to the *stage* that simply sees the IT project being 'signed-off'. Views of implementation as a wider *process*, as put forward in this chapter, are emerging in the literature on organisational behaviour. Some studies are linking the ideas from the organisational behaviour area of management with the research into technology. Of these, the following two books can be recommended:

Scarbrough H, **Corbett J M** 1992 *Technology and Organisation: Power, Meaning and Design* Routledge Series in Analytical Management, London
Walsham G 1993 *Interpreting Information Systems in Organisations* John Wiley & Sons, Chichester

References

Avison D E, **Fitzgerald G** 1988 *Information Systems Development: Methodologies, Techniques and Tools* Blackwell Scientific Publications, Oxford
Daniels A, **Yeats D A** 1971 *Basic Training in Systems Analysis* 2nd edn, Pitman, London
DoE 1987 *Handing Geographic Information*. Report of the Committee of Enquiry chaired by Lord Chorley, HMSO, London
Eason K 1988 *Information Technology and Organisational Change* Taylor & Francis, London
Gibson C, **Nolan R L** 1974 The four stages of EDP growth. *Harvard Business Review* **52**: 74–88
Giddings T 1991 Ingredients for successful GIS implementation: a Hong Kong case study. *Proceedings of the AGI Conference* Birmingham, UK, pp 1.10.1–4
Grimshaw D J 1988 The use of land and property information systems *International Journal of Geographical Information Systems* **2**(1): 57–65
Grimshaw D J 1991 Geographical information systems as part of the corporate information strategy. *International Journal of Information Management* **11** (4): 292–7
Grimshaw D J 1992 Towards a taxonomy of information systems: or does anyone need a TAXI? *Journal of Information Technology* **7**: 30–6
Grimshaw D J, **Kemp B** 1989 Office automation in local government. *Local Government Studies* March/April: 7–15
Grindley K 1991 *Managing IT at Board Level* Pitman, London
Grunden K 1986 Some critical observations on the traditional design of administrative information systems and some proposed guidelines for human-orientated systems

evolution. In Nissen H-E, Sandstrom G (eds) *Quality of Work versus Quality of Information Systems* Lund University, Sweden

Healy M 1987 *Office Systems Implementation: The Critical Success Factors* July, IBM UK, Portsmouth

Hirschheim R, Klein H K 1992 A research agenda for future information systems development methodologies. In Cotterman W W, Senn J A (eds) *Challenges and Strategies for Research in Systems Development* John Wiley & Sons, Chichester, pp 235–56

Hobson S A 1991 Critical success factors in the choice of design methodology for corporate geographic information systems. Unpublished dissertation for the degree of MBA, University of Warwick, Coventry, UK

Kappelman L A, McLean E R 1991 The respective roles of user participation and user involvement in the information system implementation process. *Proceedings of the Twelfth International Conference on Information Systems* 16–18 December, New York, pp 339–49

Kling R 1992 Behind the terminal: the critical role of computing infrastructure in effective information systems development and use. In Cotterman W W, Senn J A (eds) *Challenges and Strategies for Research in Systems Development* John Wiley & Sons, Chichester, pp 365–414

Land F F, Le Quesne P N, Wijegunaratne I 1992 Technology transfer: organisational factors affecting implementation – some preliminary findings. In Cotterman W W, Senn J A (eds) *Challenges and Strategies for Research in Systems Development* John Wiley & Sons, Chichester, pp 65–82

Le Duc M-C 1992 A design methodology for geoinformatic systems. *Computing, Environment and Urban Systems* **16**: 403–13

Long L 1989 *Management Information Systems* Prentice-Hall, Englewood Cliffs, NJ

Lucas H C 1975 *Why Information Systems Fail* Columbia University Press, Columbia

Lucas H C 1990 *Information Systems Concepts for Management* 4th edn, McGraw-Hill, New York

Machiavelli N 1968 *The Prince* Cambridge University Press, Cambridge, UK

Medyckyj-Scott D, Cornelius S 1991 The move to GIS: some empirical evidence of users' experiences. *Proceedings of Mapping Awareness '91* Birmingham, UK, pp 115–37

Openshaw S, Cross A, Charlton M, Brunsdon C, Lillie J 1990 Lessons learnt from a post mortem of a failed GIS. *Proceedings of the AGI Conference* Brighton, UK pp 2.3.1–5

Paschoud J, Bell A 1993 Quality GIS applications – easier said than done? *Proceedings of the AGI Conference* Birmingham, UK, pp 1.4.1–5

Pye R, Bates J, Heath L 1986 *Profiting from Office Automation: Office Automation Pilots Final Evaluation Results* KMG Thomson McLintock, Department of Trade and Industry, London

Strassmann P 1984 *The Information Payoff: The Transformation of Work in the Electronic Age* Free Press, New York

Sutherland A R, Galliers R D 1991 Information systems management and strategy formulation: the stages of growth model revisited. *Journal of Information Systems* **2**: 89–114

Tapscott D, Caston A 1993 *The Paradigm Shift: The Promise of New Information Technology* McGraw-Hill, New York

Willcocks L, Mason D 1987 *Computerising Work: People, Systems Design and Workplace Relations* Paradigm Press, London

Part Three

Using Geographical Information in Business

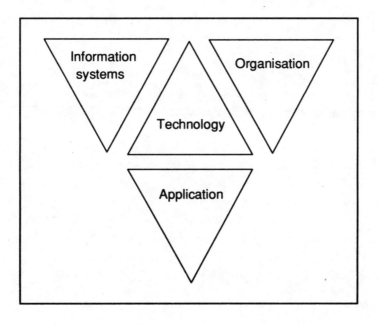

8

Application capabilities

'. . . The summits of various kinds of business are, like the tops of mountains, much more alike than the parts below – the bare principles are much the same; it is only the rich variegated details of the lower strata that so contrast with one another. But it needs travelling to know that the summits are the same. Those who live on one mountain believe that their mountain is wholly unlike all others.'

Walter Bagehot (1963)

Preamble

The basic capabilities of GIS are reviewed in relation to some questions and guidelines of their applicability to business. Examples of what GIS can do are given. These are then built on when particular case studies of the use of GIS to assist business decision making are analysed in Chapters 9–11.

The capabilities of GIS are changing all the time as technology advances and hitherto uneconomic applications become possible at a price that users can afford to pay. In this sense the boundary of where GIS is applicable is changing all the time. So why is it important to consider capability? There is some chicken and egg reasoning here. In Parts One and Two it has been argued that the business objectives and strategy need to drive the GIS. On the other hand, how does the business know what are the possible applications of GIS if they are not aware of its capabilities? The main objective of this chapter is to address this dilemma by outlining the main capabilities of GIS. Capability is defined as the utility or usefulness of GIS to do things. It is often the basis upon which comparisons of software products are made. In the literature there has previously been an emphasis on functionality, defined as the operations carried out by GIS (Maguire and Dangermond 1991). Capability is preferred as a term because it shifts the emphasis from technology functions towards use for an application.

There is an initial temptation to think of all GIS as being the same. At one level they are, at another there are vast differences of capability. This is, in the terms of the quotation from Bagehot, rather like seeing all the mountains as the same unless you happen to live on one.

Defining capabilities required

What are the application capabilities that your business is looking for? The answer to this question will differ between industries and between specific levels of application such as operational, tactical and strategic. Some general guidelines can be given. The guidelines are formulated in two ways: firstly by answering some basic questions about your business, and secondly by examining the potential for GIS applications in your industry. The following questions modified from Dobson (1993) are a way of beginning to understand which GIS functions are required by your application.

1. Is your business concerned with land cover, for example forest? This will help to determine the need for remote sensing, video, global positioning system (GPS) or aerial photographs.
2. Does your business examine its domain in orthogonal fashion? If the answer is affirmative then the chances are that a GIS will be useful.
3. Are you concerned with spatial or attribute data? Requirements for data will suggest the need for GIS or not.
4. What is the scale of geographic phenomena that your business needs to work with, for example facility or plant, community, city, region, country or global? The answer will help determine requirements for accuracy, source and availability of data.
5. Does your business have to investigate functional relationships between phenomena in a given spatial area? For example, the effect of distance or drive time on number of customers visiting a store.
6. Is change over time important? Current GIS often do not handle the time dimension well. This is likely to be an area that is expanded in terms of added functionality in the near future.
7. Is your business concerned with three-dimensional relationships, for example the volume and dimensions of mineral deposits and their overburden? If so there will be a need for some three-dimensional modelling capability.
8. Do you need to analyse the relationship of two or more spatial areas? For example, the relationship between two competing potential shopping centres or the flow of traffic or goods on a road or railway.

Answers to the above questions are a good starting point for defining application capabilities. Your particular business may answer 'yes' to only one of the questions. In which case the type of GIS required will be fairly simple. At the other extreme, if your business requires all the above capabilities your GIS requirements will be very complex.

A second way of defining capabilities required is to look at the type of business. Francica (1993) has divided business into two types: the 'geographically rooted' and the 'geographically challenged'. Table 8.1 gives some examples of business in each type – these are meant for illustration rather than as a comprehensive list. The geographically rooted industries are those that depend on geography; for example, alumina can only be extracted where the deposits of the ore are located in certain ways. The case study of Alcoa (see Chapter 9) falls into this category. The geographically challenged are those industries where geography has not been a traditional input into decision making. Business in this category is challenged to see how GIS might help improve decision making.

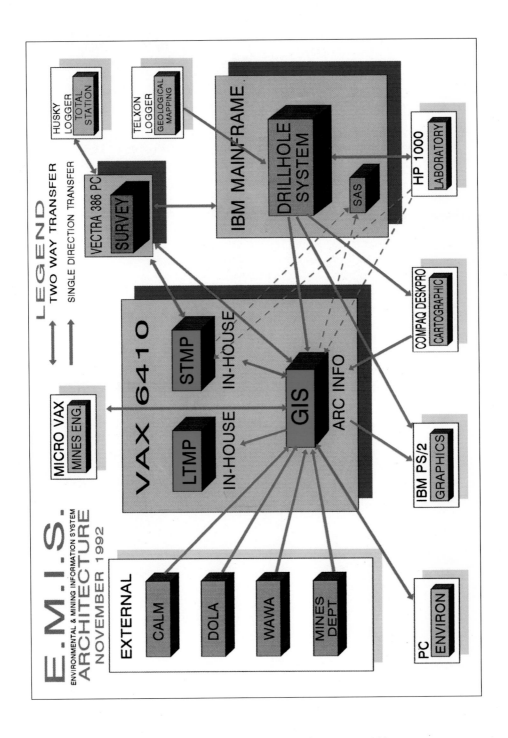

Plate I Environmental and mining information system architecture

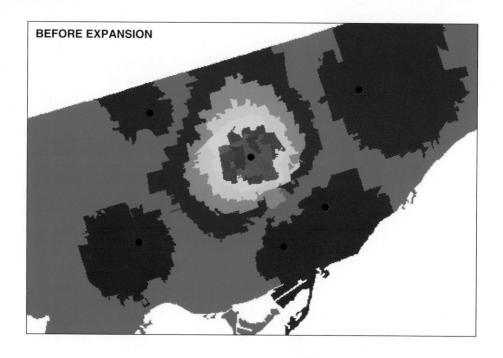

BEFORE EXPANSION

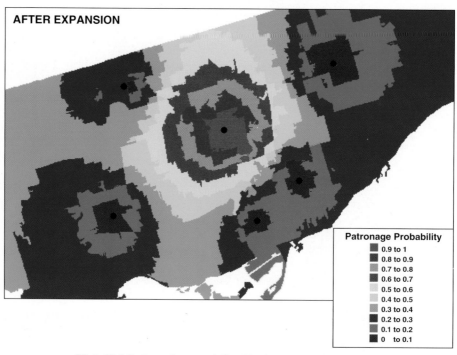

AFTER EXPANSION

Patronage Probability

- 0.9 to 1
- 0.8 to 0.9
- 0.7 to 0.8
- 0.6 to 0.7
- 0.5 to 0.6
- 0.4 to 0.5
- 0.3 to 0.4
- 0.2 to 0.3
- 0.1 to 0.2
- 0 to 0.1

Plate II Likely trade areas defined by iso-probability contours
(From Compusearch Micromarketing Data and Systems)

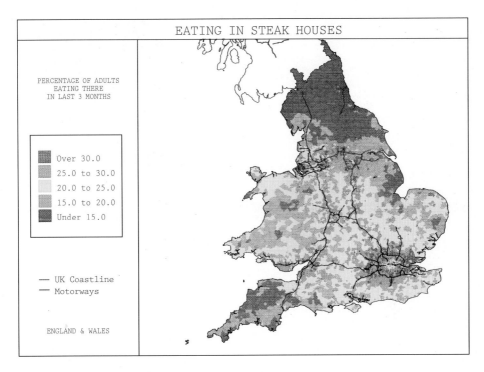

Plate III Thematic map of 'Eating in Steak Houses'

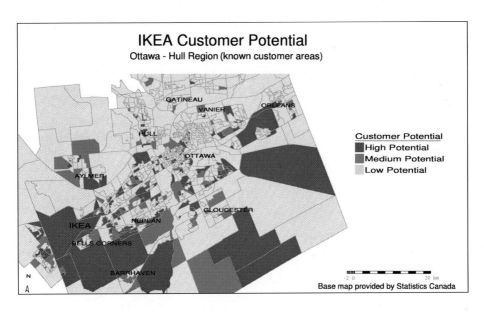

Plate IV IKEA customer potential (*Source*: O'Shaughnessy and Haythornthwaite 1993)

Plate V Trade area map of competing stores (Arby's) (*Source*: Reid 1993)

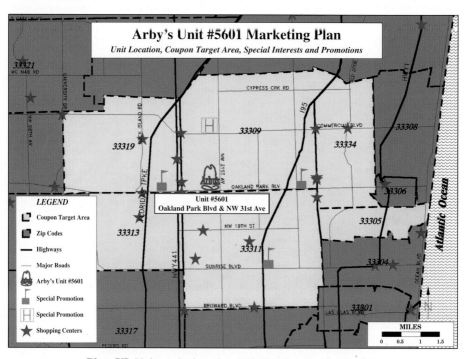

Plate VI Unit marketing plan (Arby's) (*Source*: Reid 1993)

Table 8.1   The applicability of GIS

Geographically rooted	Geographically challenged
Transportation	Retail
Mineral extraction	Banking and finance
Estate management/agency	Manufacturing
Telecommunications	Health
Agriculture	Tourism

Source: Adapted from Francica (1993).

What can GIS do?

One answer to this question is to refer back to Chapter 2 where a model of the components of a GIS was discussed (Figure 2.3). As with any information system, the GIS must have a way of capturing data, validating and editing that data, storing, manipulating and analysing it. There are many ways of describing such functions in the literature and indeed in vendor manuals for specific systems. In an effort to agree some common terminology Maguire and Raper (1990) have put forward a classification scheme which will be used here as a basis for discussing GIS capability. Table 8.2 shows the basics of this classification.

Table 8.2   Capabilities of GIS

	Geographical	Attribute
Capture	Raster	Keyboard
	Vector	OCR
Transfer	System independent	System independent
	System dependent	System dependent
Validate and edit	Add	Add
	Delete	Delete
	Change	Change
Store and structure	Raster	Flat File
	Vector	Relational database
Restructure	Change data structure	Change data structure
Generalise	Smooth	Smooth
	Aggregate	Aggregate
Transform	Affine	Linear
	Curvilinear	Non-linear
Query	Search	Retrieval
	Overlay	
Analyse	Network ·	
	Overlay	
Present	Maps	Tables
	Graphs	Reports

Source: Adapted from Maguire and Dangermond (1991).

The capabilities shown in Table 8.2 range from the very simple map presentation features to the complex, general geographic data-handling capabilities. Software packages developed for the large corporations, for example utilities (those that have traditionally used maps as a base for their operations) will typically have generic capabilities. On the other hand such systems are quite complex. Sola (1993) argued that the market for business applications in the GIS area was open to be filled with simple, economical and focused applications offering less functionality. Certainly business applications have to be focused, or what might more generally called problem focused. However, it is arguable that business requires less functionality. These ideas are expressed in Figure 8.1 which shows that business GIS need to be both simple and high in capability. The kind of capability may well differ from those seen in the generic GIS.

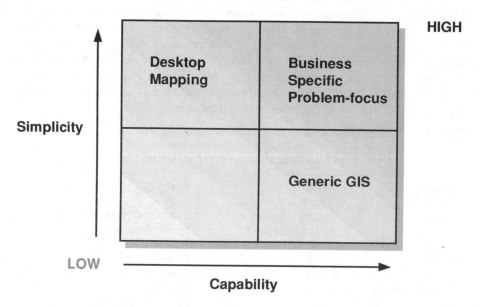

Figure 8.1 Capability trends

The most important capabilities of GIS from a business user's point of view can be grouped into three areas. Presentation of data in map form is the most obvious and immediately attractive capability. Secondly, an ability to query data. Thirdly, the capability to perform spatial analysis. These three areas are illustrated in Figure 8.2.

The capabilities of GIS can be considered under the following categories, which have been ordered so that those with the greatest mapping functions are considered first and gradually the list moves towards an emphasis on spatial analysis capabilities.

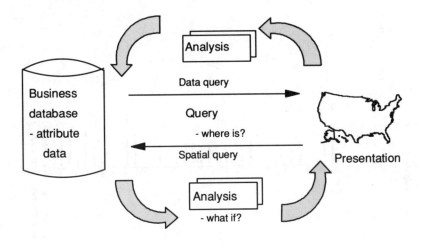

Figure 8.2 GIS capability model

Presentation mapping

According to Landis (1993) presentation mapping is the most important capability for about 90% of users. All GIS must have this feature to even warrant the name GIS; it is, however, only a necessary condition, not a sufficient condition for the title. The key feature of presentation mapping is the ability to display attribute data on a map. Often such programs are called visualisation systems because they help users to visualise the spatial patterns in their data. A useful analogy here is to think of business graphics as offering users the ability to see patterns in data via displays such as pie charts or histograms and the presentation map offers a way of understanding spatial patterns. An example would be for a bank to display a map showing the distribution of branches throughout a country.

The major limitation of presentation mapping is that it is generally a one-way process, to display data rather than to act as a method of query for that data.

Thematic mapping

Thematic maps have the additional feature of being able to display attributes in relation to points, lines or polygons. For example, the bank logo (which was simply displayed in a presentation map) might be displayed at the branch location, at a size related to the profits of that particular branch. In this example the profits (attribute) is related to the point on a map.

TASTES REGIONAL REPORTS 1992

Title: 1992 RESTAURANT TYPE & WINE
Target Zone:20 MINS CHELMSFORD (DEMO)

Client: SPA Marketing Systems
Base Zone:GB (GB)

Ref: Examples ******* 15/12/92

	--Target Zone-- COUNT	RATIO	--Base Zone-- COUNT	RATIO	--Target/Base-- PENETRATION	INDEX
EATING OUT: RESTAURANT TYPE						
Restaurant: Ever	112746	100.0%	30618872	100.0%	0.00368	100
Hamburger bar	23395	20.8%	4933834	16.1%	0.00474	129
Steak House	39912	35.4%	8174869	26.7%	0.00488	133
Chinese	29694	26.3%	7774729	25.4%	0.00382	104
English	53774	47.7%	16088084	52.5%	0.00334	91
French	8483	7.5%	1809240	5.9%	0.00469	127
Greek/Turkish	5836	5.2%	1399101	4.6%	0.00417	113
Indian	26860	23.8%	7156118	23.4%	0.00375	102
Italian	22435	19.9%	5670522	18.5%	0.00396	107
DRINKERS OF TABLE WINE						
Wine in a box	7053	5.0%	1675982	4.1%	0.00421	123
Sparkling	13227	9.4%	3531166	8.6%	0.00375	109
Low Alcohol Wines	1791	1.3%	480349	1.2%	0.00373	109
Drink Table Wine at home	51662	36.7%	12706079	31.0%	0.00407	119
Bottled table wine	60283	42.8%	14818288	36.1%	0.00407	119
French Red	15843	26.3%	3278841	22.1%	0.00483	119
French White	16592	27.5%	3535588	23.9%	0.00469	115
German White	27060	44.9%	6255245	42.2%	0.00433	106
Italian Red	5023	8.3%	1176631	7.9%	0.00427	105
Italian White	6588	10.9%	1624888	11.0%	0.00405	100
Spanish Red	2536	4.2%	503517	3.4%	0.00504	124
Spanish White	2876	4.8%	708669	4.8%	0.00406	100
Yugoslavian White	2806	4.7%	697286	4.7%	0.00402	99
Australian	1696	2.8%	306480	2.1%	0.00553	136
Californian	1391	2.3%	219775	1.5%	0.00633	156
DRINKERS OF FORTIFIED WINES						
Sherry - British	15287	10.9%	5383615	13.1%	0.00284	83
Sherry - not British	17343	12.3%	4261287	10.4%	0.00407	119
Aperitifs	3238	2.3%	674710	1.6%	0.00480	140
Vermouth	8985	6.4%	2372293	5.8%	0.00379	110
Port	13630	9.7%	2933041	7.1%	0.00465	136
Madeira	3451	2.5%	794223	1.9%	0.00435	127

(INDEX bar chart scale: 0 — 50 — 100 — 150 — 200 — 250 — 300)

Figure 8.3   Tabular report on 'eating out'

A further example will serve to illustrate the value that thematic maps can add to tabular data. There are many market research databases available (some further discussion on geodemographics is given in Chapter 10). An extract from Target Group Index data is given in Figure 8.3 to show the numbers of people within a 20-minute drive time of Chelmsford eating out at various restaurant types. By looking at the data and reading the bar chart on the right we see that steak houses have the highest market penetration. How does Chelmsford relate to other areas of the country? There would be a lot of tabular data sheets to examine before an overall picture could be established. However, with a map, for example Plate III, it becomes easy to see the geographic pattern of adults eating at steak houses.

Data query

Every business has many databases containing attribute data. In Chapter 2 the point was made that 90% of business data is geographic (see Table 2.1 for examples). For example, suppose a retail business has a customer database that includes the postcode for each customer. It also has a property assets database showing the location of stores. A manager may wish to know where customers who spend more than 100 per visit live. Without a GIS the database query could produce a table, sorted by postcode, of customers. There would be a lot of data in such a table and most managers would find it difficult to translate this into

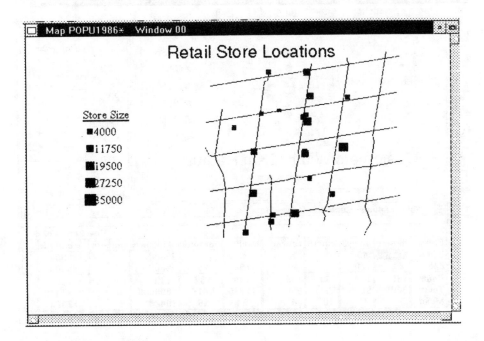

Figure 8.4 Example of a data query

meaningful information. The power of GIS is that it adds the context of the map, thereby translating that data into powerful information. The retail manager could produce a map, for example the one shown in Figure 8.4, showing retail outlets with the symbol size in proportion to the size of the store.

Spatial query

From here, down the list of capabilities, are true GIS. The capabilities discussed above are often referred to as desktop mapping. Spatial queries are driven from the map back to the database (see Figure 8.2). In other words the typical user would point (using a mouse or other pointing device) at a place of interest on a map. The GIS searches the database, for example for a retail manager who is displaying store locations and competitor locations on screen. By pointing at a competitor location the details held on the database could be displayed in a window. This might include competitor name, address, trade type, floorspace, etc. In a similar way a user might move about the screen to select any point of interest.

A slightly more sophisticated type of spatial query would involve defining an area of interest (rather than simply a point). For example, suppose our retail manager wishes to know how many and what type of customers travel from within a 2 kilometre radius of the store. Figure 8.5 shows how a GIS can display such

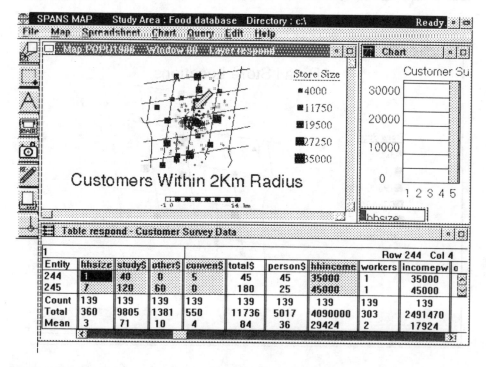

Figure 8.5 Spatial query: search for customers within 2 km radius

information. Here there are three windows open, the map shows stores and customers, the spreadsheet below the map shows attributes of customers such as household size (hhsize), total spending (total$), household income (hhincome), etc. The customers within the defined area of interest have been highlighted in the spreadsheet and a subtotal is given. On a colour screen the GIS would show these customers in (say) red whilst customers travelling further might be shown in (say) blue.

If your business interest was in estate agency (real estate), then in addition to the windows shown in the Figure 8.5 example, by pointing to a particular property it would be possible to open a window showing a photograph – or even a video of that property. The capability here is really to integrate different types of data: text, numeric, image and map.

Search by distance only can be misleading. The result depends on so many other geographic factors such as the road network, traffic conditions, terrain and so on. The capability of a GIS to use drive time can be very important for users in marketing for example. Drive-time databases (see for example Buxton and Morris 1993) can be purchased from data agencies or they can be built up by getting out there and driving and timing. Since drive-time databases are now available as part of a number of GIS packages the latter approach cannot be recommended. The essential drive-times are built from a road network (lines and nodes) and assumptions about speed attainable between each node. If road conditions change then these assumptions may be changed in the database. The advantages of using

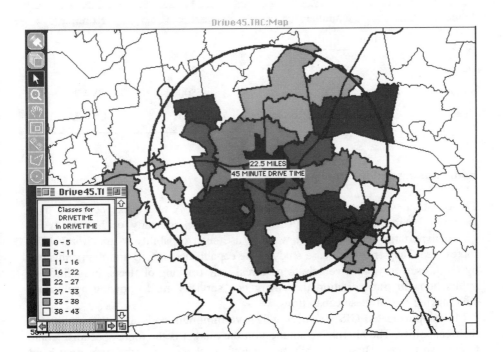

Figure 8.6 Trade area by distance or drive time?

drive time over distance are graphically illustrated by Figure 8.6. The map in Figure 8.6 shows a 45-minute drive-time trade area giving a population of 664 119. A query by distance, using 22.5 miles would give a population of 503 265 which is a difference of 32%.

Database integration

For most business applications the key to unlocking the capability of GIS is through a link to existing internal databases. A typical example of this would be a company with a customer file containing addresses with postcodes. To unlock the geography in the data (by mapping it) a boundary file is required. Given that the customer file probably does not contain all customer postcodes – some people inevitably cannot remember them – it may also be necessary to have an address or street to postcode conversion file. In many countries there are data products available to convert addresses to postcodes. Another consideration here is the level of accuracy required. Table 8.3 shows that there are, in the UK, four levels of postcode. (In the USA it is common to use the zip code whilst further detail is possible with the zip+4.)

Table 8.3   Postcodes

Name	Number	Households	Example
Area	120	183 000	CV
District	2 600	8 200	CV4
Sector	9 000	2 500	CV4 7
Unit	1.6 million	15	CV4 7AL

Route finding and minimum path

The question 'what is the shortest way to get from A to B?' is one asked by a variety of businesses – it is not just the transportation company, or the sales force. The transportation company will want to use such capability to monitor vehicle routes (see Chapter 9 for a case study). The capabilities of GIS are often enhanced by GPS, used (say) in a vehicle to give real-time tracking of fleets. In addition to applications in transportation the emergency services are a growing application area making use of these capabilities.

Most sophisticated GIS packages will have minimum path algorithms built into their capability. The alternative solution on the market is the more specialist 'route finder' software. These are highly focused packages, (in the top right-hand quadrant of Figure 8.1) offering specific solutions to the basic problem of 'what is the shortest route?' and 'how long will it take?' In the UK, Europe and the USA, AutoRoute is an example of this kind of package. It is used by over 20 000 companies in the UK (NextBase 1993). Route-finding software has the capability

Figure 8.7 Optimised route schedules for a sales force (from Nextbase)

of providing the quickest, shortest and preferred routes. The preferences can be determined by the user or by the organisation to include constraints on things like avoiding low bridges, and to optimise visits on (say) a day's schedule in the best order for the shortest driving time and calculating the costs. Figure 8.7 illustrates the capability of optimising routes for a sales force, given a schedule of customer visits.

On their own the capabilities of such software is useful to a range of business users. However, their real power is unleashed when internal databases are linked to the route planning programs to form a complete system. So important capabilities here are the interfaces to databases. For example, can you link your own databases without having to copy them or hold them in multiple formats? Standard interfaces, such as structured query language (SQL), may be an important capability. These factors should be taken into account as part of the information strategy.

Buffering

As a term, buffering has been introduced from the environmental sciences. It is used there to mean an area of land between some competing land uses such as industry and residential. More generically, buffering can be described as defining a zone of influence around a point, line or polygon. Here GIS offer the capability of defining a fixed distance from any of these features. For example, a buffer defined as a kilometre distance from a point would be drawn as a circle. If the buffer was defined as kilometres from a rail or highway, a corridor would be drawn on the map. A buffer around a polygon would take the same shape as the polygon.

An application in the insurance industry might be to identify risk areas by defining zones or buffers around features like rivers to denote flood risk. In the retail industry a simple trade area model could be established using buffers. More sophisticated ways of analysing retail markets are returned to later in the chapter.

Most generic GIS packages offer buffering capabilities. Their sophistication varies with respect to features which allow things like buffering of concave shaped polygons (Landis 1993).

Point in polygon analysis

Using standard zones for analysis, like postcode or census enumeration district, is all very useful for some purposes. However, there will often be the occasion when the predefined zone does not fit the zone required for the business analysis needed. For example, suppose a company wishes to reorganise its sales territories – postcode boundaries may be rather arbitrary so it wishes to define its own zones. From the addresses contained in the customer file, records can be geocoded and then assigned to an area whose boundary is (say) based on drive time. An example of sales territory allocation is shown in Figure 8.8.

Most of the generic GIS packages can perform point in polygon analysis and some of the specifically focused application packages are built around this capability.

Overlay

One of the most instantly impressive capabilities of GIS during demonstrations is their ability to overlay attributes. In Chapter 4 during discussion of geographical data models it was suggested that the raster model offered simpler and faster overlay analysis. The overlay capabilities may take a number of different forms. Landis (1993) has argued that although multiple layer overlays are in common usage by public sector applications, they are less frequently required by private sector users. Hopefully the examples here and the case studies in three Chapters 9–11 will show that this view must change.

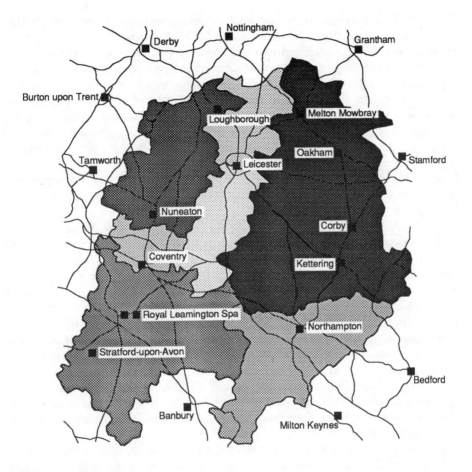

Figure 8.8 An example of a sales territory allocation

Maguire and Dangermond (1991) define overlay as the process of comparing spatial features in two or more map layers.

Proximity analysis

According to Landis (1993) only a few GIS packages can perform proximity analysis directly. The questions answered by proximity analysis are of the kind: what geographical features are near other features? Such questions can also be answered using a buffer to define the area of proximity, for example 0.5 km, and then overlaying a second map layer containing the map features required.

Spatial analysis

Very few GIS packages offer any kind of spatial analysis. Openshaw (1991a) states that a typical GIS will contain over 1000 commands but none could be regarded as offering spatial analysis functionality. One alternative approach is to perform the modelling using statistical software or specially written programs and then simply use the GIS for presentation of results. Iterations of the model would then be displayed. There has also been a detectable trend in the development of spatial analysis capability in GIS in the years since Openshaw made this statement. Certainly there are packages available that offer some spatial analysis routines.

Using GIS for decision support was a topic discussed in more detail in Chapter 5 where there was some discussion about using models to support the retail location decisions. The focus of discussion in Chapter 5 was on supporting decision makers in organisations whilst here we return to the topic of GIS capability.

So, spatial analysis capability of GIS has not, to date, been delivered by the main software packages available on the market. Further evidence of this is contained in the *1993 International Sourcebook* (Eynon 1992: Table 2.2) which compares 204 capabilities of more than 270 GIS software packages available. Spatial analysis and modelling capabilities are not included in the list. What kind of spatial analysis routines are practically required? These will vary according to the particular application domain. For illustration, it would be useful to take a closer look at the retail location problem again. Lea and Direzze (1993) argue that the main reason for non-use of GIS in the retail planning environment is lack of functionality, packaging of systems and scarcity of inexpensive high-quality data sets. In terms of Figure 8.1 what Lea and Direzze (1993) are arguing for is systems with high simplicity and high capability, that is what we have defined as problem focused systems. For another perspective on this issue see one of the case studies in Chapter 9.

The 'wish list' of capability put forward by Lea and Direzze (1993) includes regression models and gravity models. The present state of the market is largely dominated by GIS which does not include these capabilities, therefore the retail analyst has to use statistical software to model and then change to a mapping package to view the output. This state of affairs is unsatisfactory.

Gravity models

Despite what has been said earlier, some GIS software does include gravity modelling. Data inputs to such models are quite extensive, for example survey data on the number of trips taken from each demand area to each market. Probable trade areas are allowed to overlap which is a much more realistic approach than simple trade area models. Iso-probability contours are illustrated in Plate II.

Using GIS capabilities

Whatever GIS capability or group of capabilities is used in your business application there is almost sure to be map output that will be proudly presented to decision makers. As with any presentation tool there are ways of using maps to persuade. A map is essentially built from a set of generalisations about the real world. Factors such as colour, scale, level of data aggregation, labels and legends will affect the way the map user sees your message. Geographers, and those with some cartographic training, will have spent a great deal of time studying the art and craft of map design. It is impossible to do the subject justice in the short space available here, however it is important to raise some issues and common pitfalls to avoid.

One of the joys of using GIS is the ease with which maps can be designed and built. The computer offers the ability to draw and redraw maps until the user is satisfied. But does the user really understand what has been drawn? The problem here is similar to that faced by a nave data analyst using a sophisticated statistical package to analyse a survey and producing significance tests and correlations churned out by the computer but bearing little value in reality. The aim of this section is to raise your awareness of some of the problems of map design.

Map generalisation has been defined as 'the selection and simplified representation of detail appropriate to the scale and or purpose of a map' (ICA 1973). The obvious question to ask is 'what rules can be used to help me generalise?' The possibility of using expert systems ideas to embody rules in GIS has been a research area challenge but Muller (1991) points out that the results are uncertain to date. Robinson (1960:132) seems to have summed up the situation by saying that 'cartographic generalisation will remain forever an essentially creative process, and it will escape the modern tendency towards standardisation'. So we might conclude that the gems of wisdom that it is possible to pass on to the non-geographer business user of GIS are limited to pointing out some of the main issues.

One map is not enough

The capability of GIS, as we have said, makes map making deceptively simple. A very attractive looking map can be made relatively quickly. It should be remembered that it is always possible to produce many maps from the same data. In terms of data exploration using maps it is therefore good practice to produce many maps.

Areal aggregation of a ratio such as the average number of cars per household, taken from the census, will convey a different impression depending upon the area chosen, for example postcode area, district, county or region. What is the spatial distribution within the area chosen? Can homogeneity be assumed? The map maker must be aware of such questions and be prepared to qualify honestly the conclusions that might be made from the maps produced.

Classification is critically important when producing thematic or choropleth maps. For example, Figure 8.3 uses five classes, why not four or six? Most GIS packages will produce maps using automatic classification as a default option. The user needs to be wary and to find the best representation of the data.

Point data map or choropleth? Quite startlingly different results can be demonstrated in the maps shown in Figure 8.9. John Snow, a London physician working on the cholera epidemic in 1854, suspected that water might be the carrier of the disease. People carried water from pumps located closest to their homes. His map reproduced in Figure 8.9 showed the deaths from cholera, clearly showing a cluster around the Broad Street pump. The handle from the pump was removed and his suspicion was confirmed when the number of new cases decreased. As an exercise in map presentation the three smaller maps below show how different areal aggregations can mask the patterns.

Effective use of colour can help convey the message or detract from it. With the range of palettes available on good resolution screens and printers the choice may be overwhelming. Again defaults can be used, but also misused. Some basic knowledge of the effect of colour on perception is helpful. Colour is perceived in three ways: hue, saturation and value. Hue, from violet to red on the electromagnetic spectrum, represents colour as we normally speak of it in everyday conversation. Saturation is usually measured in percentage terms in GIS packages. So a hue with 100% saturation is strong, intense and brilliant. Value can equally apply to shades of grey – it represents light and dark. How does the map designer choose an appropriate mix of hue, saturation and value? On a recent course which attempted to give me the rudiments of cartographic design the one thing that was a constant debate with fellow students was the choice of colour. This goes to show that there is no range of hues that can be agreed upon to demonstrate a range of values from high to low.

Monmonier (1991) says that the critical question to ask is 'does the map use colour to portray differences in intensity or differences in kind?' Maps showing different kinds of features, for example the standard Ordnance Survey map showing roads, rivers, contours, etc., benefit from using different, sometimes contrasting, colours for each feature type. However, when using a map to indicate the intensity of a particular variable (see Figure 8.3 for example) use of value differences of a single hue or value differences from a small range of the spectral scale are recommended for conveying meaning.

User interfaces

The first impression for the user of a GIS is via the user interface. If this appears to give the user the capability required with minimal learning of new ways of working, the system is likely to be more successful. Recently there have been substantial moves towards standardised user interfaces. On the desktop this is most evident with the adoption of Windows on a personal computer, Apple Macintosh,

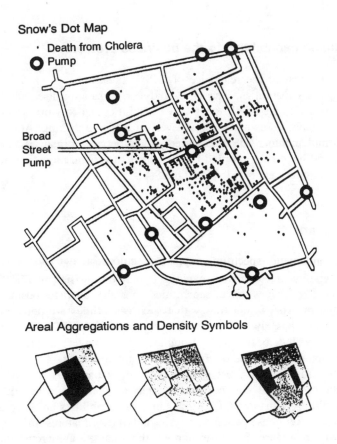

Figure 8.9 Point data map or choropleth? (*Source*: Monmonier 1991 *How to lie with maps*, reproduced courtesy of The University of Chicago Press)

or X/Windows on a workstation. Most GIS packages running under such operating environments present a fairly common look to the user.

Within this environment, however, there are substantial differences. Generic GIS are very complex, with typically over 1000 commands. Many have been written with the geographer or environmental scientist in mind rather than the business user. Figure 8.1 suggests that the trend is towards problem solving GIS that are simple to use yet offer high levels of functionality. The implication here is that GIS applications in the business environment need to be specifically tailored to fulfil decision support requirements. For example, a retail company wishing to use GIS for locational planning will not buy a generic GIS, it will look for a package that has the user interface tailored to specific needs. Such packages do exist on the market at the present time and the trend in the future is towards more of these solutions and less of the generic all-purpose GIS that we have seen brought to market in the past.

Relating capabilities to the business problem

The real test of the relevance of GIS is the extent to which business is actually using its capabilities. The case study organisations discussed in Chapters 9–11 illustrate a range of different GIS capabilities put to work to support a variety of business processes and various levels of decision making. Approaches to adopting and implementing GIS also varied widely between organisations. The patterns that emerged have been typified by the stages of growth model put forward in Chapter 2. A summary is provided in Table 8.4.

Summary

The range of capabilities of GIS is wide. Given the origins of such systems in cartography or automated mapping it is not surprising to find that many generic software packages have capabilities that the average business user will find redundant. That is not to say that such capabilities are not useful in themselves. Capability has always to be related to application. That is why the concept of capability has been used throughout this chapter in preference to the word 'functionality' that can often be found in the literature.

The emphasis at the beginning of the chapter was on raising questions that might be helpful for business people to consider when defining application capabilities. What can GIS do? A range of capabilities has been discussed with the emphasis on presentation, analysis and query features in line with the model shown in Figure 8.2. Throughout the chapter numerous illustrations of the capabilities being discussed have been presented. In the chapters that follow there will be further illustration of such capabilities in the case studies of real organisations and the story of how they are using GIS.

At some time the output from a GIS will be a map. The instant visual image presented by maps has an ability to convey meaning beyond that possible with tabular or graph data. The map also has the potential to mislead. Some warnings have been introduced to provoke thought about the design of maps and the messages that they carry.

Further study

The functions of specific software will constantly be changing as technology advances. Therefore comparisons of software packages have not formed part of

Table 8.4 Summary of GIS applications in Part Three

Case study	Business process	Decision type	Stage of growth	GIS capability
Lyonnaise des Eaux, France	Supply management Maintenance forecasting Customer complaints Water sampling Network events management	Operational	Corporate	Links to CAD
Manweb, UK		Operational	Linking	Originally excluded maps
British Gas, UK	Customer service Maintenance management	Operational	Corporate	Distributed
Miracle Foods, Canada	Customer survey processing Location analysis	Operational	Stand-alone	Digitising Links to customer database Thematic mapping
Minute Man, USA	Order entry Dispatch notes	Operational	Linking	Links to GPS
Alcoa, Australia	Mine planning Dieback disease management	Operational Strategic	Corporate	Generic GIS
Verdi Ryan, USA	Compliance with CRA Bank branch rationalisation	Tactical	Opt-out	Geodemographics Thematic mapping Spatial modelling
Car dealer, Europe	Dealer network review	Tactical	Opt-out	Geodemographics Links to databases Data integration

Table 8.4 Summary of GIS applications in Part Three (cont.)

Case study	Business process	Decision type	Stage of growth	GIS capability
IKEA, Canada	Location analysis	Tactical	Opt-out	Geodemographics Overlays Thematic mapping
MassMutual, USA	Sales territory management Market potential analysis	Tactical	Stand-alone Linking	Geodemographics Links to marketing database
Arby's, USA	Territory management Market survey analysis Market planning	Tactical	Linking	Geodemographics Thematic mapping Links to databases
Woolwich Building Society, UK	Customer marketing and sales Competitor analysis Branch rationalisation	Strategic	Opportunistic	Geodemographics Thematic mapping Links to databases
Isuzu, USA	Customer service Distribution and marketing	Strategic	Corporate	Links to databases
Conrail, USA	Business trend analysis Distribution channels Network planning	Strategic	Corporate	Data integration
Levi Strauss, USA	Business planning Distribution tracking	Strategic	Corporate	Geodemographics Links to databases

this chapter (or indeed of the book). One of the most comprehensive sources of comparison, updated annually, is:

International GIS Sourcebook GIS World Books Inc, Fort Collins, Colo

A related and very relevant area for further reading is about the interpretation of maps. Even if you feel that you can intuitively read a map there is one book that can be highly recommended. Just as statistics can be used for various purposes and can be presented in ways to support those aims, maps can also lie. If you have ever read *How to Lie with Statistics* you will know what a joy awaits when you read:

Monmonier M 1991 *How to Lie with Maps* University of Chicago Press, Chicago, Ill

Further reading in the area of spatial analysis is a specialist topic in itself. As a useful starting point the following can be recommended:

Lee C 1971 *Models in Planning* Pergamon Press, Oxford
Unwin D J 1981 *Introductory Spatial Analysis* Methuen, London
Upton G, Fingleton B 1985 *Spatial Analysis by Example* Vol 1 *Point Pattern and Quantitative Data* John Wiley & Sons, New York

Visualisation is an area of GIS research interest, with topics related to this chapter. The following references would make good further reading:

Langran G 1989 A review of temporal database research and its use in GIS applications. *International Journal of Geographical Information Systems* **3**: 215–32
Raper J (ed) 1989 *Three Dimensional Applications in Geographical Information Systems* Taylor & Francis, London

References

Bagehot W 1963 *The English Constitution* Collins, London
Buxton T, Morris M 1993 Use time, not distance, to drive your market. *Business Geographics* **1**(3): 10–11
Dobson J E 1993 GIS applications and functional requirements. In *1993 International GIS Sourcebook* GIS World Books Inc, Fort Collins, Colo, p 203
Eynon D (ed) 1992 GIS software functionality. In *1993 International Sourcebook* GIS World Inc, Fort Collins, Colo, pp 13–16
Francica J R 1993 The geographically rooted and the geographically challenged have similar needs. *Business Geographics* **1**(2): 23–4
ICA (International Cartographic Association) 1973 *Multilingual Dictionary of Technical Terms in Cartography* Franz Steiner Verlag GmbH, Wiesbaden
Landis J D 1993 GIS capabilities, uses and organisational issues. In Castle G H (ed) *Profiting from a Geographic Information System* GIS World Books Inc, Fort Collins, Colo, pp 23–54
Lea A, Direzze P 1993 The more functionality, the better the retail analysis. *Business Geographics* **1**(1): 33–8
Maguire D J, Dangermond J 1991 The functionality of GIS. In Maguire D J, Goodchild M F, Rhind D W (eds) *Geographical Information Systems* Vol 1 *Principles* Longman

Scientific & Technical, Harlow, pp 319–35

Maguire D J, Raper J F 1990 An overview of GIS functionality, *Proceedings of the Design Models and Functionality Conference* Midlands Regional Research Laboratory, Leicester, 10pp

Monmonier M 1991 *How to Lie with Maps* University of Chicago Press, Chicago, Ill

Muller J-C 1991 Generalisation of spatial databases. In Maguire D J, Goodchild M F, Rhind D W (eds) *Geographical Information Systems* Vol 1 *Principles* Longman Scientific & Technical, Harlow, pp 457–75

NextBase 1993 *Management of People on the Move* NextBase Ltd, Ashford, UK

Openshaw S 1991 Developing appropriate spatial analysis methods for GIS. In: Maguire D J, Goodchild M F, Rhind D W (eds) *Geographical Information Systems* Vol 1 *Principles* Longman Scientific & Technical, Harlow, pp 389–402

Robinson A H 1960 *Elements of Cartography* 2nd edn, John Wiley & Sons, New York

Sola L 1993 Capture the business geographics market with economical, focused applications. *Business Geographics* 1(2): 44–5

9

Operational applications

'All industries this decade will reengineer their major operations business systems in an effort to reduce operational costs and increase their ability to respond to changing market conditions. The technology platforms for automating these systems include spatial information systems'

John Pemberton (1992)

Preamble

Given the acknowledged rapid growth in the market for GIS in business, this section of the book explores current and potential applications. Using the GIS applications framework discussed in Chapters 1 and 2, Part Three evaluates the contribution GIS is making and could make in the future to business decision making at an operational, tactical and strategic level.

At the level of business operations management tasks focus on how to manage the facilities and assets of the organisation. This might involve, for example, a telecommunications company managing the network of nodes and lines around a particular country. A parcel delivery service company would need to optimise the routes for collection and delivery, manage parcel distribution centres, etc. In both these examples geographic data is a vital input to the decision-making process. This chapter analyses a number of case study organisations to examine the role of GIS in operations management. The cases are taken from a range of different industries and countries to illustrate the key issues of using GIS to support operational decisions. Why is GIS successful in some organisations and yet rejected in others? What are the benefits of GIS? How can GIS be best implemented? What data sets are used? These, and other, questions are explored with the help of the real cases.

The first applications of GIS technology were government agencies like the local planning authority or national mapping agencies like Ordnance Survey. In the terms used in Chapter 2, these are applications which involve little spatial analysis and a great deal of automated mapping function. Generally such systems have been referred to as AM/FM (automated mapping/facilities management) and there are several organisations and conferences devoted specifically to such issues. Paper maps in such organisations were commonplace repositories of operational information. As a matter of routine, managers would consult a paper based map to answer questions like when did we last maintain the highway between junctions 3 and 4? Using such operational maps as the basis of a GIS was essentially a simple step of automating the map.

Most businesses do not have operational maps, therefore the straightforward route of automating the business process from a set of paper records is not an obvious option. Yet most businesses do carry out their operations in defined geographic space. Herein lies the potential of GIS to assist the manager in running the operations of the business. For operational applications, the nature of that spatial data is likely to be narrowly focused (data breadth) and detailed (high data depth) as explained in Chapter 4.

Automated mapping/facilities management

The largest users of GIS are governmental agencies, followed by utility companies. An illustration from the North American market shows that out of the $5 billion spent on GIS in North America in 1991, the water, gas and electric utilities and telephone companies spent over $1.5 billion (CSR Inc. 1992). A survey of 1300 utility executives in 1992 found that 86% had GIS projects under way (AM/FM International Association 1992). A similar picture could be painted in other countries, with organised AM/FM associations covering Europe, Australasia and Japan.

Existing record keeping in the utilities are held on maps. Such maps have been accumulated over the years with different professionals such as engineers and planners adding features to the paper map base. Inevitably, the maps become illegible, congested in areas of frequent change and the accuracy of many maps has been questioned. Rector (1993) states that the estimated error rate within the telecommunications industry is as high as 35%. Such high errors are due to transcription and reporting errors. The maps are almost always out of date because of the time it takes to process change data. The usefulness of the map base as a source of information for decision making is thus reduced.

The transport and distribution industries also rely on map-based data in order to move goods and services in an efficient manner. Movement by land, sea or air provides slightly different challenges in respect of the data available and GIS solutions possible. In this chapter we will include discussion of sea navigation and land route planning systems.

Electronic navigation

A common problem in a wide variety of industries is how to navigate from location A to location B. Potential applications of navigational systems include transport, distribution, parcel courier services and emergency services. Market analysts have estimated that sales of navigation systems for automobiles will grow from US$5 m. in 1990 to US$100 m. in 1994 (Frost and Sullivan 1989). The private motorist will clearly benefit from car navigation systems that are already available in the USA, Japan and Germany (White 1991). However, for the purposes of this chapter we will concentrate on uses of navigational systems by corporations.

Applications of GIS technology to navigational routeing and distribution problems have been greatly enhanced by recent developments of global positioning systems (GPS). As a precursor to the discussion about specific case studies it is worth discussing the general nature of GPS. The essence of GPS is that it provides latitude and longitude, altitude and time for any point on the earth. The accurate position generation for fixed or mobile assets by people 'in the field' allows attribute data to be collected and instantly related to the spatial reference. How does this work and what equipment is required?

The original and largest GPS is that undertaken by the US Department of Defense. By February 1993 there were 22 satellites in operation, with a further 2 being required before full coverage is offered (Kruczynski and Jasumback 1993). The satellites continually broadcast a time signal using an atomic clock. A receiver uses the time signal to calculate the distance to the satellite. Accuracy available ranges from 100 m to 1 cm (these relate to horizontal measurements achievable 95% of the time). The accuracy of the data depends on a number of factors and is worthy of consideration in relation to the type of application being considered. For example, a vehicle tracking or fleet management system will require less accurate data than a utility company wishing to position its pipelines or cables.

Whilst writing the manuscript for this book several packages containing source material were delivered to my home in Warwick. These packages came from Australia, the USA and Canada via companies like Federal Express. Gazing out of my study window for inspiration I happened to notice that one of the couriers had travelled past. A short time later there was a phone call asking for directions from a driver who admitted he was lost. How would GIS have helped?

Navigating the oceans of the world was, at one time, a simple question of how to get there and back. Today's mariner must additionally plot an energy-efficient course, avoid other vessels and remain cost-effective. The advent of GPS has had a major impact on the application of GIS to ship navigation.

An electronic chart display and information system (ECDIS) developed by Matrix Technologies Inc. (Strong 1993) enables navigators to view hydrographic data on screen and GPS can update the position of the vessel. A key feature is the integration of several data sources, for example, the hydrological charts, sonar readings and weather information, into a single display. Views of the previous and intended track can be seen at the touch of a button. For added safety, a 'man overboard' feature allows the vessel to retrace its track to allow the rescue of anyone who has fallen into the sea.

Case studies

A number of case studies illustrate issues raised by the use of GIS for operations management. The cases have been drawn from a variety of countries including

France, Germany, the UK, Canada, the USA and Australia, and a number of different industries, including utilities, transport and mining. Together these cases illustrate the following key issues:

1. Is a digital map base required, and if so, what scale and accuracy are needed?
2. How and to what extent should GIS be linked to the other ITs used and to the information management strategy of the organisation?
3. What are the benefits from adopting and using GIS and how are such benefits measured?
4. What are the data issues in terms of cost, availability and transfer?
5. How is GIS related to the stage of growth of the organisation in terms of its use of IT?
6. What is the impact of new technology such as GPS on GIS?

Minute Man delivery

Minute Man is a courier service operating in the Los Angeles area of California, USA. The company offers customers a choice of two-hour, four-hour and same day delivery for loads that might be anything from small envelopes up to 8000 lb weight (Badillo 1993). The GIS part of the company information system is integrated with order entry and despatch notes.

The 45-van fleet of vehicles is equipped with a GPS receiver mounted on its roof. The GPS gives precise positioning of all vehicles which benefits both the dispatchers and the drivers. The dispatchers do not have to rely on memory to recall where vehicles are at any point of time. Dispatchers can select the most appropriate vehicle type located closest to the collection point. Drivers have a map display unit in the vehicle which helps route them by the most efficient way to the next scheduled delivery or pick-up point. After receiving new delivery instructions, the driver hears a beep and confirms receipt by pressing one key. Previous voice communications are no longer required. This is a major benefit because voice was often confusing when many drivers were using the same radio channel.

All transactions are recorded by the system, so the drivers no longer have to keep handwritten notes. The company benefits by increasing the productivity of the drivers and optimising the utility of the vehicle fleet. The customer benefits from a more reliable service with shorter delivery times.

This case example has been facilitated by GPS technology being available at a price which allowed an economic application to the vehicle fleet management and routeing issues. In the USA the Defense Department Navstar GPS uses satellites that orbit 11 000 miles above the earth. Each satellite broadcasts time data and data to describe its path. Receivers then determine location by calculating the distance between themselves and the satellite. Accuracy of 16 m is possible by locking on to four satellites. Further accuracy, to centimetres, is possible by additionally using data from a stationary receiver. The GPS converts the longitude and latitude coordinates into specific locations on the digital map display.

Routeing applications for dangerous goods in Germany

Finding a relatively safe route for the transportation of goods like petrol and gas has long been a problem for transport managers. A new impetus was given, in Germany, by a new law (7/7a GGVS) which came into force in April 1992 and requires individual documentation of routes for the transportation of dangerous goods to be carried in the vehicle (Freckmann 1993).

A simple PC-based software package called MAP&GUIDE, running under Windows, gives access to a road network of 250 000 km in Germany. Other European road networks are available, in readiness to meet the requirements of European legislation. Features of the length of road segments include 12 speed classes, descents greater than 5% and a road hierarchy. The software calculates a danger factor for each road segment based on the length of the road and its associated dangers.

Fleet monitoring facilities are also available via GPS. Using these systems it is possible to adjust a route dynamically to take account of changing traffic conditions or other unforeseen hazards. Similar software is available in other countries, for example in the UK a PC based package called Autoroute provides road networks throughout Europe, with database links for holding attribute data on any specific point (node) or road (network). In the USA there is a package called RouteSmart. An application of this package to a newspaper delivery problem resulted in reported savings of 10–18% in total travel distance (Bodin *et al.* 1992).

Lyonnaise des Eaux, France

This international group is active in water, gas and electricity supply, sewerage and refuse disposal, street lighting, telecommunications, funeral services and urban cleaning. In 1986 the group developed a policy for GIS with the objective of optimising the networks it was responsible for all over the world (Alla and Trow 1990). At present GIS is operational in a number of locations including Barcelona, Monaco, Macao, Lille and Lyon.

The first GIS installed by the group was at Parisienne des Eaux in 1988. The development was primarily undertaken for operations support to the following functions:

- supply interruptions management for planned works;
- forecasting of maintenance works;
- customer complaints management;
- water sampling and analysis management;
- network events management.

These functions represent important operational activities vital in the day-to-day running of the organisation. The data collected, stored and used by the GIS is required by other administrative and management systems so it was important to integrate the GIS into the corporate information systems. Figure 9.1 shows the GIS within the corporate information system. The corporate system facilitates the storage and processing of many data types, including engineering drawings, maps and attribute data. The linking of the CAD system, used to hold engineering drawings, with the GIS allows users to find a locality on the map and then zoom down to the detailed drawing of a pipe junction.

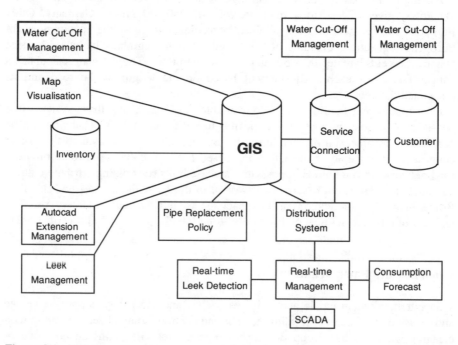

Figure 9.1 Parisienne Des Eaux corporate information system

Some items of the attribute data are collected and updated by field staff using hand-held computers. Examples of such data collection would be data about water leaks, repairs or water quality samples. These items of data are updated as events happen. There is further potential here to link the systems to real-time monitoring systems so that leaks might be detected more rapidly.

From Figure 9.1 it is clear that the GIS is central to many business processes. Many users, in different parts of the organisation, require access to the databases. Improved customer service and response times can be given by the improved access to customer data. Flexibility, ease of access, data management facilities and good response times are important criteria when selecting the appropriate technology to deliver the GIS in such an environment. The system chosen is an object-oriented database which runs on the company VAX architecture machine. Table 9.1 shows that some of the objects relate to attributes and some to geographic entities. The map base source comes from the Parisian Cadaster Service at 1 : 500 scale. Networks are related schematically to the street axis.

Table 9.1 Database objects

Geographic entities

Base map	Street	Footpath	Bridges	Wharves	Railways	River Seine
Sewers	Stairways	Manholes	Sewerage devices			
Drinking water	Pipes	Nodes	Valves	Service connections		

Attribute data

Valve	Identification number	Type	Diameter	Status	Installation data	Number of turns for closing

This case illustrates how GIS has been at the heart of an improvement in the management of operations at the Paris Water Company. Using GIS in this way to improve operations management does not preclude uses for other managerial purposes, for example for strategic planning. Such uses typically come later, after some years of operation. Examples of such systems will be discussed in Chapters 10 and 11.

Manweb, UK

Manweb is an electricity distribution company in the UK, supplying an area of 12000 km^2. including the urban areas of Liverpool and Merseyside and the rural area of North Wales. Prior to the GIS project, records on computer related to substation plants, for example, type of plant, scheduled maintenance, when and where installed. Paper-based records related to the location of overhead and underground networks at various voltages are available for the operational engineers in three formats (Roberts *et al.* 1990):

1. Maps at 1 : 500 and 1 : 1250 which record underground cables and overhead lines used to locate plant for maintenance and operational purposes.
2. Maps at 1 : 5000 to provide an overview of the network and assist planning.
3. Schematic representations of substation plant used for operational purposes.

When investigating the potential and costs of GIS Manweb were aware, in 1989, that the storage of digital map data at two scales would be both expensive and consume much storage space. The phasing of application modules using GIS therefore took into account costs and data availability. The first application did not require a map base, simply a schematic representation. Later modules included a map base when costs and benefits allowed. The case represents a good example of an operational application where the organisation had many and diverse paper maps yet was able to achieve benefits from using GIS without implementing a detailed digital map base.

British Gas, UK

British Gas is a UK utility company supplying gas to customers nationwide. There are 12 regions with 100 district offices. It has approximately 225 000 km of gas mains. A digital records project started in 1981 and is not expected to be fully completed until 1995 (Ives 1993). This large GIS project is part of a still larger total engineering information system. At British Gas there is no doubt that the GIS project is part of the corporate-wide information management strategy. The fact that GIS provides spatial reference to data means that previously unlinked data can be integrated (Finch 1992).

The largest proportion of users are operational, for example engineering staff located at district offices. The database is distributed so that each district office has fast access to both maps and attribute databases. The system has been designed to be flexible, so that if the district geographical areas change it is a straightforward matter to change the digital maps held at that district level. Overall the digital records cover the equivalent of 90 000 map sheets.

Operational enquiries of the database can be made using a variety of criteria, for example customer name or property address. Questions like 'where is the pipeline outside this property?' can then be answered. If an engineer needs to be dispatched to identify a leak or effect a repair then the job instructions can be issued immediately.

A frequent occurrence is that British Gas needs to excavate a highway to examine a pipeline that may have fractured, or to renew a section of pipe as part of an ongoing maintenance programme. In such circumstances it is very important to know the whereabouts of the water pipes and electricity cables. Cutting through an electricity cable can be an expensive and dangerous mistake.

In the UK it is a requirement for the utilities to keep each other informed of the location of their networks (Mahoney 1991). Data transfer must obviously be done to certain standards and in the UK the agreed standard is the national transfer format (see Chapter 2). A national initiative to coordinate the operation of utilities was started in 1977 with the formation of the National Joint Utilities Group (NJUG). The group aims to provide improved service levels to the public by minimising inconvenience of roadworks, saving money and improving safety.

A digital records trial at Dudley Metropolitan Borough in the West Midlands of the UK aimed to build a joint data bank for both local government and the utilities (Yarrow 1987). The two most practical outcomes of this trial were an agreement on data transfer standards and a specification for a simplified digital map (NJUG 1986a).

Miracle Food Mart, Ontario, Canada

The food retailing business is a very competitive one. It is important to business success to know both your own customers and the competition. The main business issues are about how the retailer can meet the needs of their customers in terms of store location, product mix, level of service and price. Data gathered to help address such issues must be done on a regular basis and fed into the decision-making process.

Miracle Food Mart is a major supermarket chain operating in Ontario, Canada. There are about 200 Miracle stores in Ontario. Regular customer surveys are undertaken at the major supermarket sites. The traditional approach to their analysis involved staff in mapping customers on paper-based maps. Before GIS there were four to five people engaged in the analysis of store customer surveys. This has been reduced to two people. With the manual method of analysing store surveys there was always a backlog of surveys to analyse. The basic reason for investing in GIS was that it would lead to a productivity increase. Now, the store survey can be processed in about two hours.

An investigation into the suitability of GIS was started by an enthusiastic champion working in the Estates Department. The essence of the first idea was to save money by automating the collection and storage of survey data for use in location analysis and store planning. In 1988 Miracle and Tydac did a pilot project involving 70–80 stores. Tydac were selected as a GIS supplier (SPANS) because they offered a raster-based mapping system which would run on an IBM PC hardware platform under MS-DOS. The system was therefore capable of integration with the technology available and used in the Estates Department of Miracle Food Mart.

In 1991 Miracle was acquired by A&P. Since that time there has been little enthusiasm for using GIS. The management style of Miracle allowed for individual initiative whilst A&P adopt a hierarchical style. With the main office in New Jersey there appears to be some communications problems. A&P had little experience with IT, for example there were no PCs in use before the acquisition; also IT is part of the Finance Department. In terms of our stages of growth model (see Chapters 3 and 4) the time scale dimension indicates an organisation with little corporate coordination of IT policy, where technical skills are in short supply and where the likely response will be 'what is GIS?'

The main uses of GIS are for locational research involving assessment of new sites and the processing of customer surveys for existing stores. A simple and straightforward approach is preferred, using trade areas defined by distance not travel times. Gravity models were tried but rejected because it was difficult to calibrate the models reliably.

Store surveys are carried out on an *ad hoc* basis at all stores, with the aim of collecting approximately 1000 responses per store. Each response is coded to the respondents' home address via their postcode. A file containing the centroids of each postcode converts the survey into point data.

In the early days all the maps, of all the urban areas of Ontario were digitised in-house. At the time of visiting the Estates Department there was still a digitiser in the champion's office. This was a very labour-intensive activity.

Census tract boundaries and demographic data are mapped. Each census tract represents about 5000 people. From the census information is known about average spending per capita on groceries (currently about C$30.00 per week). Sales by people living in census areas are known from the customer survey data. Putting this together then gives an idea of how well a store is doing compared to expected sales levels in an area.

Map output at Miracle was discussed at board level and at some meetings a PC was present so that analysis could be run interactively. Maps at A&P go to the merchandising department but there is little feedback. The marketing manager in New Jersey asked for a report on GIS capability a year ago, the champion in the Estates Department is still waiting for a response! Analysis is done on a personal computer using SPANS running under DOS. This is preferred to the OS/2 version because of problems experienced with printing under OS/2. A link to dBase is used, to provide customer and competitor data. However, files have to be converted for use in SPANS, therefore duplicates of files have to be kept. This has been found to be frustrating by the main user and is in any event far from good data management practice.

The introduction of a map visualisation software package by SPANS was seen as offering the potential of spreading the applications around others within the company. However, SPANS MAP does not solve the data management or printing problems and therefore is not perceived as an improvement. SPANS have announced a version of the product that will run under Windows and will therefore solve some of the problems perceived. The Estates Department are now considering changing to a different software package. On the short list are MapInfo, AtlasGIS and Tactician. Advantages of such systems are that they run on a PC under DOS or Windows. Printing is thus straightforward. Data management must be good in any new package – to offer the direct use of dBase files. One of the important dBase files is data about competitors. This is data that has been collected over the years.

Demographic profile systems are not currently used. The one person in the Estates Department spends about 20% of his/her time on GIS. At the time of the pilot project in 1988 this was all of the time. Therefore, the steep learning curve was manageable.

What does all this say about future use of GIS? Are there any lessons for other organisations to take away from this experience? The case for using GIS was clear, map production and analysis could save time over the manual methods. In this sense it was a straightforward case of an operational support system. The champion was able to develop a 'stand-alone' kind of application. However, the lack of high-level project sponsor (see Chapter 7) meant that further development of the GIS was given a very low priority. The low experience level of IT use by the company taking over Miracle Food Marts inhibited the linking of information systems to benefit the business strategy. Clearly the decision to take over certain stores had not been done on a systematic geographic basis. Yet such decisions are by their nature inherently geographically intensive.

Alcoa of Australia

Clearly, any extractive industry must have maps in order to conduct its business. Maps will show not only surface features but also the underlying geology. Landownership, access roads, drill hole data and much more will all be traditionally related to paper-based maps. A prima-facie case for investigating the use of GIS would rest on supporting the business operations. Alcoa undertook a feasibility study of GIS in 1989 and was implementing a large-scale GIS two years later (Barber *et al.* 1989).

Alcoa is a major aluminium producer with assets over A\$3.4 billion (Alcoa 1991). It operates three bauxite mines, three alumina refineries, two shipping terminals and a gold-mine in Western Australia and two aluminium smelters, a brown coal-mine and a power station in Victoria (Alcoa 1989). This case will concentrate on the bauxite mines business in Western Australia (Figure 9.2). The three mines in the Darling Range produce 15% of the world's alumina (Barber *et al.* 1989). There are reserves of approximately 2500 million tonnes of bauxite in a 4200 km^2 area within state forest to-the south-east of Perth.

The business problem

Current annual production of bauxite is about 22 million tonnes which requires the clearing of 500 ha of forest per annum. The forest is a unique, indigenous hardwood forest, dominated by the jarrah and marri species. The jarrah tree is susceptible to a fungus called *Phytophthora cinnamomi* more commonly referred to as dieback which causes the death of jarrah and many other under-storey species (Batini 1973). Large areas of the forest are already affected by this fungus. The challenge to Alcoa is to prove that it can mine in the forest without the fungus spreading. The fungus lives in moist soils and in the roots of host plants. It spreads freely under high moisture conditions and is readily spread by water or in the wet soil which adheres to vehicles (Elliott and Wake 1990). The forest area has a number of conflicting land-use pressures. Close to the metropolitan area of Perth there are pressures for recreational activities. The population of Perth also depend on the area for about 70% of their potable water supplies (Mauger 1987).

All the mining activity is within the state forest area. The ore occurs in areas which vary in size from 1 to 100 ha. The operational process involves exploration to identify the ore deposits, forest logging and clearing, topsoil removal, overburden removal and then bauxite mining using trucks and loaders. Following the completion of mining, the overburden and topsoil are returned, and the trees and under-storey seeded (Nichols *et al.* 1985).

Fundamental to the success and future survival of the business is the continued mining of bauxite deposits from the Darling Range in Western Australia. Continued access depends upon community acceptance of the mining operations, and this can only be maintained if the operations are conducted in a socially and environmentally responsible manner (Slessar 1988). Hence, the management of the jarrah dieback issues presents the business with a unique operational challenge.

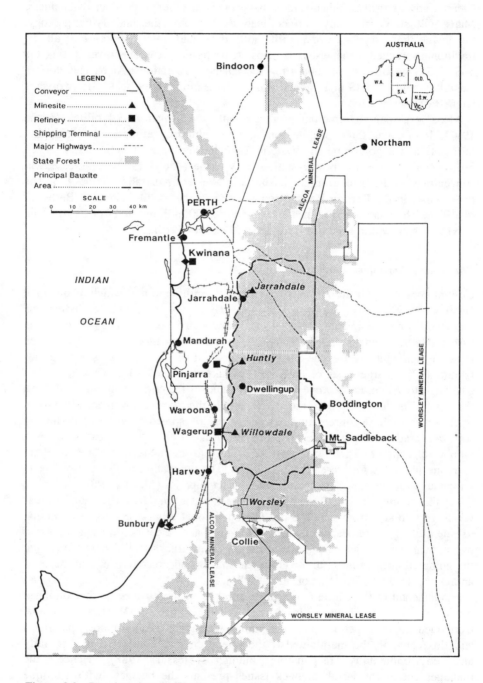

Figure 9.2 Bauxite mines in Western Australia

The Alcoa mining strategy decided in 1986 to consolidate Del Park and Huntly into one large mining operation. This meant mining the area to the north and east of the existing Huntly mine. The incidence of dieback in these areas was lower than previously encountered, therefore it became crucial to develop an operational plan to ensure dieback would be controlled at all stages of mining and rehabilitation.

Effective procedures for the prevention of the spread of the dieback fungus were therefore essential in order to maintain access to the mine areas. Detailed operational procedures were developed and agreed with the Department of Conservation and Land Management (CALM 1989). These procedures would generate a large amount of data which would have to be interpreted by those taking decisions on a day-to-day basis about mining activity.

The demand to analyse and store these greatly increased volumes of data led to the consideration of GIS. For the purposes of dieback management the maintenance of accurate maps is essential. Frequent changes are needed to monitor the changing patterns of disease. Regular updating of mine sites and forest access is also important as is the monitoring of all pre-mining activities like logging, drilling and fuel reduction burning. Changes in the timing of any of these operations could have a significant impact economically or on the environment (Elliott and Wake 1990).

The task of storing all this data and using it effectively for operational management of the mines led Alcoa to consider using IT. Before recommending a trial GIS, Alcoa undertook a feasibility study. Although such studies are common practice in the information systems development field prior to a full systems development project, in the area of GIS they are less routine (Hobson 1992).

The feasibility study

The feasibility study included:

1. A thorough data requirement study – identifying all data sets used for planning, the custodian of the data and its reliability and accuracy. A number of government departments were interviewed to ascertain the availability of data sets. A great deal of digital data was already available. Contours and map bases were available from the Department of Land Administration (DOLA), environmental data from CALM and borehole data from the WA Water Authority.
2. A comparison of the costs of undertaking revised manual procedures for dieback management with those of introducing a computer-based system.
3. A cost–benefit study where the benefits were classified as cost saving, cost avoidance and intangibles. Cost savings were possible by rationalising existing computer systems, and greater efficiency of the environmental planners and mine surveyors. Cost avoidance was possible by eliminating the need to employ more cartographic staff. Intangible benefits were assessed with the help of Parker's (1982) taxonomy of intangible benefits (see Chapter 6).
4. An assessment of the possible systems architectures. Central and distributed

architectures were evaluated. The distributed approach was rejected because of a perceived high systems administrative overhead at each location.

5.   An outline implementation plan. The period after the feasibility study would include a site reference study, full functional specification, pilot study, final purchase and implementation of the full system.

The post-feasibility study started with a site reference study. Although there were many organisations in Australia that had used GIS for about four years (i.e. from about 1985) there were no other mining companies using GIS at the time (in 1989). The possibility of undertaking a full systems specification was considered. In most other domains of information processing in business some kind of systems development methodology would be adopted, such as structured systems analysis and design methodology (SSADM) (see Chapters 6 and 7). However, Alcoa decided that such a path had not proved to be successful in the GIS area because of the lack of understanding of geographic information and geographic processing (Barber *et al.* 1989).

Trial project

The next substantive step was to have a trial project in preference to a pilot study (see Chapter 7 for a full discussion of pilot studies and other approaches to implementation). The purpose of a trial project was to provide a test for GIS to show real benefits to the business. As a specific test area the trial project chosen was to perform the dieback management planning for Huntly mine for the next five years. The trial project lasted for three months.

The budget for the trial project was limited, and a small consultancy fund was established to meet training costs and ensure the project was managed properly. Hardware was loaned from Digital (a Microvax II) and ARC/INFO software was provided by ESRI Australia Pty. An extensive evaluation of GIS software packages, undertaken by the Department of Conservation and Environment of South Australia, found that ARC/INFO was the only system used by large organisations in Australia. Being recommended by these organisations made it the natural choice for the pilot project. Central IT staff are involved in setting up menus and screens, however it is the mining staff who control the system.

According to Barber *et al.* (1989) users felt the project was so successful they did not want it to end. Overall, the following benefits were achieved: solved real planning problems, achieved significant tangible benefits including: reduced forest clearing by 3 ha in the area of interest and optimised haul road alignment thereby reducing construction costs. Additionally, the project demonstrated a real working GIS to the users. Experience gained enabled progress to be made towards a full implementation of a GIS.

Data analysis followed the conventional approach of building a data model for each functional area, for example, Figure 9.3 shows an entity relationship model for the clearing subsystem. In geographic terms, each of the entities identified in Figure 9.3 has either point, line or polygon attributes. These entities became the layers in the GIS listed in Figure 9.4. Overall, it was estimated that the database

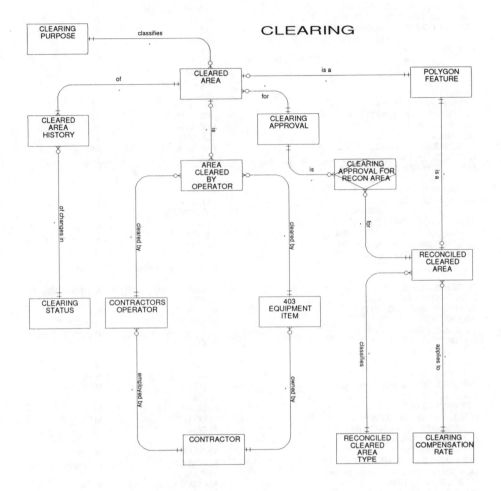

Figure 9.3 Data model for the clearing subsystem

would be about 800Mb. In 1993 the GIS database is approximately 2.5Gb. The GIS subsystems were then defined by mapping the layers in a matrix with the functional areas, as shown in Figure 9.5.

LAYER	ORGANIZATION RESPONSIBLE	PRIORITY
MINERAL LEASE	ALCOA	H
ALCOA METRIC GRID SYSTEM	ALCOA	H
ALCOA IMPERIAL GRID SYSTEM	ALCOA	M
SURVEY CONTROL - ALCOA DERIVED	ALCOA	H
- GEODETIC	DOLA	
CONTOURS - 5m	DOLA	H
- 10m	DOLA	
- 1m	ALCOA	
ROADS	DOLA/CALM	H
LAND PARCELS	DOLA	H
CALM FOREST LEASES	CALM	M
STATUTORY BOUNDARIES	DOLA/CALM	M
HYDROGRAPHIC	DOLA/CALM	H
UTILITIES	DOLA/SEC	M
MISC. TOPO FEATURES	DOLA/CALM	M
LATERITE UNITS	ALCOA	M
LOCAL SURFACE GEOLOGY	ALCOA	M
REGIONAL SURFACE GEOLOGY	ALCOA	L
MINING REGIONS	ALCOA	M
INFRASTRUCTURE - LOCAL	ALCOA	H
- REGIONAL	CALM/DOLA	
ALCOA WATER FACILITIES	ALCOA	L
ALCOA ELECTRICAL FACILITIES	ALCOA	L
PLANNED DRILLING COVERAGE	ALCOA	H
DRILLHOLE LOCATIONS	ALCOA	H
	DRILLHOLE SEAMS	ALCOA
	H	
DRILLHOLE SAMPLES	ALCOA	M
EXPLORATION ORE UNITS	ALCOA	M
DEVELOPMENT ORE UNITS	ALCOA	H
PRODUCTION ORE UNITS	ALCOA	H
MINE PLANNING BLOCKS	ALCOA	H
GRADE CONTROL BLOCKS	ALCOA	H
SHIFT MINED AREAS	ALCOA	H
MONTHLY MINED AREAS	ALCOA	H
CLEARING AREAS	ALCOA	H
RECONCILED CLEARING AREAS	ALCOA	H
SOIL STOCKPILES	ALCOA	
STRIPPED AREAS	ALCOA	M
DRILL AND BLAST AREAS	ALCOA	M
LANDSCAPED PIT CONTOURS	ALCOA	L
REHABILITATION AREAS	ALCOA	H
DIEBACK AREAS	ALCOA/CALM	H
SHEARER DIEBACK HAZARD AREAS	ALCOA/CALM	H
DOWNSLOPE DIEBACK RISK AREAS	ALCOA	H
HAVEL VEGETATION	ALCOA/CALM	H
FOREST PRIORITY AREAS	ALCOA	H
FOREST BURNING AREAS	CALM	M
GROUNDWATER BOREHOLE	ALCOA	M
CONSERVATION & RECREATION RESERVES	CALM	H
VEGETATION API	CALM	L
LOGGING COUPES	CALM	M
HARDWOOD BLOCKS	CALM	M
CALM REFERENCE GRID	CALM	M
VEGETATION	AGRICULTURE	L
SOILS	AGRICULTURE	L
DISEASE RISK AREAS	CALM	H

\data\gww\93-456

Figure 9.4   GIS data layers

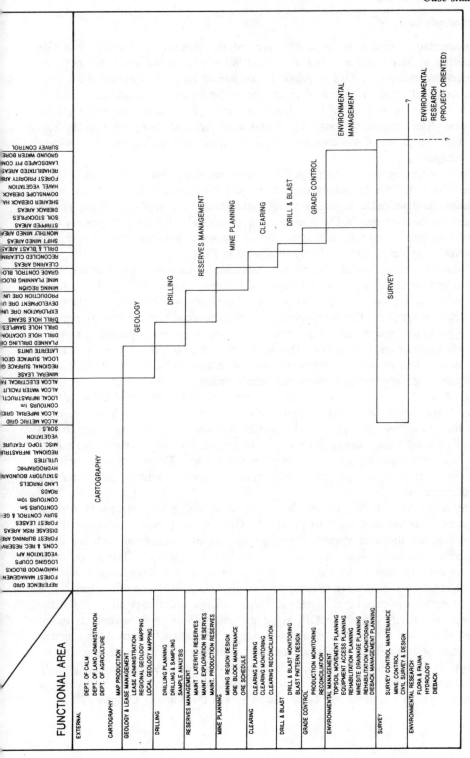

Figure 9.5 GIS subsystems

Implementation

Implementation was seen as a vital part of the process of developing a GIS capability in Alcoa. Indeed, Barber *et al.* (1989 p. 69) put the point succinctly as: 'the implementation of GIS in Alcoa is considered more of a management issue than technical'. The management of change in the organisation has been overseen by a steering committee with a charter to set objectives, review and facilitate progress. The committee consisted of two managers and two professionals from the following areas of the company: environmental, mining, cartographic, survey and computing.

Day-to-day progress of the project was undertaken by four work groups. These were responsible for the achievement of project milestones in the following areas: hardware and software acquisition and installation, GIS implementation, survey system installation and VAX system development. The full project process took about two years. The GIS is simply part of the wider environmental and mining information system which is clearly illustrated in Plate I.

The management of dieback and the associated procedures agreed with CALM necessitate a close working relationship between Alcoa and CALM. Alcoa currently funds about nine CALM staff to collect and analyse data in relation to dieback management. The development of an operational mining strategy requires mine planning, operational requirements and environmental parameters to be brought together and understood. The ability of GIS to overlay a number of maps is crucial in this process: for example, ore distribution and clearing, dieback lines, drainage, landscape and soil return, and rehabilitation.

In Alcoa GIS are used by around 29 users, and this is being added to all the time. Some users are limited by the system to running menu-driven systems directing their use to certain job-specific routines. Other users have gained confidence with the system and are able to answer not only routine operational questions but also ask *ad hoc* queries of the system. There is a small central team responsible for programming, systems access control and database administration.

The Alcoa case study illustrates an organisation with a very mature IT support structure. This enabled them to produce a GIS that met their specific needs by developing an in-house system. Such system naturally integrated with the other corporate information systems ensuring good data management. Through the wide involvement of people in various job roles a team was able to develop the technical GIS and also serve to spread the news about GIS to potential users.

Starting as an operational system to record data at specific point or about the geology in specific areas the GIS at Alcoa was able to grow beyond its initial conception when the business demands changed. The business strategy highlighted the issue of managing the dieback of the jarrah forest in a way that would be acceptable to the public and ensure that reserves of alumina could be continually exploited. The system became critical to the business mission, it became a strategic system and more will be discussed around this topic in Chapter 11.

Overview of operational applications

At this stage of the chapter it would be useful to review the themes and messages arising from the case studies. Earlier in the chapter a number of key issues were identified which can now be used to structure the discussion.

Is a digital map base required, and if so, what scale and accuracy are needed?

This is a very important question. A feature of all the case studies reviewed here is that all the organisations kept paper-based maps showing records of assets ranging from gas pipelines through to mineral deposits. The organisations had all recognised that the management of assets and resources in geographical space was an important feature of operations management. However, it does not necessarily follow from this that gains will be made by 'computerising' the maps. Only a proper and full analysis of the business processes will reveal the extent to which maps are or are not the subject of change data.

The Manweb example is interesting here because a GIS was developed initially without a map base. Simple, schematic representations were sufficient for the first applications. Only later did it become necessary to have a digital map base to scale.

In the utility industry examples, the accuracy of the map base was very critical because of the operational need to dig up roads for the purposes of repairs and maintenance. In the vehicle-routeing and retail-analysis examples accuracy was less critical. The important point is to be aware of the decision making that is being based upon the map data.

How and to what extent should GIS be linked to the other information technologies used and to the information management strategy of the organisation?

It is evident that in all the examples reviewed here, with the exception of the retail industry and the routeing examples, the GIS was integrated with other operational information systems. In the utilities, the GIS is typically linked to records of maintenance jobs. In the mining example GIS is integrated with mine planning, restoration and drill-hole data systems.

In essence, the greater the volume of data processed that has a spatial dimension the greater will be the need to integrate any GIS capability with other operational information systems of the business.

What are the benefits from adopting and using GIS and how are such benefits measured?

As we should expect from any operational information system, the initial impetus to bring in IT is to gain efficiency benefits. Such benefits are measured in terms of doing what the business is doing with less resources. These benefits are manifest in cost savings which tend to be tangible benefits. Nevertheless, when GIS is

199

implemented many businesses have found benefits beyond those originally thought of to justify the system. These intangible benefits were most evident in the case of Alcoa where systematic identification of a whole range of benefits had taken place.

What are the data issues in terms of cost, availability and transfer?

This is one of the issues that varies greatly depending on which country the application is in. Part of the success of the Alcoa example can be attributed to the availability, at the right price and format, of data from a number of external agencies like CALM, WALIS and WAWA. The national policies in Australia also helped to provide a framework to support data transfer and guidelines for data custodianship and pricing (see Chapter 2).

In the UK, the utility examples demonstrated that availability of digital maps from Ordnance Survey was a constraint on the implementation of GIS.

How is GIS related to the stage of growth of the organisation in terms of its use of information technology?

The utility and mining examples clearly had well-established support and factory applications in the information systems portfolio. Some examples had centralised IT departments and some were more distributed, but all exhibited some maturity in terms of the stages of growth model. In these circumstances there were the skills needed to develop the information management strategy, taking into account the need for spatially related information.

What is the impact of new technology such as GPS on GIS?

The advent of a new technology opportunity is always something the business needs to watch out for. In Chapter 4 the ways of integrating technology planning into the information management process were reviewed. In some businesses, the new technology will be GIS itself, for examples of this see Chapter 11. In others it will be a related, enabling technology. We have seen here in this chapter examples of how GPS have enabled transport and distribution companies to really use GIS to the full. The capability of pinpointing resources, assets or vehicles in real time in the geographic space opens up many new opportunities of using GIS. Parcel courier service companies like the Minute Man reviewed here have been able to use GPS technology to improve service delivery.

Summary

When GIS are used to support the basic business processes that are carried out on a day-to-day basis they can be said to be operational systems. Typically such operational systems will be fully integrated with other business information systems like order processing and dispatch. A selection of case studies from different countries and different industries has been discussed and reviewed here to highlight some key issues in the development of successful GIS.

All classification systems are incomplete in some way and cannot always represent discrete information systems. Some systems will start out by being operational systems and then grow and change in their functions and uses to become what might then be termed tactical or strategic systems. This is a gradual and inevitable process of development.

The Alcoa case provides a good example of a system which started as an operational system and then grew to become a strategic business system. The reasons for this happening will be discussed in Chapters 10 and 12.

Further study

The algorithms involved in vehicle routeing and scheduling problems may be of particular interest to readers with an interest in operational research. The following references are a good starting point for further study.

Bodin L, Golden B L, Assad A, Ball M 1983 Routing and scheduling of vehicles and crews: the state of the art. *Computers and Operations Research* **10**(2): 63–211
Golden B L, Assad A 1988 *Vehicle Routing: Methods and Studies* North-Holland, Amsterdam

References

Alcoa 1989 *Alcoa Australia* October, Alcoa of Australia Limited, Melbourne, Victoria, Australia
Alcoa 1991 *Annual Report* Alcoa of Australia Limited, Melbourne, Victoria, Australia
Alla P, Trow S W 1990 Implementation of GIS: a way to optimising utilities operations. *Proceedings of the Second Conference of the Association for Geographic Information* 22–24 October, Brighton, UK, pp 3.2.1–6
AM/FM International Association 1992 Executive directions in AM/FM/GIS: 1992 survey results. *AM/FM/GIS Networks* **8**(5), October/November: 10
Badillo A S 1993 Transportation and navigation. In Castle G H (ed) *Profiting from a Geographic Information System* GIS World Books Inc, Fort Collins, Colo, pp 161–76
Barber G G, Wake G G, Hutchinson R G 1989 GIS – The Alcoa experience: a summary of justification, selection and implementation procedures used by Alcoa of Australia. *Proceedings of the Seventeenth Australasian Urban and Regional Information Systems Association* November, Perth, WA, Australia, pp 60–73
Batini F E 1973 *Jarrah Dieback – a Disease of the Jarrah Forest of Western Australia* Bulletin No. 84, Forest Department, Perth, WA, Australia
Bodin L, George F, Levy L 1992 Vehicle routing and scheduling problems over street networks. *Proceedings of the First Conference on GIS in Business and Commerce* 11–13 May, Denver, GIS World Inc, Fort Collins, Colo, pp 31–42
CSR, Inc 1992 Market summaries. *AM/FM Market Data Reports* January

CALM *Manual of the Forest Priority System and Developmental Prescriptions for Dieback Control in Good Quality Forest during Bauxite Mining* February, Department of Conservation and Land Management, Perth, WA, Australia

Elliott P E 1991 Dieback mapping and interpretation process. Internal Paper, April, Alcoa of Australia, Applecross, WA, Australia

Elliott P E, Wake G W 1990 The integration of environmental management into mine planning using a geographical information system: the Alcoa experience. Internal paper, Alcoa of Australia, Applecross, WA, Australia

Finch S 1992 GIS in the infrastructure. In Cadoux-Hudson J, Heywood D I (eds) *Geographic Information 1992/93* The Yearbook of the Association for Geographic Information, Taylor & Francis, London, pp 135–8

Freckmann P 1993 Route calculation for dangerous goods transports with a graphical information system. *Proceedings of the Fourth European Conference on Geographical Information Systems* Vol. 2, 29 March–1 April, Genoa, Italy, pp 1132–8

Frost and Sullivan 1989 *The US Non-Entertainment Automotive Electronics Market* Frost and Sullivan Inc, New York

Hobson S A 1992 Critical success factors in the development of GIS. Unpublished MBA project, Warwick Business School, University of Warwick, May

Ives M J 1993 The British Gas digital records system. *Mapping Awareness and GIS in Europe* 7(3), April: 25–7

Kruczynski L R, Jasumback A 1993 Forestry management applications of the Navstar global positioning system: United States Forest Service experiences. *Proceedings of the Fourth European Conference on Geographical Information Systems* Vol. 2, 29 March – 1 April, Genoa, Italy, pp 1139–48

Mahoney R P 1991 GIS and utilities. In Maguire D J, Goodchild M F, Rhind D W (eds) *Geographical Information Systems* Vol 2 *Applications* Longman Scientific & Technical, Harlow, pp 101–14

Mauger G 1987 *Planning Future Sources for Perth's Water Supply* Report No. WP33, Water Authority of Western Australia, Perth, WA, Australia

Nichols O G, Carbon B A, Colquhoun I J, Croton J T, Murray N J 1985 Rehabilitation after bauxite mining in south western Australia. *Landscape Planning* 12: 75–92

NJUG 1986a *Proposed Data Exchange Format for Utility Map Data* National Joint Utilities Group, London

NJUG 1986b *Specification for the Digitisation of Large Scale OS Maps* National Joint Utilities Group, London

Parker M M 1982 Enterprise information analysis: cost–benefit analysis and the data managed system. *IBM Systems Journal* 21(1): 108–21

Pemberton J 1992 *Operations Automation Strategies Overview* April, Gartner Group, London

Rector J M 1993 Utilities. In Castle G H (ed) *Profiting from a Geographic Information System* GIS World Books Inc, Fort Collins, Colo, pp 193–208

Roberts G V, Park G W A, Cottle E J T 1990 Manweb's implementation of a mapless GIS. *Proceedings of the Second Conference of the Association for Geographic Information* 22–24 October, Brighton, UK, pp C2.1–3

Slessar G C 1988 Management of strategic environmental issues – Alcoa's bauxite mining operations in Western Australia. *Australian Mining Industry Council Environmental Workshop* 18–23 September, Darwin, NT, Australia

Strong S 1993 The electronic ocean: a new wave in navigation technology. In *Decks Awash – Special Report: Electronic Navigation* Matrix Technologies Inc, Newfoundland, Canada, pp 3A–5A

White M 1991 Car navigation systems. In Maguire D J, Goodchild M F, Rhind D W (eds) *Geographical Information Systems* Vol 2 *Applications* Longman Scientific & Technical, Harlow, pp 115–25

Yarrow G J 1987 Joint utility mapping. *Proceedings of NJUG '87 First National Conference* National Joint Utilities Group, London

10

Tactical applications

'. . . a quiet, grave man, busied in charts, exact in sums, master of the art of tactics.'

Walter Bagehot (1858)

Preamble

More than 100 years ago Bagehot conjured up an image of a tactician as a backroom character busy with calculations and charts (which can historically be interpreted as sea maps). So maps have a long history of contributing to tactical decisions. The word 'tactics' is defined as 'the art of disposing military or naval or air forces in actual contact with the enemy' (*Concise Oxford Dictionary*: 1317). Translating this into the more common usage in civilian business arrives at a definition something like the art of distributing resources to gain competitive advantage in the market.

There may have been a brief period in the history of industrialisation when location did not matter. Increasingly, in today's global market managers have to face questions about where to place assets and other resources of production. Gone are the days of Winnie the Pooh who exclaimed: 'we will build it there because that's the place we first thought of it' (Milne 1926).

Today's managers are more likely to be guided by three principles governing where to place resources: location, location and location (Jones and Simmons 1987). Yet locational decisions are only one example of tactical applications of GIS in business. The general characteristics of tactical decision making were reviewed in Chapter 2 where it was described as relating to semi-structured decisions characterised by 'what if?' kinds of modelling.

The first uses of IT in business, as was discussed in Part One of this book, were for operational systems. This chapter examines uses of GIS that are tactical in nature. In terms of the taxonomy discussed in Chapter 2, the *tasks* of tactical applications are semi-structured decisions made by middle managers. In terms of the *time frame* dimension, tactical applications – depending as they do on data from other parts of the business – are likely to be developed at a more mature stage. In terms of the *technology*, the options are widening rapidly as the cost is reduced and the facilities offered are increased. For tactical applications, the nature of spatial data is likely to be either wide-ranging (data breadth) and detailed (high data depth) or narrow (data depth) and summarised (low data depth) as explained in Chapter 4.

Such systems support a range of decision-making activities in a range of different industrial sectors of the economy (see Table 8.4). Instead of a mindset of automating business processes the successful development of tactical applications is more likely to be aimed at increasing the effectiveness of the business by 'doing different things', rather than 'doing things differently'. Many businesses are naturally reluctant to talk about applications of IT which they perceive as giving them some edge over competition in the market. Conference proceedings are most frequently populated with stories from academics and vendors, with only a small number of actual users telling their stories. Evidence from market research organisations like Dataquest (1993) will provide figures on the use of GIS software by industry. However, there is a dearth of academic research which is empirically based to give an overview of GIS applications at the tactical level. The survey by Grimshaw (1992) of building societies in the UK gives an overview of GIS applications in one particular industry sector. Chapter 3 used that empirical data to help calibrate a model of the growth of GIS in organisations. In this chapter it provides a useful starting point for a discussion of more detailed case studies spanning a wide range of industrial sectors.

Geodemographics and marketing

A survey of GIS in business users, carried out in the autumn of 1992 by Dataquest, found that half the business users said that geodemographics was their primary application (Hale 1993).

Demographics have been used in marketing for many years. However, the term *geo*demographics is relatively new. It has been defined by Brown (1991) as 'the development and the application of area typologies that have proved to be powerful discriminators of consumer behaviour and aids to market analysis'. The ability of GIS to take raw data, relate it to customer databases and present information on maps has represented a major impetus to the growth of applications in marketing. As a term, 'geodemographics' should not be confused with 'geographics'. Geographics is of a much more recent vintage and can be traced back to Bill Baldwin, editor of Forbes (Sherwood Bryan 1993a). The term 'business geographics' is also coming into use with the launch of a magazine with that title from GIS World Inc., who define it as an application of GIS technology (Sherwood Bryan 1993b). The advent of new terms and debates about their meaning is a hallmark of a rapidly changing and expanding market. In one sense the debate is sterile, in another sense it illustrates a change of emphasis from the full function GIS (as used for environmental applications – see Chapters 2 and 3) towards geography as one solution to business information issues and the problem-focused GIS as discussed in Chapter 8.

The data issues underlying geodemographics, their availability and cost in different countries have been discussed in Chapter 4. An example of GIS used for decision support in the marketing area was discussed in Chapter 5. In this chapter a range of case studies follow which are aimed at illustrating uses of GIS for supporting tactical decision making.

Case studies

A number of case studies illustrate issues raised by the use of GIS for supporting tactical decision making. The cases have been drawn from a variety of countries including the UK, Canada, the USA and Australia, and a number of different industries, including retailing, financial services, motor vehicle dealerships and fast-food franchises. The uses of GIS are also diverse: they include marketing, location planning, trade area analysis, cannibalisation, merger/acquisition analysis and regulatory compliance.

The case studies have been ordered to illustrate the stages of growth model advanced in Chapter 2. Starting with a company facing the business challenges of new legislation and a merger, the 'opt-out' stage is illustrated via the case of Verdi Ryan – a data agency and consultancy called in by a big banking corporation to illuminate their geographical data. The case of the European car manufacturer is the story of a company calling in consultants to help bring together geographic data sets from different European countries. The application is at the 'stand-alone' stage yet it made use of consultants, which is more typical of the 'opt-out' stage. The reason for this is that bringing together European-wide geographical data requires some special expertise. In the future this will almost certainly not be the case as more businesses in Europe demand to understand the market across the traditional frontiers.

The third case, IKEA, highlights an interesting scenario of a company 'opting out' for some data analysis, pursuing a demonstration GIS and in the end rejecting the use of GIS. MassMutual is the largest case study in this chapter; it shows how over the years the company have progressed in their use of geographic information. Arby's show a well-established GIS user on the boundary between 'linking' and 'opportunistic' stages. Finally a short case of W. H. Smith & Sons illustrates a company buying in modelling expertise to solve a specific business problem.

Together these cases illustrate the following key issues:

1. How dependent is a spatial DSS on the underlying analytical model?
2. How and to what extent should GIS be linked to the other ITs used and to the information management strategy of the organisation?
3. What is the most effective way of using the customer database with the GIS?
4. What are the benefits from adopting and using GIS and how are such benefits measured?
5. What are the data issues in terms of cost, availability and transfer?
6. How is GIS related to the stage of growth of the organisation in terms of its use of IT?

7. What is the impact of new technology, such as desktop mapping and EIS, and multimedia on GIS?

Verdi Ryan Associates, Williamsville, NY, USA

An important part of the GIS market-place is the role played by data agencies and consultants (see Chapter 4). The very existence of the 'opt-out' stage of the growth model (see Chapter 2) assumes that there are consultants available with GIS services to offer both large and small corporations. The purpose of this case study is to illustrate the role of consultants by using one particular firm operating in the US market. Verdi Ryan is a small (currently five professional staff) research and planning firm specialising in the quantitative analysis of markets and delivery systems for financial services providers (Verdi Ryan 1993a).

Compared with retail sector businesses, financial institutions have a major advantage in terms of the ease of applying GIS. The advantage is that internal customer records will already hold the zip code or postcode, giving the potential to spatially analyse them. Data is therefore comprehensive, compared to the customer survey work that has to be undergone in the retail sector, producing partial statistics that may not represent the accurate customer profile.

We imagine then that most financial institutions know who their customers are and where they live. Traditionally, however, business was organised on an account basis. Several accounts (all with different numbers) were difficult to relate to one another if held at the same address. The financial deregulation, which has taken place in most western economies since the mid 1980s, served to increase competition and has forced the organisations to adopt a customer focus. Along with this change in the business strategy has come a change in the information systems from account base to customer base.

Banks specifically and financial institutions generally have used some form of geographical analysis, for location problems like where to site ATMs, for many years. More recently the location problems have been more about which branch to close or which branch to remodel as many countries have experienced 'over-banking in the High Street'. In 1991 NorWest bank merged with another bank. This gave them some duplication in the branch network and some gaps in other areas. In total the bank has about 500 branches in 14 different states. The bank wanted to rationalise its branch network.

The second business drive toward GIS was the need to comply with the Community Reinvestment Act (CRA) 1990. Although in force for a number of years, the revised regulatory requirements introduced in 1990 make it increasingly difficult to demonstrate compliance. To help business comply with the Act their are some federal guidelines which use 12 assessment factors to help determine fair lending policies. Half of the assessment factors have a geographic element. Figure 10.1 shows the CRA assessment factors in relation to the major questions and issues of the community, the regulations and the financial institution.

CRA ASSESSMENT FACTORS	VERDI RYAN REPORT

Number 1: To ascertain the credit needs of the local community	**CREDIT NEEDS ASSESSMENT SURVEY**
	Primary credit demand survey
	          chart/map applications received
	Secondary national survey data
	          local community group studies
	          housing stock, neighborhood condition

Number 5: To outline the geographic distribution of the bank's credit exentisons , applications, and credit denials.	**GEOGRAPHIC DISTRIBUTION REPORT** -Geo-code HMDA loan types I-IV to 1990 census geography -Geo-code all lending activity to 1990 census geography -Aggregation of each loan type within 1990 census tract designation -Map creation at a regional scale outling the spatial distribution of HMDA data by approval and denial rates -Tabular reports by census tract that outline the distribution of HMDA data by total number of applications, approvals and denials
Number 6: Evidence of discriminatory or other illegal credit practices.	**GEOGRAPHIC DISTRIBUTION AND MARKET SHARE REPORT** -Ascertain portion of total loans the institution may possess within a market -Examine household penetration rates of total accounts/branch trade areas -Creation of ratio of loans to deposits
Number 7: The bank's record of opening and closing offices and providing services at offices	**TARGET AREA DELINEATION REPORT** -Delineate Federal Target Areas based on 1990 Census reports and geography -Plot trade areas and penetration rates for all branches -Establish historical trend of loan penetration -Assess historical lending patterns in the target areas
Number 9: The bank's origination of residential mortgage loans, housing rehabilitation loans, home improvement loans, small business loans within a community	**REGIONAL LENDING REPORT,** **GEOGRAPHIC DISTRIBTUION REPORT** -Plot all lending activity by type -Examine in comparison to loan demand -Creation of lending potential by area -Formulation of Neighborhood Condition Index -All items in Geo Distribution Report
Number 2: The extent of the bank's marketing and special credit related programs to make community members more aware of credit services available.	**SPECIAL PROGRAM EVALUATION** -Evaluates the progress of specialized credit programs that may have already been insitituted by the bank. -Outlines potential means to improve program effectiveness

Figure 10.1   Geographical data analysis requirements of the CRA (from Verdi Ryan Associates)

COMMUNITY CONCERNS	REGULATORY CONCERNS	INSTITUTION CRA POSITION
How is access to lending and lending information provided? 1. What is the branch presence? 2. What advertising programs are in place? 3. What special lending or communications programs are in place?	How is credit demand ascertained in the local community? How are credit needs being met by the institution? How are credit needs being met in the low to moderate income areas?	The institution does have an understanding of community credit needs. These credit needs were assessed through research and community outreach programs
What is the evidence the institution can provide to document its lending activity in the community? Are approval or denial rates biased in any way?	What is the geographic distribution of all lending in relation to all areas that are considered by the institution to be its primary trading area? What is the approval and denials rates within and outside of defined target areas. Is the institution utilizing 1990 census data and census geography.	The institution has analyzed the geographic distribution of all lending activity. There is no evidence of discriminatory lending practices in terms of lending. The institution is utilizing current socio-economic data and geography in its analysis
What is the criteria for loan approval? Are they applied uniformly. Are deposits gathered in the community but lending does not occur in the same areas?	Are loan denials directly related to race of applicant, the neighborhood, or any other criteria not related to credit or not uniformly applied to all applicants? Is there evidence of redlining?	Loan to deposit ratios are similar regardless of the geographic area. Loan approval criteria does not include racial factors or neighborhood factors. The institution has provided its fair share of lending in target areas
What is the criteria for closing a branch office? What is the proximity of other branches? How is access to financial services affected?	How many branch offices have opened and closed in the target areas? What was the impact on the community by closing offices? Has there been a restriction of access to information regarding lending programs?	Detailed arguments outlining branch closings. Develop a plan to address community concerning the impact of closing an office.
What is the institution's lending record in the community? Particularly mortgage lending? Are there programs to generate access to mortgage lending?	What is the accuracy of HMDA data related to geocoding? Does the institution have knowledge of the spatial distribution of all of its lending with respect to the target areas? What is the methodology for target area creation?	The accuracy of geo-coding HMDA data is consistent with Federal guidlines. Analysis of HMDA data and other lending activity is detailed and comprehensive and has resulted in program generation to improve results in target areas.
How often does the institution meet with the community? How involved is the institution with community concerns?	What is the number and composition of special programs in relation to increasing awareness of lending within the target areas.	Document the impact of past programs. Outline and commit to future lending programs.

SCHEDULE 5

NEW ORLEANS MSA
SELECT SOCIO–DEMOGRAPHIC DATA BY TRACT

PARISH NAME	CENSUS TRACT	HOUSEHOLDS 1990 CENSUS	1990 HOUSING UNITS	%OWNER OCCUPIED	VALUE OF OWNER OCCUPIED HOUSING		MEDIAN INC. 1990	TARGET AREA DESIGNATION
					>$125,000 HOUSING UNITS	MEDIAN VALUE OWNER OCCUP		
JEFFERSON	020101	1,429	1,507	60.56%	60	$80,800	$26,472	NON-TARGET
JEFFERSON	020102	1,459	1,510	73.51%	320	$101,800	$36,194	NON-TARGET
JEFFERSON	020201	961	1,122	31.55%	216	$150,300	$34,806	NON-TARGET
JEFFERSON	020202	1,460	1,889	8.15%	0	$43,900	$23,083	TARGET
JEFFERSON	020203	2,667	2,743	76.67%	1084	$133,700	$40,541	NON-TARGET
JEFFERSON	020301	1,235	1,251	95.84%	551	$123,400	$50,778	NON-TARGET
JEFFERSON	020302	2,031	2,089	71.95%	613	$120,100	$33,721	NON-TARGET
JEFFERSON	020303	1,425	1,461	85.76%	107	$83,400	$34,092	NON-TARGET
JEFFERSON	0204	1,196	1,207	95.03%	377	$107,900	$42,635	NON-TARGET
JEFFERSON	020501	3,023	3,170	66.21%	688	$111,300	$40,689	NON-TARGET
JEFFERSON	020502	2,287	2,450	56.08%	3	$57,500	$31,132	NON-TARGET
JEFFERSON	020503	4,577	5,010	41.96%	918	$125,900	$36,075	NON-TARGET
JEFFERSON	020505	647	725	57.66%	1	$50,100	$16,743	TARGET
JEFFERSON	020506	1,929	1,986	49.09%	20	$85,400	$28,500	NON-TARGET
JEFFERSON	020507	1,794	1,876	61.89%	25	$70,600	$35,382	NON-TARGET
JEFFERSON	020508	1,930	2,017	84.38%	67	$58,900	$29,205	NON-TARGET
JEFFERSON	020509	2,576	2,773	62.93%	18	$67,400	$29,216	NON-TARGET
JEFFERSON	0206	1,480	1,741	27.52%	4	$56,800	$30,191	NON-TARGET
JEFFERSON	0207	731	935	46.95%	4	$52,000	$18,022	TARGET
JEFFERSON	0208	644	784	40.69%	8	$54,100	$15,521	TARGET
JEFFERSON	0209	506	636	34.75%	6	$53,100	$15,068	TARGET
JEFFERSON	0210	1,030	1,112	62.68%	20	$63,300	$23,378	NON-TARGET
JEFFERSON	0211	948	1,016	69.98%	10	$61,400	$22,407	NON-TARGET
JEFFERSON	0212	954	1,028	45.91%	1	$64,900	$22,685	NON-TARGET
JEFFERSON	0213	1,069	1,097	89.33%	13	$72,600	$38,609	NON-TARGET
JEFFERSON	0214	792	809	91.47%	3	$83,200	$37,827	NON-TARGET
JEFFERSON	0215	1,222	1,576	25.93%	0	$65,900	$21,171	TARGET
JEFFERSON	0216	2,850	3,123	31.03%	10	$81,800	$28,755	NON-TARGET
JEFFERSON	0217	2,279	2,393	57.08%	85	$84,400	$30,070	NON-TARGET
JEFFERSON	021801	1,515	1,614	35.32%	50	$89,200	$24,004	NON-TARGET
JEFFERSON	021802	3,090	3,705	3.51%	1	$79,700	$20,596	NON-TARGET
JEFFERSON	0219	779	916	31.22%	18	$85,200	$29,960	NON-TARGET
JEFFERSON	022001	2,114	2,435	12.28%	8	$81,700	$30,543	NON-TARGET
JEFFERSON	022002	1,362	1,491	67.94%	69	$84,600	$31,564	NON-TARGET
JEFFERSON	022101	619	633	90.21%	202	$114,800	$33,029	NON-TARGET
JEFFERSON	022102	1,609	1,652	34.56%	56	$89,900	$20,952	NON-TARGET
JEFFERSON	0222	1,138	1,185	76.37%	90	$86,900	$30,968	NON-TARGET

Figure 10.2 New Orleans MSA: select socio-demographic data by tract (from Verdi Ryan Associates)

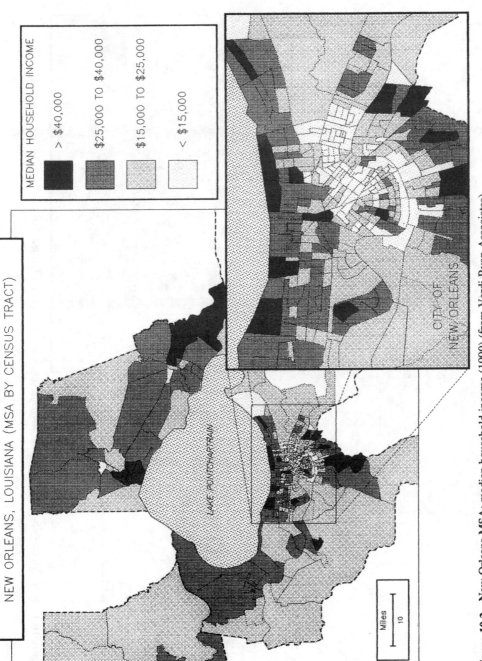

MEDIAN HOUSEHOLD INCOME (1990)
NEW ORLEANS, LOUISIANA (MSA BY CENSUS TRACT)

MEDIAN HOUSEHOLD INCOME

> $40,000

$25,000 TO $40,000

$15,000 TO $25,000

< $15,000

LAKE PONTCHARTRAIN

CITY OF
NEW ORLEANS

Miles

10

Figure 10.3 New Orleans MSA: median household income (1990) (from Verdi Ryan Associates)

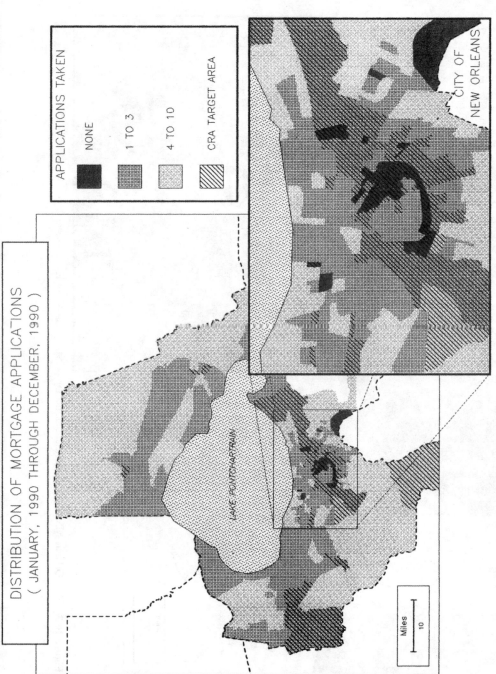

Figure 10.4 New Orleans MSA: distribution of mortgage applications (from Verdi Ryan Associates)

Demonstrating compliance with the Act involves understanding the geographic distribution of loan approvals and rejections. Data from internally held customer files is mapped, by census tract against key socio-economic and demographic variables from the census, as can be seen in Figures 10.2 to 10.4.

There is a central IT department which lacks the skills and knowledge of GIS. The vice-president of marketing became the project sponsor. Initial ideas for the use of GIS came from an external consultancy firm, Verdi Ryan, based in Williamsville, New York state. The bank is now considering bringing GIS in-house. It wants to be able to offer services centrally for the decentralised marketing departments to purchase themselves.

European-wide dealer network for a car manufacturer operating in a niche market

European car manufacturers are facing a changing business environment. The main opportunity comes from the formation of the single market in 1993. On the other hand, the main business threat is that block exemption for dealers will be abolished in 1995.

With these business issues in mind Company X decided to review its dealer network of 1500 dealers throughout Europe. The system chosen to do this had to be portable to give to the dealers themselves ultimately. It also had to be suitable for all countries.

Finding a consultant who had expertise in all countries in Europe proved to be impossible. Nevertheless, consultants were appointed to advise on maps. The software chosen for the task was MapInfo. Data would include car registration details, socio-economic data and dealer data. The system was to be used to define dealer catchment areas. Typically these are large geographical areas because the manufacturer is operating in a niche market. The main outputs from the system have been thematic maps of dealer performance and areas of dealer potential. The main benefit has been that maps make things easy to understand. The flexibility of having a system is that it is possible to do 'what if' kinds of scenario building.

However, there have been drawbacks too. The software is not user-friendly. The project has been very time-consuming and there have been data format problems. Future developments of the project are likely to include moving to a more friendly software environment, for example, ARC/INFO for Windows. Also, it is hoped to link the system to in-house databases currently held on an IBM AS/400 machine. Implementation is currently a sensitive commercial issue because some hard decisions involving rationalising the dealer network will have to be taken. Therefore, at the present time the company have requested to remain anonymous.

IKEA, Ottawa, Canada

The managing director of IKEA in Ottawa has rejected the use of GIS for planning the location of a new store. Yet, paradoxically, Rob Rogers is enthusiastic about the importance of finding the best location. The meeting room on the first floor of the Ottawa store has the walls covered in maps, with coloured dots and pins stuck in them to indicate shopping centres, competitor stores and target population groups. Would most businesses in this situation not turn to a GIS solution? (See for example the story of another retail store, the Miracle Food Marts case in Chapter 9.) As a business, IKEA have always prided themselves on seeing problems as opportunities and finding that slightly different route to a solution. On the basis that much can be learnt from studying where GIS is not being used as can be learnt from studying where it is being used, it is worth exploring this case study further.

The IKEA mission is strongly influenced by its Swedish originator, Ingvar Kamprad who said, 'we shall offer a wide range of home furnishing items of good design and function, at prices so low, that the majority of people can afford to buy them' (IKEA 1984). Putting this mission into practice has led to the striking blue and yellow stores built on cheap land and averaging around 12 000 m^2 in size. How is the location decision arrived at?

It is recognised by IKEA that location is an important factor in success. Potential sites are selected on the basis of three criteria:

1. A minimum population base of more than 1 million living within a one-hour drive time;
2. Inexpensive land (IKEA own their own sites);
3. Proximity to a major road – 99% of customers travel by car.

Coming down to the micro level, the important thing is to be able to recognise who IKEA customers are. Normal IKEA practice is to do customer surveys about four times a year. Each survey will be based on interviewing about 1000 customers. One of the important geographical data collected is the respondents' postcode. A study undertaken by Compusearch, a leading market research and GIS consultancy/data agency operating in Canada, in June 1990 defined the Ottawa customers as:

1. Young (26–34) middle-class families with children in recently built single or semi-detached housing and townhouses with household income of about C$49 900 per annum.
2. Young to middle age (35–44), well-educated families in high-value houses with household income upwards of C$80 000 per annum.
3. Young lower income singles in apartment dwellings.

The data agency, as the next step, produced maps to indicate where these three customer groups lived. In terms of the stages of growth model of GIS, IKEA could be said to be at the first 'opt-out' stage. An interesting question here is why IKEA has not progressed to the next stage.

The current Ottawa store, opened in 1979 in the suburb of Bells Corner, is small by IKEA standards and this is thought to affect the average time spent at the store by customers. The average family visit to IKEA lasts between four and five hours. In Ottawa this average figure is only one and a half hours. The small size of the store influences some of its key characteristics; for example, it restricts the range of goods that can be displayed, it means that a restaurant and shop cannot be provided, and car parking is limited.

One of the key business issues currently facing the management is where to relocate the store. Rob Rogers takes the view that customers will travel to the IKEA store from anywhere in the metropolitan urban area. Analysing the competition is an important factor in most business location decisions, especially in the retail sector. Yet IKEA feel that they are sufficiently different that they have no real direct competition. The population size of the Ottawa area is such that there is only scope for one IKEA store. This is normal practice – there being few examples in the world where IKEA have opened more than one store per metropolitan area. Hong Kong, with a population of 6 million, is the major exception to this rule, with four stores (IKEA 1992).

To test the feasibility of using GIS to help the location decision, Erin O'Shaughnessy undertook a study as part of her graduate work at the University of Carleton (O'Shaughnessy and Haythornthwaite 1993). In order to make an estimate of the store trade area, O'Shaughnessy did a survey of 309 customers as they left the store. Most of these customers, 82%, live within the Ottawa–Hull area. The study concentrated on those respondents in the metropolitan area for the purpose of analysing their socio-economic characteristics. There was a very high correspondence of customer to the types already defined by IKEA (see above). Some 36.6% were young middle-class families living in semi-detached housing, and 32.7% were in the young to middle-aged group living in high-value houses.

Using a GIS called SPANS from Tydac Technologies a number of census variables were input as attribute data. The attributes were expressed as a percentage of the enumeration district total. Census data for the following variables was supplied by Statistics Canada from the 1986 census.

1. Private home ownership;
2. Population age 25–34 and 35–44;
3. Household size of two or more persons.

The geographic base map was created from boundary maps of the Ottawa–Hull census metropolitan area supplied by Statistics Canada. The study area comprised 895 enumeration areas. Customer postcodes, collected from the survey, were linked to enumeration area postcodes via a postal code conversion file supplied by Statistics Canada. The Canadian postcode is six digits long (compared to the UK eight digits); the first three are known as the forward sortation area (FSA) and the last three digits are local delivery units identifying blocks of the city. Survey respondents could then be mapped as in Figure 10.5 which shows the wide catchment area of the store.

More interesting than maps of current customers are maps that show potential customers. Where should the business be targeting marketing? Plate IV shows areas of customer potential defined by the three demographic variables from the census data. The variables have been combined and equally weighted. The western part of the metropolitan area, where IKEA is currently located, provides the majority of the existing customers (see Figure 10.5). However, there are areas of

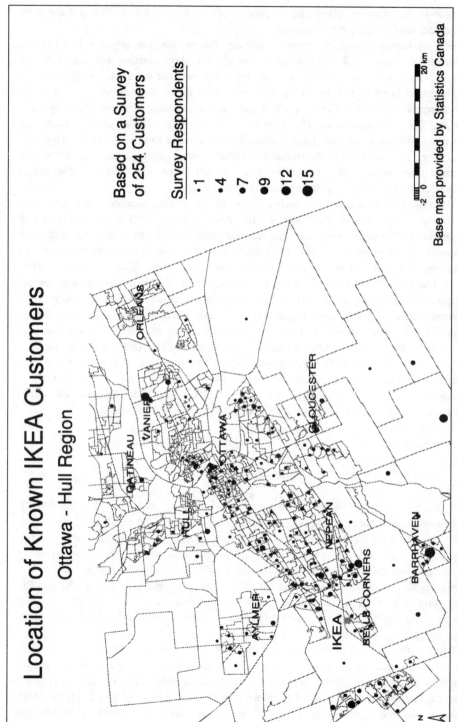

Figure 10.5 Location of known IKEA Customers (*Source:* O'Shaughnessy and Haythornthwaite 1993)

high potential in the eastern areas. The distance and drive time from these areas may currently be too great to attract large numbers of customers.

So how does this GIS feasibility study help IKEA decide on a new store location? The analysis suggests that a move eastwards would attract customers from areas of high potential in the east. Yet the move should not be too far from the existing customer base in the west. The analysis of O'Shaughnessy and Haythornthwaite (1993) has concentrated on macro location factors. At the more detailed site level, additional attribute data such as land values, zoning and physical features, could be analysed to help refine the search for a specific site.

In practice, Rob Rogers has made a decision to move to another site in Ottawa, without the benefit of GIS analysis – IKEA is to move to a site off the Queensway. It will benefit from improved car access and larger car parking facilities. An additional key factor in the decision was the availability of the property at a reasonable price. In the case of IKEA it could be argued that the sophistication of a GIS would be overkill in terms of providing more analysis than was required in order to make the relocation decision.

Employing a data agency to undertake market analysis, including mapping of customers, is indicative of a company at the 'opt-out' stage of using GIS. By way of an interesting diversion the project undertaken by O'Shaughnessy and Haythornthwaite (1993) provided another perspective on the location decision. Again this was a perspective that, although it had full company cooperation, was external to the company. The costs of introducing such a GIS into the company outweighed the perceived benefits. The needs of the company were essentially very focused and confined to one specific business problem area. Possibilities for using GIS in the future would depend upon the price of GIS declining and the range of applications to the particular business situation expanding. Both of these prospects are quite likely to happen in the future. So IKEA provides a case study of an organisation at the brink of moving to the next stage of using GIS.

MassMutual Life Insurance Company, Springfield, USA

MassMutual is an insurance company specialising in life policies, based in Springfield, Massachusetts, USA. As a company, MassMutual has assets of about $30 billion, making it about twelfth in size within the US life insurance market. It has about $100 billion of life policies in force – ranking ninth in the industry.

The MassMutual case illustrates a company that has used GIS since 1986. As such it is interesting to interpret the path followed by MassMutual in relation to the stages of growth model advanced in Chapter 2. The 'opt-out' stage began in 1986 when the services of a data agency – CACI – were used for market segmentation. Customer files were given to CACI who used Profile America to create nine standard predefined reports. These included reports on market penetration by geographic area (county level), product (12 categories) and market segments (44 ACORNs). The reports were mainly used for analysis of territories and sales management (Greeley 1993).

MicroVision AREA PROFILE REPORT

BY EQUIFAX NATIONAL DECISION SYSTEMS
PREPARED FOR
YOUR COMPANY

BEACON ST. & HARVARD AVE.   SITE
BROOKLINE, MA.   COORD:

		DESCRIPTION	3.0 MILE RADIUS HSHLDS	PCT	BASE 1991 HSHLDS	PCT	INDEX
MVG01	1	UPPER CRUST	1455	0.9	906204	1.0	89
MVG01	2	LAP OF LUXURY	0	0.0	1803921	1.9	0
MVG01	3	ESTABLISHED WEALTH	198	0.1	2604852	2.8	4
MVG01	4	MID-LIFE CRISIS	793	0.5	783409	0.8	56
MVG01	5	PROSPEROUS ETHNIC MIX	1	0.0	2615351	2.8	0
MVG01	6	GOOD FAMILY LIFE	0	0.0	1519612	1.6	0
MVG06	7	COMFORTABLE TIMES	91	0.1	820497	0.9	6
MVG04	8	MOVERS AND SHAKERS	7714	4.6	2308796	2.6	185
MVG03	9	BUILDING A HOME LIFE	7	0.0	476906	0.4	1
MVG02	10	HOME SWEET HOME	40	0.0	5361646	5.7	0
MVG02	11	FAMILY TIES	0	0.0	4250824	4.5	0
MVG04	12	A GOOD STEP FORWARD	19749	6.3	1976750	2.1	304
MVG09	13	SUCCESSFUL SINGLES	5103	3.0	548187	0.6	615
MVG01	14	MIDDLE YEARS	330	0.2	121992	0.1	149
MVG04	15	GREAT BEGINNINGS	671	0.4	1401087	3.6	11
MVG02	16	COUNTRY HOME FAMILIES	0	0.0	5225763	5.6	0
MVG02	17	STARS AND STRIPES	0	0.0	1685123	1.8	0
MVG02	18	WHITE PICKET FENCE	0	0.0	5584986	6.0	0
MVG03	19	YOUNG AND CAREFREE	420	0.2	366271	0.4	63
MVG06	20	SOCIAL SECURITY	305	0.2	1902968	2.0	9
MVG06	21	SUNSET YEARS	355	0.2	511341	0.5	38
MVG02	22	AGING AMERICA	7	0.0	2806883	3.0	0
MVG02	23	SETTLED IN	454	0.3	4770332	5.1	5
MVG08	24	METRO MINORITY FAMILIES	25	0.0	1679267	1.8	1
MVG03	25	BEDROCK AMERICA	26	0.0	3213322	3.4	0
MVG07	26	MATURE YEARS	0	0.0	1168392	1.2	0
MVG05	27	MIDDLE OF THE ROAD	323	0.2	418370	0.4	43
MVG03	28	BUILDING A FAMILY	359	0.2	1474443	1.6	13
MVG05	29	ESTABLISHING ROOTS	154	0.1	442721	0.5	19
MVG06	30	RETIREMENT AGE	642	0.4	878492	0.9	40
MVG06	31	GOLDEN TIMES	0	0.0	672719	0.7	0
MVG04	32	METRO SINGLES	23806	14.1	2272814	2.4	580
MVG07	33	LIVING OFF THE LAND	0	0.0	1854538	2.0	0
MVG04	34	BOOKS AND NEW RECRUITS	4757	2.8	905674	1.0	291
MVG02	35	LATE-LIFE LABOURERS	0	0.0	4569644	4.9	0
MVG09	36	METRO ETHNIC MIX	1643	1.0	1390900	1.5	65
MVG09	37	MOVING AHEAD MINORITIES	41473	24.5	538821	0.6	4257
MVG02	38	BACK COUNTRY	0	0.0	5637733	6.0	0
MVG04	39	ON THEIR OWN	6062	3.6	3243539	3.5	103
MVG04	40	TRYING METRO TIMES	0	0.0	2766993	3.0	0
MVG08	41	SOUTH OF THE BOARDER	12	0.0	705404	0.8	1
MVG08	42	HANGING ON	0	0.0	2019013	2.2	0
MVG08	43	LOW-INCOME BLUES	131	0.1	264127	0.3	22

BASE DEFINITION STATE/COUNTY: UNITED STATES

Figure 10.6   MicroVision area profile report

A number of problems and limitations arose from the experience with the CACI systems. The level of geography, at the county level, was rather coarse, particularly in heavily populated urban areas. The cost of the services of CACI was not cheap and the types of reports were predefined. Therefore, running interactive 'what if' kinds of questioning was not possible. A review of the system was initiated in 1992. Over that six-year period there were now many more geodemographic systems on the market with improved features and facilities. The 1990 census had just been issued and therefore it was a timely moment to reconsider the market segmentation analysis systems.

The systems review had a number of key objectives. Firstly, reduce the costs by limiting spending to the purchase of data and then linking to internal databases in-house. Secondly, to allow more flexibility so that *ad hoc* queries could be done at anytime. Thirdly, to use a smaller geographic area for analysis. The zip code or where possible the zip+4 would be preferable. Fourthly, to be able to analyse data at the agency level, not just the company level – this is particularly important where agencies share the same territory.

A full feasibility study, with a cost–benefit analysis and information requirement study, was not undertaken. In practice only two GIS software packages were evaluated before purchase of InfoMark in November 1992. InfoMark is a Windows product of Equifax NDS Inc. and is based on an ARC/INFO shell. A decision was made quickly. The system chosen had good support from the vendor and was in fact the cheapest (at around $35 000).

InfoMark was purchased with its compatible market lifestyle data set called MicroVision. The clusters in MicroVision were developed with a financial services focus, making it the leading segmentation system in the insurance industry. There are 90 lifestyle clusters which collapse into 37 insurance clusters which further collapse into 8 insurance segments based on a nine-digit zip code (zip+4). Figure 10.6 shows an example of a MicroVision area profile report. The data is supplied on CD-ROM enabling larger data sets to be accessed than with the previous hard disk system. Additionally a zip+4 data directory was purchased to allow the MicroVision codes to be transferred to internal files.

Bringing the GIS facility in-house takes MassMutual to the 'stand-alone' stage of the growth model. The project champion was Judith Greeley from the marketing department. Although MassMutual have their own IT staff at a devolved (department) level in the company, it was preferable to choose a package rather than allowing the internal IT staff to develop the system. It proved to be easier to get budgets for purchasing than for systems development.

The plan for integrating the system with other internal information systems was outlined in four phases reproduced below:

Phase I: Extract and import internal sales data from marketing database (MDB) into the InfoMark system

Actions

1. *New business.* Extract a file from the MDB of number of policies, $ amount of premium by:
   - zip code (about 30 000 five-digit zip codes)
   - product type (six product categories)
   - agency (95 agencies)

2. *In force business.* Extract a file from the MDB of number of policies, monetary ($) amount of premium by:
   - zip code (about 40 000 five-digit zip codes)
   - product type (six product categories)
   - by agency (95 agencies)

Import the two files as user-created InfoMark files which will give us the ability to calculate total business and new business penetration rates. LIMRA's MarketMap data is already built into InfoMark so we can calculate agency/company market share as well. Update quarterly.

Rationale

This is the quickest and most efficient method to get up and running with company and agency-level marketing-oriented reporting applications. With this accomplished we are able to create meaningful customised 'turnkey' market penetration, market performance and market potential reports which can be accessed by home office sales executives as well as agency staff.

Phase II: Use phase I data to create a market potential and market performance scale (in Lotus 123 outside MDB and InfoMark)

Create a spreadsheet by zip code to calculate 'potential index', 'performance index' and 'market score' (Table 10.1).

Import potential index, performance index and market score into InfoMark for each zip code. These values will now be available to incorporate into the next level of 'turnkey' agency reporting.

Table 10.1 (a)

A Zips	B No. of policies	C $Premium	D No. of households	E Potential index	F Performance index	G Market score
12345	1 000	$1 500 000	6 500	Calculated from a formula utilizing Financial Forum and MarketMap	Calculated as (No per 1 000 households in area) indexed to national average and premium per policy in area indexed to national average	Calculated sales as a factor of E and F, e.g. (2D)+(E)/2 to create a linear value for ranking area based primarily on potential and secondarily on market performance

(b) Rank by market score

Zips	No. of policies	$Premium	No. of households	Potential index	Performance index	Market score
12357	6 123	12 000 000	750 000	300	149	250
12347	2 500	4 000 000	800 000	300	85	228
12353	5 500	10 000 000	750 000	300	61	220
12345	2 500	1 500 000	650 000	200	59	153
12359	7 348	14 400 000	900 000	125	149	133
12361	2 750	10 000 000	450 000	100	184	128
12349	300	750 000	30 000	75	185	112
12351	2 400	5 000 000	1 000 000	95	94	95
12355	1 000	500 000	750 000	50	30	43

One Application
A visual presentation can be made with this data for an agency by perceptual mapping or graphing zip codes into the following four quadrants based on the relationship between each area's market potential and market performance (see Figure 10.7).

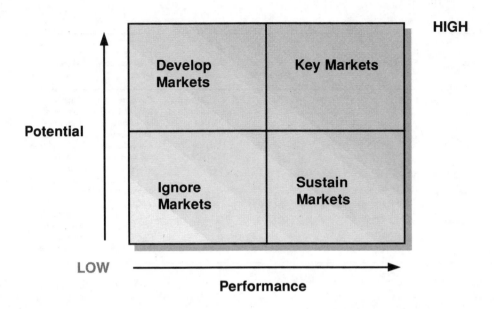

Figure 10.7 Perceptual map of zip codes

Rationale
At this point we will be able to rank and categorise geographies – although not yet market segments within. We will be able to create simple, easy-to-understand geographic market potential, market penetration reports for strategic information-based marketing decision making. This now lays the groundwork for incorporating the MicroVision segmentation system into our analysis.

Phase III: Begin the process of incorporating the market segmentation system into the market potential equation by attaching the MicroVision directory to the sales data in the MDB

Company-level analysis
- Create a sequential file from the MDB of 1992 New Business (by product type [12] and by MicroVision code #[37], policy counts and premium amounts).
- Extract from InfoMark a file with MicroVision counts by total US geography to determine penetration per 1000 households by MicroVision Code.
- Merge the two files and run simple SAS tests against the file to determine the correlations and significance levels between MicroVision codes and (1) propensity to buy MassMutual and (2) monetary ($) amount of premium by five product categories.
- Create MassMutual company-level MicroVision profiles for each of the five product categories. This will depict the relative likelihood of each MicroVision

segment in terms of (1) propensity to purchase and (2) an index of their relative premium level.

- Incorporate these profiles into a new 'customised' market potential equation to replace the one using MarketMap and Financial Forum data in the Phase II Lotus spreadsheet. Update InfoMark with the new market potential and market score.
- Deliver profile data to direct marketing vendor for incorporating into the selection process for lead generation/direct marketing programs.

Agency-level analysis
- Create an identical sequential file from the MDB of 1992 new business adding agency-level detail.
- Rerun SAS test to create an individualised agency-level MicroVision profile by product for direct marketing department.

Rationale
This will create the critical link between our market analysis and the home office sponsored marketing support programs.

Phase IV: Bring MicroVision coded (Mass Mutual) MM sales data into InfoMark PC

Go back to Phase I and add a MicroVision dimension to the sales data being imported into InfoMark. This could increase the size of the import file by about 10 times. We may be unable to achieve this goal before upgrading system hardware. We may choose instead to contract Equifax Decision Systems to put on to a CD-ROM for us.

Rationale
This is the last application in the CACI developed system which had to be developed by MassMutual.

Following this plan will take MassMutual to the 'linking' stage of the growth model. Now, having proved a number of benefits the company is looking towards improving its GIS capabilities. This may require some new software package; at a recent conference Judith Greeley was seen evaluating new GIS software packages. Could this be the early signs of a prospective move to the 'opportunistic' stage?

Future plans include devolving a copy of the database to the operational agency marketing department for the production of standard reporting applications. This would represent a move to the last stage in the growth model, namely the 'corporate' stage.

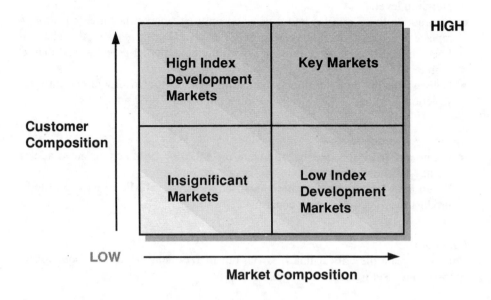

Figure 10.8 Perceptual map of customer composition

Arby's Restaurant, Miami Beach, USA

Arby's Inc. is in the fast-food business in competition with McDonalds, Pizza Hut, Dunkin Donuts, Kentucky Fried Chicken and many others. There are currently over 2000 restaurants in the USA and Canada, and about 90% of these are franchise outlets. Recently an outlet has been opened in London, UK. In contrast to the IKEA case study, Arby customers will want short drive times. As John Freehling (1993) director of development research puts it: 'What is so fast about fast food if it takes forever to get to the restaurant?' Typically 50% of customers drive 5 minutes or less and 75% drive 11 minutes or less to get to Arby's. Figure 10.9 shows the relationship of drive time to percentage of customers.

A number of key business issues are geographically dependent. Three key applications of GIS were used to evaluate and test the capabilities of GIS at Arby's:

1. *Franchise administration and territory management.* The traditional approach involves drawing territories on paper maps, with the sales unit identified by a dot. The business process of agreeing new franchisees means searching files and paper maps to ensure that the proposed location of a new unit is not within an existing franchisee protected territory. Identifying potential trade area overlaps is important for avoiding 'cannibalism'. Improved accuracy of

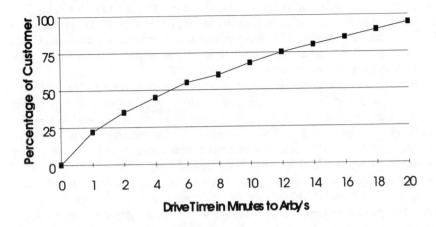

Figure 10.9   Drive times to Arby's (*Source*: adapted from Freehling 1993)

these maps and easier duplication of printing maps were two of the main reasons for adopting GIS. Bringing together attribute data in files, for example name of franchisee, the term, the royalty rate, with the territorial boundary data held on the paper maps has served to reduce the time it takes to process applications for new franchise locations.

This part of the GIS use is in a sense asset management which was considered as part of the operational applications of GIS in Chapter 9. The reason for consideration here in this chapter is that the main motivation for GIS was to assist in the tactical decisions of opening new franchises and developing marketing plans for stores.

2. *Market surveys.* Several surveys are undertaken each year of the market and potential market. The researcher visits a unit and notes the location of competitors. The main uses of these surveys fall into two groups: firstly, to help the franchise sales department sell new territories and secondly, from a strategic point of view, to help to develop the business development plan. Plate V shows a trade area map of competing stores.

3. *Desktop marketing system.* Before venturing into GIS, Arby's had four desktop marketing systems. These held demographic, lifestyle and competitor location data. In terms of costs, the first-year GIS costs were almost identical to the costs of the desktop marketing systems (Reid 1993a) and this included the cost of keeping two of the desktop systems that were running in parallel with the GIS. Over three years Arby's estimated that changing to GIS would reduce costs by 20%. On the benefits side there were clearly established gains in terms of the increased capability of the GIS.

Arby's have a well-established information systems group which gives support to all areas of the business, running many operational support applications like stock control, payroll and electronic point of sale. However, the initiative for using GIS did not come from this information systems group, rather it has been championed by Hal Reid, the vice president of development and research. Hal came to Arby's in 1986 with a background at Popeye's where he was responsible for introducing the first GIS in the fast-food industry.

Several software packages were tested in-house before purchase. The ability to show people the capabilities of a GIS and produce map output was a powerful persuader. Support from the top was also seen as an important reason for successful adoption of GIS. The two applications used by Hal Reid to persuade his boss of the utility of GIS were the franchise management and market survey enhancements. Other applications were being considered.

One tactical application, shown in Plate VI is the development of local marketing plans for each unit. A map of the trade area can be subdivided into customer groups, for example large employers and special promotional activities such as selective discounting can be applied to that group. Essentially this is target marketing based on knowledge of customers and potential customers and where they live or work.

Given that the main uses of GIS have been for tactical decision support, it should not be surprising that the managers with responsibility for decisions with a high intensity of geographic data are those most likely to champion GIS developments. The dangers of the champion leading the development is that GIS may simply become an 'island of technology' with little relationship to other information systems in the organisation. At Arby's, this trap has been avoided by linking some of the attribute databases to the geographic bases. So the territory management system includes a database of details of franchisees and assets related to the geographic 'point' or unit address. This database was extracted from an existing system running on a mainframe computer (Reid 1993b).

The Arby's case illustrates a fast-food business operating in an international environment. Location of units has always been a key business decision based in the past on hand-drawn maps and demographic data. The impetus for GIS came from an internal champion in the development research department who was able to introduce relatively simple off-the-shelf GIS by demonstrating cost savings and enhanced capabilities. In terms of the stages of growth model introduced in Chapter 2 Arby's are at the 'linking' stage. Hal Reid is showing signs of moving to the 'opportunistic' stage but can he carry the rest of the organisation with him?

'I was recently looking for something else to which I could apply GIS' (Reid 1993c). As part of the operational management of each store there is a PC-based information system, taking information from the cash registers, which helps to schedule labour, track inventory and automatically generate routine paperwork. After close of business each day a program would transfer data to the corporate mainframe and also create a file of 'yesterday' data. Now suppose the regional operations managers, responsible for the day-to-day management of several units, had access to the 'yesterday file' for each unit within their region. Further suppose that this data could be accessed via a map on a PC which showed streets and Arby's locations. By clicking a mouse on any unit the manager would be able to access the database to review daily sales and costs. Graphics could enhance the impact by relating the size of the Arby's logo to (say) normal, high or low daily sales.

The 'opportunistic' idea was there, but was it a technology looking for an application or was it genuinely useful for the regional managers? Certainly, according to our model the strategy was technology-led. Was there sufficient business gain in terms of strategic goals to make the application worthwhile and did the development team have the marketing skills to sell the application to the prospective users?

W. H. Smith & Sons Ltd, UK

Operating in a mature market where there are many competitor stores offers its own business challenge in terms of analysing the problem of whether to open or close stores. W. H. Smith & Sons is a well-known UK retailer with more than 400 stores selling newspapers, books and magazines. It has its own specialist stores selling records and videos (Our Price), card and stationery (Paperchase) and specialist books (Waterstones).

Roper (1993) states that W. H. Smith were increasingly frustrated at their inability to accurately forecast sales for newly opened stores. A study in 1987 showed that about half of the stores opened had performed above budget and the other half below. The business challenge, simply put was, could sales be predicted more accurately? Could new locations be identified? How would opening a new store affect an existing store in the locality?

The location planning manager decided that because it was not possible to purchase an off-the-shelf package solution to these problems it was necessary to ask a consultancy firm to tailor-make the appropriate software. Using some standard packages like dBase IV together with some specifically written modelling and mapping software, GMAP delivered a system which is currently used to find locations offering potential for new stores. This is an example of a problem-specific GIS that has been built to meet a need that required knowledge of spatial interaction modelling.

The benefits of the system are difficult to quantify but it has been said (Roper 1993) that if two stores are sited profitably then the investment in GIS will have been recouped.

Overview of tactical applications

At this stage of the chapter it would be useful to review the themes and messages arising from the case studies. Earlier in the chapter a number of key issues were identified which can now be used to structure the discussion.

How dependent is a spatial decision support system on the underlying analytical model?

The nature of tactical decision support has been well characterised in the immortal question, 'what if?' In other words a questioning approach, typified by management being sceptical of the first answer which might come out of the computer, is the norm. Iteration of a model, changing assumptions and so on, are an important part of the process of reaching tactical decisions. So it is important to have computer-based support which truly supports such typical methods of working and decision making. In this sense the model and the flexibility allowed by the modelling software are a very important part of success.

From the review of application capabilities in Chapter 8 it became clear that spatial analysis and modelling capabilities are one of the areas of GIS software that is in need of further development. What do the case studies reviewed here tell us about the importance of spatial modelling in practice?

Locational analysis is one of the traditional decision areas to which modelling has been applied. All the case studies in this chapter included some consideration of locational issues. The approaches were markedly different. The simple approach of IKEA, based on population and distance trade areas, is in contrast to the approach of W.H. Smith & Sons who adopted spatial interaction modelling. To a large extent the differences in approach can be explained by the different business environments being faced by these companies.

Those organisations that have adopted the more sophisticated models have used a data agency or consultancy to develop the software for them. The risks associated with this strategy were considered in Chapter 7. In terms of GIS, starting with simple solutions, getting more complex only when business benefits have been demonstrated, has a lot to commend it.

How and to what extent should GIS be linked to the other ITs used and to the information management strategy of the organisation?

By definition the tactical applications are those that are the most independent of the three types of applications being considered. The evidence for this can be expressed in terms of the stage of growth reached. From Table 8.4 we see that most of the tactical applications are at the 'opt-out' stage. The two case study organisations that have reached the 'linking' stage are beginning to see some benefits from linking GIS with other information systems. Yet the main drivers towards adoption of GIS could not be said to be corporate. In other words there is little evidence amongst these case study organisations that GIS has been identified as an essential part of the information management strategy. This conclusion should not be taken to mean that there is no potential to do this. Only that to date, from the limited number of case study organisations, the approach to tactical applications has been largely on a 'bottom-up' basis.

What is the most effective way of using the customer database with the GIS?

In all the organisations studied here the customer database was an important component of the whole GIS. The key to unlocking the potential of the customer database lies in the ability to geocode the customer address. The cases illustrate slightly different ways of doing this, dependent on the country and the availability of data in that country. Essentially, the method is to convert addresses into point data that can be used by a GIS. Some organisations give their customer files (or more likely extracts from them) to a data agency or consultant to analyse according to some predetermined method. Others have linked their GIS to customer files in-house and begun to explore the value of that data.

What are the benefits from adopting and using GIS and how are such benefits measured?

The benefits of using GIS for tactical decision support are often expressed in terms of effectiveness gains. This compares to the case studies discussed in Chapter 9 which were mainly justified in terms of efficiency benefits. In terms of the business benefits GIS are being used to help market analysis, segmentation and location decisions. Some of the benefits here are difficult to quantify in hard money terms but the value added to the business may be substantial

What are the data issues in terms of cost, availability and transfer?

Out of all the issues considered, this is the one that varies most widely according to the policies and institutional factors operating in particular countries. In all the case studies in this chapter the most commonly used publicly available data set was an address to postcode conversion file. This data is widely available in Canada, the USA, the UK and most EC countries studied here. Availability of common data formats across Europe is a current issue and was clearly a problem area for the car dealer case study.

How is GIS related to the stage of growth of the organisation in terms of its use of IT?

The examples discussed in this chapter illustrate almost the full range of stages of growth. A summary is given in Table 8.4. Organisations such as Arby's and MassMutual have developed through various stages of the model.

Most organisations that have considered using GIS to help with tactical decision support have started at the 'opt-out' stage. This is essentially because of the fact that the decision areas have been thought by the business to be sufficiently discrete to allow for the development of isolated, or independent, solutions.

What is the impact of new technology, such as desktop mapping and EIS, and multimedia on GIS?

To the extent that GIS is being used to integrate data from different sources and that GIS is also being used as a way of integrating information systems, technology offering multimedia can be expected to be of importance in some application areas. None of the case study organisations really made use of these new areas. However, there is evidence from other sources that, for example, the integration of video and still image photographs into GIS is having an impact on real estate applications (Castle 1993). At the other end of GIS usage, it can be expected that simple desktop mapping will find applications where full-scale GIS is not appropriate. Maps, used as outputs from systems in this way, are likely to become an increasing feature of a range of business information systems. These trends are in fact likely to reduce the barriers between what we now know as GIS and all other business systems.

Summary

The use of GIS to assist managers making semi-structured decisions or 'what if?' kinds of modelling have been reviewed in this chapter. The case studies discussed have illustrated a range of applications, from different industries and different countries, of GIS for supporting such tactical decisions.

The overall pattern that emerges is of GIS applications originating as 'opt-out' systems that later prove useful to the organisation. Bringing systems in-house, initially as 'stand-alone' and later as 'linking' systems, gives the organisation further benefit that often goes beyond efficiency gains to add value to the business.

It seems likely that applications in this category of 'tactical' will benefit from future releases of GIS software that have been specifically focused to solve specific business problems. More spatial analysis features will also be useful in this area.

Further study

Many of the tactical applications discussed in this chapter involve marketing. For those readers specifically interested in marketing applications of GIS a thorough understanding of market research concepts and techniques is recommended. The following books should provide a useful starting point.

Baker M J (ed) 1992 *Perspectives on Marketing Management* Vol 2, John Wiley & Sons, London
Beaumont J R 1991 *An Introduction to Market Analysis* CATMOG 53, Geo Books, Norwich, UK
Dibb S, Simkin L, Pride W M, Ferrell O C 1991 *Marketing: Concepts and Strategies* (European edn), Houghton Mifflin, London

Spatial analysis and spatial modelling have formed part of the discussion in this chapter. The detail of the actual modelling process has not concerned us here. For readers who wish to follow up the modelling ideas the books recommended for further reading at the end of Chapter 5 would make a good starting point.

References

Bagehot W 1858 Estimates of some Englishmen and Scotchmen, *The First Edinburgh Reviewers*

Beaumont J R 1991 Managing information: getting to know your customers. *Mapping Awareness* 5(1): 17–20

Brown P J B 1991 Exploring geodemographics. In Masser I, Blakemore M (eds) *Handling Geographical Information: Methodology and Potential Applications* Longman Scientific & Technical, Harlow, pp 221–58

Castle G H 1993 Real estate. In *Profiting from a Geographic Information System* GIS World Books Inc, Fort Collins, Colo, pp 85–104

Dataquest 1993 *GIS Strategies* The Dataquest/GIS World Market Report, GIS World Inc, Fort Collins, Colo

Freehling J 1993 Using drive times to construct trading areas. *Proceedings of GIS in Business '93 Conference* Boston, GIS World Books Inc, Fort Collins, Colo, pp 261–4

Greeley J 1993 GIS applications in life insurance: one company's experience. *Proceedings of GIS in Business '93 Conference* Boston, GIS World Books Inc, Fort Collins, Colo, pp 171–6

Grimshaw D J 1991 GIS – a strategic business tool? *Mapping Awareness and GIS Europe* 5(2), (March 1991): 46–8

Hale K 1993 GIS in business: market trends. Paper presented at GIS in Business '93 Conference, 7–11 March, Boston, Mass

IKEA 1984 *The Future is Filled with Opportunities, or the Philosophical Story about IKEA* Inter-IKEA, Humlebaek, Denmark, December

IKEA 1992 *The IKEA World 92/93* IKEA International, Denmark, October

Jones K, Simmons J 1987 *Location, Location, Location* Methuen, Toronto, Canada

Milne A A 1926 *The House at Pooh Corner* Methuen, London

O' Shaughnessy E, Haythornthwaite T 1993 Retail location analysis using GIS. *Proceedings of the Canadian Conference on GIS* Ottawa, 23–25 March pp 25–38

Reid H G 1993a Retail trade. In *Profiting from a Geographic Information System* GIS World Books Inc, Fort Collins, Colo, pp 131–52

Reid H G 1993b Big and small, blue and red. *Business Geographics* 1(2): 16

Reid H G 1993c Big and small, blue and red: we threw too much 'tech' at you. *Business Geographics* 1(3): 14.

Roper C 1993 Spatial interaction modelling helps W.H. Smith pick better store sites. *GIS Europe* 2(3): 40–2

Sherwood Bryan N 1993a Off the map. *Business Geographics* 1(1): 10–11. GIS World Inc, Fort Collins, Colo

Sherwood Bryan N 1993b What are 'business geographics' anyway? *Business Geographics* 1(1): 24–5. GIS World Inc, Fort Collins, Colo

Verdi Ryan 1993a *Community Reinvestment Act Planning and Reporting Process* Verdi Ryan Associates, Williamsville, NY

Verdi Ryan 1993b *The Development and Implementation of an Enhanced Geographic Database and Information System* Verdi Ryan Associates, Williamsville, NY

Verdi Ryan 1993c *The Verdi Ryan Approach to Retail Banking Delivery Network Optimization* Verdi Ryan Associates, Williamsville, NY

11

Strategic applications

'. . . the art of gaining competitive advantage . . . by unlocking the spatial information in your company's databases'.

Donald F. Cooke (1993:15)

Preamble

The art of gaining competitive advantage is one practised on both a local and a global scale. There are many factors that contribute to a particular company's ability to gain such an advantage in the market: effective use of spatial information is just one.

The wider context of gaining competitive advantage has been debated in the literature around the question: 'can information give you competitive advantage?' (Porter and Millar 1985). Chapter 3 explored the difference between competitive and strategic, concluding that strategic is something which supports the creation and implementation of the organisation's strategic business plan. The basis of using GIS strategically was outlined in Chapter 3; this chapter seeks to give examples by way of case studies of actual organisations that use GIS in strategic applications.

As in the previous two chapters, the taxonomy of information systems introduced in Chapter 3 will be used to define strategic applications and place them in relation to operational and tactical applications. In terms of the taxonomy discussed in Chapter 3, the *tasks* of strategic applications are unstructured decisions made by senior managers. In terms of the *time frame* dimension, strategic applications are likely to be developed at a mature stage. In terms of the *technology* dimension, the systems may be relatively simple.

Strategic applications help senior managers to focus on key business issues by unlocking the spatial data held in corporate databases. For strategic applications, the nature of that spatial data is likely to be wide ranging (data breadth) and summarised (low data depth) as explained in Chapter 4.

The first applications of IT were to improve productivity by cost reduction. This was the era of automation discussed in Chapters 2 and 3. The essence of strategic applications is to move away from the substitution paradigm of thought to realise the potential of IT 'to do different things', not simply 'to do things differently'. A number of recent studies have articulated this idea in somewhat different terms. Zuboff (1988) argues that the real goal is to informate not automate. Informate means to empower the workforce with tools needed to become self-directed.

A major research project at MIT (Scott-Morton 1991) argued that business needs to be re-engineered. In other words, do not automate the way things are done now. First of all modify existing procedures and operations to take account of the potential offered by IT. A rather graphic analogy is drawn by Roe (1993) who points out that roads were made from old droving tracks, often following old boundaries and certainly not going in a straight line. Surfacing such tracks provides an easy means of providing roads suitable for cars. However, the track often does not provide the best route. In a similar way, an office manual procedure provides the easiest way of developing a computer system. Yet, a new office process might be possible to take account of the full potential of the technology.

A true story might serve to illustrate the point. A local authority in the north of England was considering introducing a new computer system to assist with the processing of applications for planning permission and building control consent. Specifications of the required system were put out to tender and the resulting bids carefully considered. A well-known computer manufacturer won the bid; however, the system could not be supplied for a further two years. What should the local authority do? They decided to wait, and in the mean time to modify the existing manual procedures in readiness for the arrival of the computer. Measuring the benefits achieved by the new manual procedures and comparing them to those achieved in the first year of the computer system revealed an interesting statistic: 60% of the benefits had been as a result of the new procedures.

Strategic systems are the exciting end of the business. The survival of the business depends on them. With that excitement comes risk, the risk of trying something new and failing is ever present and most people will not need reminding of the tremendous costs of failure of information systems. For example, Bank of America are reported to have lost $20m. and more importantly about 30 of its best customers after scrapping its masternet system.

Executive information systems/desktop mapping

Executive information systems (EIS) have received a great deal of publicity and hype in recent years. Their essential feature and purpose is to help support the information requirements of board-level managers. Typically such systems make use of graphical presentation of data. A natural extension of this is to introduce more maps to illustrate the spatial relationships of key data items.

With the trend towards faster and cheaper hardware has come the development of desktop mapping packages which provide good map display features. The usual limitations of such software is rather simple analytical features and poor links to databases. Nevertheless such software does have its contribution to make towards the increasing acceptability of using geographical information and the practicability of bringing such features to a wider number of users at reasonable cost.

Case studies

A number of case studies illustrate issues raised by the use of GIS for strategic decision making. The cases have been drawn from a variety of countries including the UK, the USA and Australia, and a number of different industries, including finance, transportation, motor vehicles and mining. A summary of the business process, decision type, stage of growth and GIS capability of these case organisations was given in Table 8.4. The cases are ordered to illustrate the stages of growth model discussed in Chapter 3. The 'opportunistic' stage is illustrated by the Woolwich Building Society whose advanced technology department identified GIS as a technology that could be used by the business. Isuzu, Conrail, Levi Strauss and Alcoa illustrate more 'corporate' approaches to the identification, development and use of GIS. In all these cases the use of GIS is firmly rooted in the business strategy.

Together these cases illustrate the following key issues:

1. What is the balance required between mapping and spatial analysis?
2. How and to what extent should GIS be linked to the other ITs used and to the information management strategy of the organisation?
3. What are the benefits from adopting and using GIS and how are such benefits measured?
4. What are the data issues in terms of cost, availability and transfer?
5. How is GIS related to the stage of growth of the organisation in terms of its use of IT?
6. What is the impact of new technology, such as EIS and desktop mapping on GIS?

Woolwich Building Society, UK

The Woolwich Building Society is one of the top three building societies in the UK with assets of around £23 billion. In terms of mortgage lending, traditionally one of the main parts of the business, it ranks as the third largest lender with £2.7 billion worth of mortgage lending in 1992 (Annual Report and Accounts 1992). Further background about the building societies was discussed in Chapter 3.

What's in a name?

The ideas behind GIS were first used by building societies during the 1960s and 1970s for identifying new branch sites. These systems, which relied upon the use of census data, produced little mapping output. People employed in the environmental and public service sectors might have an understanding of the term 'geography' and geographical data, but, to most business people the term 'geographical information system' is of little meaning (Grimshaw 1989). Certainly, at the Woolwich Building Society, little use is made of the term 'GIS' – systems are described according to their applications and include 'customer', 'product' and 'branch' databases.

In recent years, there has been an increasing realisation that data is one of the most important resources possessed by an organisation. Accordingly, emphasis has been placed in gaining maximum return from this resource, especially in those areas catered for by the GIS industry. Clearly GIS has a major role to play as competition within the financial sector intensifies due to the economic climate. Markets for many financial products have reached saturation point and organisations are seeking to consolidate their market share, contracting in an attempt to reduce non-supportable cost–income ratios.

As part of the process of recognising the problems and identifying the possible solutions provided by a GIS, the Woolwich Building Society is conducting a series of pilot studies within the business. The ultimate objective is to implement a system that will meet all critical business requirements.

Introduction of GIS to the Woolwich Building Society

At the Woolwich Building Society, several applications of GIS have been identified by the advanced technology department. This department has as its objective the research of new technologies and the demonstration of their value to the business areas. Development of GIS has been aided by the siting of both the IT and business functions at the same location – the Corporate Headquarters. Hence, exchange of information is rapid and effective, which may contrast with organisations who have decentralised their IT and research activities away from planning, marketing and other head office functions.

Planning processes for business and information systems at the Woolwich Building Society are relatively advanced. The information systems group contains a number of planning departments who are consulted by the business when reviewing long-term objectives. Whilst GIS will have a profound impact upon the development and execution of business objectives, it is not perceived as having a major influence upon IT planning. The reasoning behind this is that PC-based GIS applications can function independently of 'live' and production systems, which are business critical and require careful planning. Further, GIS software has been developed with emphasis upon human–computer interfaces that are easily utilised by business professionals and so require minimal support from computing departments.

As a result of a series of successful presentations to the business, GIS has been well received and has consequently been given a high priority for implementation. The most significant benefits were outlined to the business as falling within the two main areas defined as operational systems and strategic systems, which we will look at in greater detail.

GIS as an operational tool

In line with the key aim of consolidation of market position, one of the most relevant applications of GIS lies in the area of customer marketing and sales. This can be broken down into two main sub-areas – customer development and customer recruitment, the customer being the basic resource of any financial service organisation.

The reasoning behind customer development is that significant opportunities exist for cross-selling financial products and services to existing customers. By combining commercially available demographic data with existing customer data it is hoped that it will be possible to create unique customer profiles. An understanding of the relationship between customer characteristics and the consumption of financial products and services, should allow the generation of additional revenues from existing customers. During times of economic recession, it may be prudent to divert resources to the increasing of customer loyalty rather than attempting to attract new customers from competitors.

Whilst the existing customer base provides the source of the society's potential for organic growth, any strategy for future development necessitates the identification of potential customers. Again, by accurately profiling and mapping existing customers, it may be possible to identify suitable areas for implementing customer-recruitment campaigns.

Use of geodemographic data for GIS can provide a necessary, more focused, approach to direct marketing. As an example of this, a recent survey into GIS and mail campaigns has highlighted the importance of using customer profiling for marketing financial products and services. Three methods were assessed, being:

1. Random targeting;
2. Targeting using financial characteristics of customers as a guide;
3. Targeting using financial and socio-economic characteristics.

An analysis of marketing costs, customer response, etc., revealed wide discrepancies in the cost per lead for each of the three methods, and are shown in Table 11.1. This example clearly illustrates the benefits to be realised, for financial organisations, in using geodemographic data as a key input into any GIS.

Table 11.1   Lead costs for various methods of customer targeting

Method	'Lead Cost' (£)
No targeting	89
Financial targeting	48
Socio-economic targeting	8

Source: Pinpoint Analysis (1991).

GIS as a strategic tool

During the next decade, building societies will be confronted with tough challenges to their newly established market share, and IT will be viewed as the means to attain and increase competitive advantage (Grimshaw 1991).

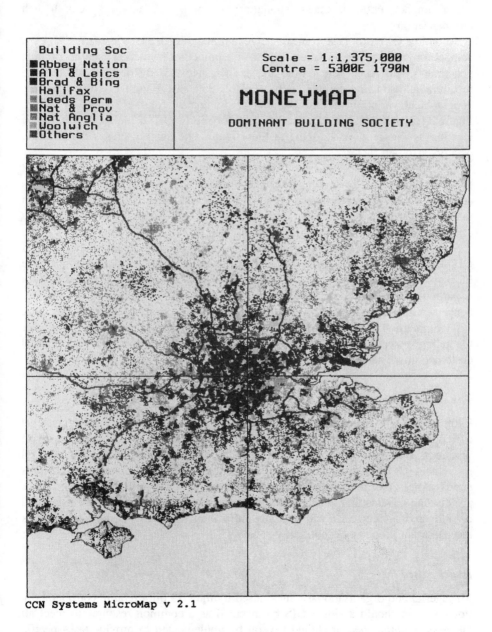

CCN Systems MicroMap v 2.1

Figure 11.1 Building society dominance in south-east England

Specifically, it is likely that GIS will rise to dominate as a key tool for strategic planning.

Firstly, GIS can facilitate high-level decision making, and help in ensuring the integrity and survival of the organisation, particularly as competitive pressures increase. There are two main areas in which GIS technology is likely to have a major impact upon business strategies – competitor analysis and branch rationalisation.

Secondly, GIS provides a means of examining, in detail, the market share a competitor enjoys. Information about a competitor's market share, product penetration, customer penetration and branch network distribution all become readily available using commercially available data sets. Figure 11.1 illustrates the geographical variation of building society dominance for the South-east region. Figure 11.2 shows the product penetration for mortgages in the same geographic location as Figure 11.1. Looking at these maps, one quickly grasps the strategic benefits afforded by GIS.

Thirdly, GIS also provides a means of defining and profiling the catchment areas for your own, or a competitor's, branches. This system of branch analysis allows for branch performance trends to be easily identified, and success in marketing financial products can quickly be quantified. Again, economic pressures stress the importance of gaining maximum value from the branch network.

Some of the smaller building societies have been quick to take advantage of GIS. Because of their relatively small customer databases, such organisations have little problem integrating GIS applications. The competitive edge afforded by GIS is particularly vital because smaller societies tend to be regional in nature, and are hence susceptible to regional downturns in economic activity. Also, they face very stiff competition from building societies with larger branch networks and greater marketing potential. This can be countered by using GIS to target potential customers more accurately.

The value of piloting

Pilot studies are being implemented not only to evaluate the various systems currently available, but also to demonstrate the applicability of GIS to head office functions. Encouraging users to participate in the evaluation process has allowed refinement of business requirements, as well as exposing comparative strengths and weaknesses of the various systems under evaluation as GIS prototypes. Use of prototyping ensures that, when final implementation does take place, the users will be delivered systems that will not only fulfil their requirements, but also possess the important property of familiarity.

Issues raised

Managerial and organisational issues raised by the GIS pilot require consideration. For instance, should a single GIS be installed as a common resource to meet all business requirements, or should several be implemented to provide task-specific applications for each of the head office functions? The final outcome will depend not only upon the business requirements, but also be impacted by the level of resources necessary for GIS maintenance and support.

Another important issue relates to the adoption of commercially available geodemographic data sets. Three categories of data sets have been identified: 'base' data such as the 1981 census; 'lifestyle' data, an example of which is CCN's MOSAIC; and 'application' data such as the banking and insurance data

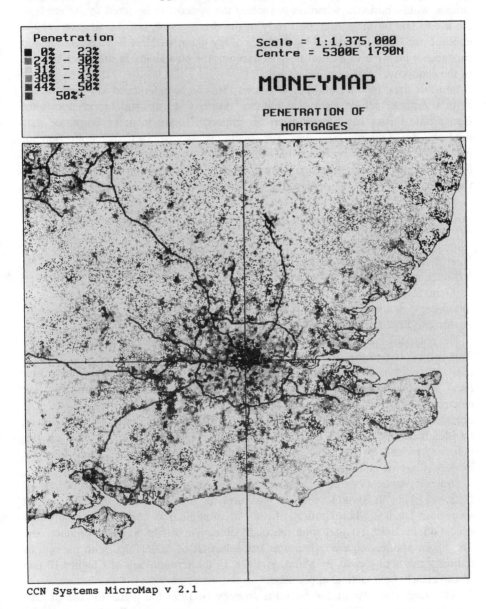

CCN Systems MicroMap v 2.1

Figure 11.2   Penetration of mortgages in south-east England

supplied, for example, FINPIN (Pinpoint Analysis 1987). Data sets selected will depend upon specific business applications, but each of the categories have a role to play in the successful implementation of GIS.

By taking a small-scale approach to the development of GIS, the Woolwich Building Society has been able to demonstrate clearly the necessity of geodemographic data in the attainment of key business objectives. Use of pilot studies within business departments enables the systems to be fitted to the needs of the users. The business may be firmly in the driving seat, but the adoption of the concept itself was introduced by the technology planners. Here is a valuable lesson for those who wish to exploit new technology for businesses in the private sector of the economy.

Items of data, held by building societies, that can be referenced to a point in the earth's surface include customer address, property details and branch locations. Geographical data has clearly been an important component of corporate data holdings by building societies for many years. In fact the collection of geographical data can be traced back long before the computer capability existed to analyse the data in geographic areas. Perhaps it is not surprising then to find that 'GIS' as a term has been played down in business use of geographical analysis.

American Isuzu Inc., USA

Isuzu is a motor vehicle manufacturing company which started in Japan in 1916. Vehicles were first imported into the USA in 1980 and now Isuzu is 37% owned by General Motors. The company operates in a niche market with competence in diesel engines and sport utility four-wheel drive vehicles. There is a long tradition of using technology in the business and this is also true of IT.

The company has a fairly sophisticated computer network operating world-wide. This gives something like 850 users access to electronic mail via PROFS. Predominantly an IBM user, the central mainframe dominance is supplemented by local area networks with 3270 gateways to access mainframe databases and electronic mail. Included on the network are all the dealers world-wide. The operational stock control system is operated in real time such that any vehicle can be identified (by the vehicle identification number (VIN) or in the case of sold vehicles, by the owner name). The importance of these points is that they are evidence that the company is a mature user of IT.

Strategic applications of GIS have to be linked to the achievement of strategic business plans. It should come as no surprise, therefore, that the GIS project sponsor at Isuzu is Mark Darling, director of strategic planning. The company first used GIS in 1989. At that time the main objective was to increase productivity. The major application envisaged was site selection of dealerships with the aim of reducing marketing costs by $50m. in 1991. In the terminology of Chapter 10 this would clearly be a tactical application.

Following a review of the business strategy in 1993 the plans for use of GIS have been updated. There are plans to develop a proprietary GIS solution with the following key objectives (Darling 1993):

- Reduce distribution and marketing costs by more effectively segmenting markets, positioning products and targeting customers.
- Exploit real-time information at the dealer level to create customer value.
- Realign internal functions/organisation to coincide with that of our customer, the dealer, and help the dealer forge a long-term relationship with the retail consumer.
- Define and expand the responsibilities of the field organisation by utilising interactive IT to enhance relationship management and diffuse the shift of power from the manufacturer to the retailer.

In terms of the five forces of competition model (Porter 1985) introduced in Chapter 3, the above statements from the Isuzu strategy are saying that the links with the customer are the most important ones. At Isuzu, Mark Darling talks about a paradigm shift in management thinking to reflect the changes wrought by the new information age. This is visionary thinking, and after all vision is the very stuff that strategy is founded upon.

The thinking behind the strategy is important because understanding the thought process highlights why geographical information can be strategic. A change of management thinking, often referred to as a paradigm shift, is taking place. This means that the successful corporation of the future will place emphasis on teamwork, global markets, customers and information rather than hierarchy, domestic markets, profits and capital. Figure 11.3 illustrates the change in emphasis that is taking place (Scott-Morton 1991).

The old paradigm, leading to business strategy based upon efficiency and

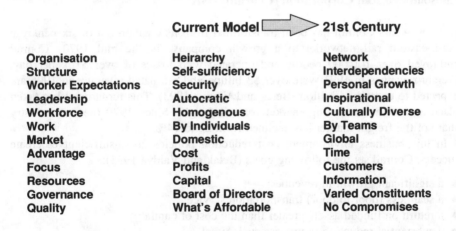

Current Model ➡ 21st Century

	Current Model	21st Century
Organisation	Heirarchy	Network
Structure	Self-sufficiency	Interdependencies
Worker Expectations	Security	Personal Growth
Leadership	Autocratic	Inspirational
Workforce	Homogenous	Culturally Diverse
Work	By Individuals	By Teams
Market	Domestic	Global
Advantage	Cost	Time
Focus	Profits	Customers
Resources	Capital	Information
Governance	Board of Directors	Varied Constituents
Quality	What's Affordable	No Compromises

Figure 11.3 Paradigm shift of management thinking (*Source*: adapted from Darling 1993)

economies of scale, can be seen to have failed many companies recently, for example, General Motors, IBM and Wang Computers. The new paradigm implies a number of new axioms:

- Markets can be segmented into diverse 'niches'. The mass market is dead.
- Mass communications are less effective than targeted advertising.
- Information captured at point of sale gives the retailer enhanced power *vis--vis* the manufacturer.
- Information from the point of sale can help forge a strong relationship with the customer.
- Maintaining state of the art technology in a wide number of areas is increasingly difficult. Strategic alliances can share the fixed costs of keeping up with technology across a wider range of activities (Ohmae 1989).
- The cost of IT has reduced to a level which makes it viable to make information available within and between organisations to the manager who needs that information.

In the above areas geographical information is fundamental to releasing the potential of new business relationships. Links with customers can only be developed with a thorough knowledge of where the customer lives and works. Market segmentation requires fine-grain census data to be analysed on a small geographic area and compared to the socio-economic characteristics of existing customers. Dealer locations and vehicle locations are essential geographical data that can be used to add value to the customer. Only GIS technology can do these things successfully. Darling (1993: 247) sums up by saying: 'It is customer segmentation, targeting, and positioning, synthesised by GIS and information technology that will be the flexible bonds to create customer value and a competitive advantage.'

Consolidated Rail Corporation (Conrail), USA

In recent years Conrail has been transformed from its creation out of six bankrupt north-eastern rail networks to a growth company. In the mid 1970s Conrail employed over 100 000 people and operated with losses of over $1m. per day. Freight revenues in 1991 were over $3 billion and estimated revenues in 1996 are expected to exceed $4 billion (Betak and Vaidya 1993). This turnaround has taken place against a contracting market for rail freight. Since 1970 the rail industry share of the freight market has declined from 22 to 14%.

In this business environment cost reduction policies are insufficient to create success. Conrail set the following goals (Betak and Vaidya 1993):

- a significant growth in revenues;
- a seamless (door to door) transportation service;
- a return on funded assets greater than the cost of capital;
- a substantial reduction in process cycle time;
- a significant reduction in operating costs.

These business goals have created the need for IT to go beyond simple automation of the labour-intensive functions towards corporate-wide strategic systems. Incidentally, it is interesting to note that Conrail have a well-developed set of support and factory information systems, for example computer-assisted train dispatching and track geometry analysis.

The words used by Betak and Vaidya (1993:276) are remarkably similar to those used by Darling (1993) of Isuzu. 'Conrail . . . must make the transition from data processing (to automate the secondary functions) to information application (to informate the organisation). GIS is envisioned as an integral and strategic component of IT initiatives.' Why is GIS so central to the achievement of the Conrail strategy? The answer is that GIS is regarded as a 'backbone system' because it offers consistent locational referencing to allow the integration of data from many sources and of many types. Vaidya (1992:140) states that the role of GIS is to 'access, share, link, display and manipulate internal and external information while maintaining the data integrity through a standardised location referencing scheme'.

Examples of the range of GIS applications are given in Table 11.2. These examples clearly show that GIS is being applied across the business in all departments. The corporate-wide information system has been dubbed a *G*eneral *I*nformation *S*ystem by Vaidya (1992).

Before introducing GIS Conrail maintained over 15 geographical reference files. Some of the geographical references used are rather specific to the railway business, for example, mile post, freight station destinations, yard names, and junctions. Naturally this led to data duplication, with data definitions being incompatible and updating sporadic. But GIS provides consistent integration of data and also of data types. Data sources include maps, CAD, GPS, aerial photographs, video images and document images. In addition, GIS provides the integration and gives the user a friendly interface to make queries, generate reports, plot maps and perform 'what if' analysis.

Table 11.2   Conrail applications of GIS

Grade crossing safety analysis

Routeing analysis with clearance, track condition and demographic data

Fixed asset inventory and utilisation management support for capital planning and maintenance

Establish data links and standardise location reference for track data, clearance, yards, junction terminals, FCC radio signal stations, pipe, wire, fibre cable, storage tanks, properties and customers

Business trend analysis

Critical corporate activity monitoring

Customer prospecting and geographical problem monitoring

Site evaluation and selection

Crisis management

Environmental property information management

Property valuation and management support

Tax and liabilities mitigation support

Tonnage tracking

Sizing of rail network with workforce and rolling stock based on market demand

Link rail network with external data to include transportation infrastructure information, demographic information and marketing information

Interlink all map applications and provide channels of distribution

---

The ability of GIS to allow sharing and integration of data has an impact on the human resource side of the business. According to Betak and Vaidya (1993) the system changes the way employees relate to customers, competitors and suppliers. This fosters the re-engineering of the business processes. A very important effect of data sharing is that it facilitates the exchange of both inter- and intra-company information. The implications for organisational change were explained by John Betak and Arun Vaidya (1993:277) as promoting the following changes:

- consolidation of functions;
- reduction in departmental functional barriers;
- cross-functional integration;
- delayering of management structure;
- emergence of a network organisation.

It is interesting to note here the recurring theme of the importance to the business strategy of strengthening links with suppliers and customers. This is in accord with an analysis of the industry using the five forces model of competition (Porter 1985 – see Chapter 3).

Table 11.3   Development of GIS at Conrail

The implementation of GIS has been incremental, following the phases below:

---

1. Evaluation of GIS alternatives consistent with Conrail's goals and objectives:
    (a) analyse goals and objectives to determine decision criteria;
    (b) evaluate major GIS vendors;
    (c) compare and differentiate vendors;
    (d) match vendors against goals and objectives;
    (e) prioritise recommendation;
    (f) develop implementation strategy.
2. GIS assessment and implementation design:
    (a) inventory of georeferenced information;
    (b) identify data problems and business needs;
    (c) prioritise potential GIS applications;
    (d) identify core GIS functionality;
    (e) develop preliminary data conversion and data integration strategy;
    (f) identify resource requirements;
    (g) perform cost–benefit analysis;
    (h) develop detailed pilot implementation plan.

Objectives of the pilot

1. Demonstration of technical feasibility at Conrail:
    (a) compatibility with IT infrastructure;
    (b) portability of multi–departmental functional applications;
    (c) connectivity for internal and external information exchange:

2. Determination of the optimal IT infrastructure required for GIS.
3. Establishing systematic methodologies for data delivery.
4. Implementing GIS functional applications.
5. Evaluating user interface requirements and training.
6. Developing a corporate–wide implementation plan.
7. Documenting tangible and intangible benefits.

GIS pilot implementation plan

1. System development:
   (a) GIS hardware and software implementation plan;
   (b) Hardware, software, telecommunications and facilities acquisition and installation;
   (c) Prototype software development.
2. Data delivery:
   (a) data acquisition, integration, conversion and loading;
   (b) data integration and conversion plan.
3. User implementation:
   (a) user orientation, training and support;
   (b) revised GIS functional requirements, based on user feedback;
   (c) user support plan.
4. Performance monitoring:
   (a) monitoring to gauge improvements in the effectiveness, efficiency, controllability and adaptability of business processes;
   (b) GIS performance monitoring plan;
   (c) revised GIS benefits assessment.
5. Project management:
   (a) comprehensive project management of all project tracks;
   (b) GIS organisational and management plan.

Source Betak and Vaidya (1993 pp 280–1)).

Although the implementation plan is essentially incremental, using pilot studies (see Chapter 7), the development of the plan to achieve corporate objectives was done on a corporate-wide basis. The corporate goals and critical success factors (Rockart 1979) were considered in assessing the role of GIS at Conrail. Commitment was sought and gained from all departments to ensure the long-term strategic value of GIS.

Local champions from departments were identified to act as change agents during the process of development and implementation. The core group of champions took every opportunity to articulate GIS solutions to corporate problems wherever appropriate. Key board-level managers acted as sponsors to the GIS project. Undertaking GIS at a corporate level is sometimes a difficult process so it was found to be essential to have the support of high-level project sponsors and a core group of champions to undertake the change management.

In summary, the key aspects of the utility of GIS at Conrail were:

● the transformation of abstract data into a visual form which allowed managers to explore potential solutions and strategies;

- to correlate data with a consistent geographical reference;
- to integrate different data types such as multi-media;
- to provide the users with a friendly interface which combines graphics and interaction.

Overall the Conrail approach has been to understand their existing data in terms of its geographical references, and to work from the overall business strategy which identified opportunities through the strengthening of links to suppliers and customers. With a corporate-wide vision GIS became a strategic tool with which to deliver integrated data to managers across a range of departments in the business. Betak and Vaidya (1993) have summarised the approach as vision-guided, management supported and user-focused.

Levi Strauss & Co., USA

Best known for the 501 jeans, Levi Strauss is in fact the largest apparel manufacturer in the world. Size alone, did not protect the business from feeling the wind of change during the 1980s. Santoro (1993), a marketing specialist at Levi Strauss, sums up the period as the 'decade of change'. The retailing business environment was one of mergers, buy-outs and acquisitions. In the American market-place companies like Wal-Mart provided one-stop shopping for a mass market. With the growth of cable television and niche magazines it became more difficult to reach a target audience with traditional marketing approaches. A higher disposable income from more dual income families led to an increase in mall order purchases because of less time being available for shopping.

Against this general changing pattern of the retailing environment, some specific factors to Levi Strauss had to be faced. The top customer of 1980, The Gap, began to sell their own-label goods. By 1989 they no longer sold any Levi products. Contraction in the number of department stores because of bankruptcy also served to reduce the number of large customers. In a very competitive market there was pressure to reduce prices, thereby reducing the profit margins for retailers.

This general and specific business environment led to an increasing number of requests at Levi Strauss for geographical analysis of the market. These requests came from both retailers (customers) and other departments of the business. In the mid 1980s such requests were analysed using geodemographics together with some internal data about customers. However, this approach based on using spreadsheets to model data imported from a number of sources proved to be time consuming, with some requests taking several weeks to answer.

With the objectives of integrating the data sources and providing interactive queries GIS was investigated. Interestingly, one of the biggest problems encountered was to get the internal data into a suitable format for GIS. Three main sources of internal data were used. Firstly the company's customer information system. Since this was designed for billing and tracking deliveries to a location number some further work was needed to enhance the data. This works well for the department of distribution and transport who wish to know which box number goes in which lorry for delivery. The existing database needed extending to incorporate the street address of customer locations (approximately 36 000), and other geographical codes such as latitude and longitude, and MSA codes.

The second internal source of data was the internal shipment file. This contained details of over a million product codes (over a three-year period this gives a file size of about 4Gb). It took several months to manipulate this data into a manageable file to use with the GIS. Basically this was achieved by aggregating the data into meaningful product code groups. For example, a men's jeans group was created from product styles (501, 550 jeans) and product groupings (men's casual).

Thirdly, data collected from a diary panel, cross-referenced by lifestyle, used to calculate potential sales by geographical area. Two sets of external data were also used in the GIS. MicroVision customer segmentation and lifestyle data together with the 1990 census data. These data sets were available from the supplier of the GIS software package. InfoMark was the chosen GIS software running on a Sun SPARC workstation. The main reason for the choice of hardware was that it was consistent with the IT infrastructure at Levi Strauss. A powerful workstation was chosen because of the fairly large file sizes that have to be processed and stored.

You may recall that MassMutual (see Chapter 10) had a similar hardware and software platform for their GIS. Why was MassMutual classified as a tactical user and Levi Strauss a strategic user? The first, and perhaps obvious, point is that it is the use or *task* that determines whether an application is tactical or strategic, not the hardware and software combination. The case of Levi Strauss is strategic because the impetus to use GIS came from an analysis of the business environment and the system is used by a wide range of senior managers. The distribution analysis system discussed in this case is used by senior management, sales and marketing management, regional marketing managers and research managers for strategic business planning, sales region development, media allocations, market and account performance tracking and test market selection for new products. Some of these tasks are tactical in nature, but the use of the system by senior management for strategic business planning makes the case for it being a strategic system overall.

The applications of GIS at Levi Strauss are currently all in the USA; however, plans are in hand to develop similar systems in Canada and Mexico. Overall, the payback to the company has been measurable in terms of reduced analysis time and the increased ability to be proactive to change rather than reactive. In a market where there is nothing so constant as change this is an important benefit.

Alcoa revisited

Alcoa was the major case study on operational applications (see Chapter 9). Why revisit the case now? As an mineral extraction and alumina processor the simple, initial case for investment in GIS rested on automating the map record keeping. A straightforward operational application. After considerable efforts in collecting, updating and processing mine operational data the GIS became embedded as a fundamental part of the business processes. When a major business problem arose, namely how to mine in areas of jarrah dieback disease, the GIS offered a strategic tool which was used to plan and to persuade the conservation lobby that Alcoa was sensitive to environmental pressures.

Overview of strategic applications

At this stage of the chapter it would be useful to review the themes and messages arising from the case studies. Earlier in the chapter a number of key issues were identified which can now be used to structure the discussion.

What is the balance required between mapping and spatial analysis?

This is an important issue when considering strategic applications. The map is clearly an important way of visualising geographical data. There is some evidence that the more traditional geodemographic map output is no longer regarded as sufficiently flexible to provide for strategic analysis. This suggests that the analysis of the geographic data and the linking of that data to more traditional databases within the organisation is the way that strategic advantage is being gained. Ultimately this is the route towards integration of GIS with other information systems in a seamless environment.

How and to what extent should GIS be linked to the other ITs used and to the information management strategy of the organisation?

In all the case studies reviewed in this chapter GIS has been linked to the business strategy. This is really a fundamental requirement for strategic applications. By definition such applications have to support one or more of the key goals (or critical success factors) of the business. In some of the organisations this link to the business had been articulated via the information strategy, in others it had not. This is an interesting observation which warrants some further discussion.

For example, in the Woolwich case there was no explicit mention of GIS in the information strategy. The reason given for this was interesting, namely that GIS as a technology was relatively free-standing and did not have a major (or strategic) impact on other ITs used elsewhere in the business. This is a view of information strategies which is essentially one dominated by the importance of IT strategy. A view put forward in this book has been (see Chapter 3) that information strategy comprises issues of technology (IT), systems (IS) and management (IM). Taking this wider view would encourage organisations to consider GIS in terms of what strategic importance for the business could be unlocked from the geographical data contained in internal files (an IS issue). In terms of the stages of growth model (see Chapters 2 and 3) the view of information strategy taken by the Woolwich can be interpreted as 'opportunistic'. More will be discussed on this specific issue below.

What are the benefits from adopting and using GIS and how are such benefits measured?

The benefits of using GIS for supporting strategic decisions are notoriously difficult to quantify. A strategic benefit is by definition one that contributes towards the achievement of the business strategy. Benefits are most likely to be measured in terms of the effectiveness of GIS to achieve 'different things', often referred to as the transformation of the business. The ultimate level of transformation identified by Scott-Morton (1991) has been difficult to identify in practice; it remains to date something of a theoretical state. In more practical terms it is likely that the benefits can be measured more in terms of value added (see Chapter 6).

What are the data issues in terms of cost, availability and transfer?

Some of the remarks made in Chapters 9 and 10 in relation to this issue are worth repeating here, namely that the cost availability and transferability of data are dependent on the circumstances of the country or group of countries that the business is analysing. Confirmation of this view is at hand when it is realised that most of the examples in this chapter come from the USA. It is in the USA that data is most widely available at a price that is economic to apply to the applications considered here. Standards have been agreed and adopted, and there is a well-developed market of data agencies who sell value-added geographical information products.

How is GIS related to the stage of growth of the organisation in terms of its use of IT?

The cases represented in. this chapter fall into two stages: 'opportunistic' and 'corporate'. What are the features of organisations that have reached this particular stage of the growth model? Can this tell us anything about the conditions that are needed before GIS may be used for strategic decision support?

All five case organisations have a very mature IT infrastructure. The business is well supported with information systems for a range of business processes. Staff have a balance of technical (computing) and business skills. There is a cooperative structure of management which helps build consensus amongst user groups and helps to support applications which users both need and want. Organisations with these kinds of characteristics are the ones who will most likely adopt GIS for strategic business support.

It is likely that GIS will become just another part of the whole information system of the organisation. The fact that it handles spatial and attribute data will be largely unnoticed by the user community.

What is the impact of new technology, such as EIS and desktop mapping on GIS?

Generally new technology can be seen to have an impact on our case study organisations. The most apparent case is that of the Woolwich where it was the technology opportunity offered by GIS which led to it being considered by the business. Technology, as we have observed earlier, is constantly changing. The price at which applications of that technology become economic for the business to adopt, therefore change over time.

Executive information systems were introduced in Chapters 1 and 2. Like many of the descriptive adjectives that precede the words 'information system', executive is something of a misnomer. The taxonomy of information systems introduced in Chapter 2 provides a more realistic way of describing and assessing information systems. The three 'T's' of task, time frame and technology combine to provide dimensions on which information systems can be discussed. Executive information systems becomes a redundant term.

The relevance for GIS can be discussed in terms of *task*. Executives or top managers will generally be concerned with unstructured decision making for strategic planning. We have seen in this chapter how GIS can fulfil some of these tasks. The issue posed is something of a red herring. A more meaningful question might be to ask how maps can be used effectively by executives. The likely scenario is for mapping to become more widely accepted as a form of output from a range of information systems. In a sense this will be a measure of the extent to which GIS is being integrated into the business.

Summary

Strategic applications are those that support the goals of the business strategy. The applications discussed as case studies here are examples of where GIS has been used to support strategic decision making in the organisation.

Chapters 9 and 10, have discussed operational and tactical applications respectively. Critical readers should already be aware that the boundaries between these concepts do not entirely represent a discrete classification. Notwithstanding this, the three categories of decision have proved to be a useful way of sustaining a discussion about GIS applications that is not bogged down in vertical industry issues.

Two cases have specifically transcended the boundaries between the chapters. The Alcoa case was largely presented and discussed in Chapter 9 as an operational example. However, as was clear in that chapter the Alcoa case also represents a strategic application of GIS.

Strategic applications of GIS are most likely to happen in organisations with a mature IT base. This can be measured in terms of the staff, skills and strategy of the stages of growth model. This model shows that the 'opportunistic' and 'corporate' approaches that are the most typical of strategic applications are most likely to occur in large organisations with mature information systems, cooperative management structures and a balance of technical and business skills.

Further study

Further study of EIS and desktop mapping are worthy topics in their own right. The following sources can be recommended.

Holtham C (ed) 1992 *Executive Information Systems and Decision Support* Unicom Applied Information Technology 15, Chapman & Hall, London
Thomas R K, Kirchner R J 1991 *Desktop Mapping* American Demographic Books, Ithaca, NY
For readers wishing to explore the strategic business concepts and ideas that underpin the strategic applications reviewed in this chapter, the further reading on business strategy listed at the end of Chapter 3 is recommended.

References

Betak J, Vaidya A 1993 GIS: a change agent in a transportation company. *Proceedings of the GIS in Business '93 Conference* 7–10 March, Boston, Mass, GIS World Books Inc, Fort Collins, Colo, pp 275–82
Cooke D F 1993 Unlock your company's databases. *Business Geographics* 1(1): 15–16
Darling M W 1993 Expoiting GIS to create and sustain competitive marketing advantage. *Proceedings of the GIS in Business '93 Conference* 7–10 March, Boston, Mass, GIS World Books Inc, Fort Collins, Colo, pp 243–7
Grimshaw D J 1989 Geographical information systems: a tool for business and industry?. *International Journal of Information Management* 9: 119–26
Grimshaw D J 1992 The use of GIS by building societies in the UK. *Proceedings of the Third European Conference on Geographical Information Systems* Vol. 2, 23–26 March, Munich, pp 988–97
Ohmae K 1989 The global logic of strategic alliances. *Harvard Business Review* **67**: 143–54
Pinpoint Analysis 1987 *FiNPiN: Solving Financial Marketing Problems* Pinpoint Analysis Ltd, London
Pinpoint Analysis 1991 *Cost Savings Achievable by Marketing* Pinpoint Analysis Ltd, London
Porter M E 1985 *Competitive Advantage: Creating and Sustaining Superior Performance* Free Press, Macmillan, New York
Porter M E, Millar V E 1985 How information gives you competitive advantage. *Harvard Business Review* July–August: 149–60
Rockart J F 1979 Chief executives define their own data needs. *Harvard Business Review* March–April: 81–93
Roe G V 1993 Don't pave over old cow paths: spatially re-engineer. *Business Geographics* 1(2): 41
Santoro P J 1993 Using GIS to map, track and attack the jeans business. *Proceedings of GIS in Business '93 Conference* Boston, GIS World Books Inc, Fort Collins, Colo, pp 93–5
Scott-Morton M (ed) 1991 *The Corporation of the 1990's* Oxford University Press, New York

Vaidya A 1992 GIS: Implementing a strategic solution. *Proceedings of the First GIS in Business and Commerce Conference* 11–13 May, Denver, Colo, GIS World Books Inc, Fort Collins, Colo, pp 139–41

Zuboff S 1988 *In the Age of the Smart Machine – the Future of Work and Power* Basic Books, New York

Conclusion

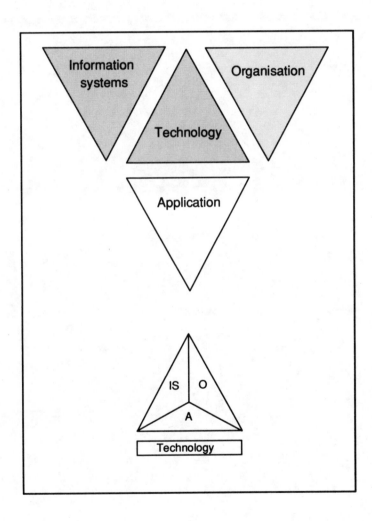

12

An integrated part of the business

'. . . business must make the transition from data processing (automating functions) to information application (to informate the organisation). GIS is envisioned as an integral and strategic component of IT initiatives.'

Betak and Vaidya (1991)

Preamble

The purpose of this final chapter is to bring together some of the main ideas of the book and to look forward to make some comment on the future of GIS. The three main parts of the book have been organised to reflect the view that GIS must be understood as more than just a technology. The base of the GIS pyramid (Figure 1.1) is technology, often referred to as the platform. The three sides of the pyramid are other important views in making up a complete system: information systems, applications and organisation. Taking the analogy further, when the whole pyramid is built and the structure is standing the base – the technology – will be invisible. This is exactly how things should be.

Themes and frameworks

Bringing GIS into business successfully depends upon a number of things happening. The quotation at the head of the chapter reminds us that automating functions is not enough and that GIS can be an integrated part of a business information system. These two ideas have been at the heart of the book. Before returning to these themes it is worth pausing to reflect on some lessons that might be learnt from the past.

To predict the future use of GIS in business is a tough task. Applications in the business domain are relatively new, although geographically referenced data has been used widely since the 1970s. Therefore, forecasts based on trends are likely to be misleading. What can we learn from the past? There are a few key reasons for the, initially, slow take-up of GIS by business:

1. Geographic data sets have been expensive, and not always available on a comprehensive basis in a standard format (data conversion can account for as

much as 90% of systems costs).
2. GIS technology has been expensive and specialist.
3. Software packages have been generic and complex.
4. GIS has been seen as the province of geographers.
5. Many businesses are accounts based not customer oriented.
6. Although the business world in general has taken on board the need to have an information strategy, few organisations include 'technology planning' within that process, thereby excluding the possibility of using new technologies quickly.

The removal of these constraints to the use of GIS is key to the growth of GIS applications in business.

This chapter will bring together the themes and frameworks used in the book. Each theme will be discussed in relation to the conceptual frameworks which are used to help understand and analyse what is happening. Also under each theme some consideration is given to the prospects for the future. The themes of the book can be summarised as follows:

- There needs to be a *paradigm shift* in the way in which the use of GIS is thought of: from the substitution to the completeness paradigm.
- A GIS was defined in Chapter 3 as a group of procedures that provide data input, storage and retrieval, mapping and spatial analysis for both spatial and attribute data to support the decision-making activities of the organisation – *GIS is moving into mainstream information systems.*
- Consideration of GIS as a business tool used to support decision making is most profitably done when *GIS is part of the information strategy.*
- *Spatial data*, comprising up to 90% of all data held by business, can be unlocked by GIS. This data can enable the business to understand patterns previously not revealed, thereby supporting decision making at various levels in the organisation.
- By adding value to customer databases, *GIS helps the business focus on the customer.*
- *Benefits management and implementation* issues need to be considered throughout the GIS project, not simply appended towards the end of the process.
- There is evidence that the *use of GIS* is spreading and that this might best be understood in relation to a stages of growth framework.

The frameworks used in the book are as follows

- GIS in the organisational setting
- taxonomy of GIS
- classification of GIS
- information strategy
- data architecture
- technology architecture
- stages of growth.
- implementation process

The paradigm shift

The traditional paradigm that has driven the use of technology into organisations is based on the idea of substitution. This is a narrowly conceived idea which restricts the range of application of IT. It leads to replacement of existing business procedures with faster computer-based ones, often on a function-by-function basis. This approach does nothing to make the business more effective or help change its direction in a rapidly changing global economy. In essence, the substitution paradigm serves to limit thinking.

The impact of this idea in the realm of GIS has been to foster the notion that if an organisation did not have a manual map based set of procedures then GIS was not going to be useful. The evidence presented in this book should be sufficient to challenge this idea. A necessary condition to allow change is for business to move to a different paradigm of thought. Viewing GIS as an information system working in an organisational setting represents a change to a completeness paradigm. The utility of this new paradigm is that it releases business from traditional ways of thought, opening up new possibilities for the application of GIS.

The framework introduced in Figure 1.1 and again referred to in Figure 3.4 conceptualises the completeness paradigm and shows the implications for GIS. When questions of information requirements are being discussed in the business the issue of identifying spatial data needs to be firmly on the agenda. Those companies who engage in technology planning and forecasting (see for example the case of the Woolwich Building Society in Chapter 11) may become aware of 'new' technologies like GIS and then these need to be taken to the business to establish whether there is a real business requirement that can use the technology. This is really an iterative process in practice. There needs to be the dual interaction of the business drivers on the one hand and the technology enablers on the other.

Applications of GIS are then identified as part of the information strategy. The whole process of systems development, implementation and organisational change will then ensue. The point is that this is very much a process to be considered in its entirety. In other words the process contained in Figure 1.1, conceptualises the completeness paradigm.

The application case studies in Chapter 9 consisted of operational support applications, and not surprisingly most of those organisations did originally have a set of maps, or indeed several sets of maps, that were automated by introducing GIS. However, even in these organisations the major benefits were seen when the GIS was integrated into the business information systems.

In other words, although starting with the functional automation motive, or the substitution paradigm, many of these organisations have moved to adopt the completeness paradigm thereby gaining more benefits for the business. The organisation shows that it 'learns' and is enabled through experience to move and develop by stages.

More will be said about applications for tactical and strategic decision support when the theme of applications of GIS in business is reviewed below.

GIS moves into mainstream information systems

In the conclusion to the seminal work of reference on GIS, editors Rhind, Goodchild and Maguire (1991: 324) speculate that 'GIS may disappear as a "free-standing" activity in many organisations as its functionality becomes encompassed by those business-oriented systems, such as those for market analysis, and it becomes part of a wider management information system.' The choice of words, it was pointed out in Chapter 1, are unfortunate in the sense that management information systems have generally been discredited in the information systems literature. In fact there is much debate, and some little confusion still, about a whole range of terminology in the information systems field. Terms such as decision-support system, expert system and executive information system tend to have different meanings in different authors' minds. Rather than perpetuate a sometimes esoteric debate, a taxonomy of GIS was put forward in Chapter 2 which uses a set of consistent concepts. The major utility of these concepts is that they allow a debate and analysis of GIS over time. It recognises that information systems are growing and changing, dynamic systems responding and changing in response to stimuli from the organisation.

The taxonomy of GIS is a useful conceptual framework, integrating a number of previously separate concepts. The three 'T's', *task*, *technology* and *time frame* can be used to place the information systems existing within an organisation and also to seek out stakeholder group views as to where the organisation might aim in the future. Used in this way the framework can become a useful management tool. It often helps to build consensus in organisations about priorities and gives managers a common consistent view of objectives. The time frame dimension integrates the stages of growth idea which was introduced in Chapter 3 and used to analyse and discuss the application case studies in Part Three. The framework is another part of the completeness paradigm in that it provides a way of conceptualising GIS within the organisation and highlighting the factors that contribute to differences in diverse organisations. Thereby it is a helpful framework in terms of analysis. Importantly it is also a way of seeing GIS as other information systems are seen.

Why are GIS likely to be integrated into business information systems in the future? Firstly, there is a changing attitude towards GIS. People employed in the environmental and public service sectors might have an understanding of the term 'geography' and geographical data, but, to most business people the term 'geographical information system' is of little meaning (Grimshaw 1989). How GIS is introduced into the organisation is crucial. For example, at the Woolwich Building Society, in the UK (see Chapter 11) little use is made of the term 'GIS' – systems are described according to their applications and would include 'customer', 'product' and 'branch' databases.

Secondly, GIS applications are moving from operational support through decision support to become strategic systems in many organisations (see Chapter 11). Examples of the uses of GIS in the business domain come within all three of the task classifications: operational, tactical and strategic, in contrast to uses in the environmental domain which are typically based on the need for operational information. Tactical applications rely on good modelling capabilities. The demand for greater modelling and spatial analysis capability is likely to increase and lead to each GIS software vendor marketing specialist business modules for their software package. In terms of the capability trends framework of Chapter 8 (Figure 8.1) we will see more problem-focused, business-specific software packages that combine simplicity with high levels of capability.

Thirdly, crucial data for the business GIS, for example census and postcode (zip code) boundaries, are becoming available in a more accurate, readily accessible format, at a cost which reflects the increased demand. Most advanced economies in the world are now aware of the potential of land-based information and are coordinating efforts, at government level, to supply data in standard formats (see for example ALIC 1990). This trend is expected to have a significant impact in the next few years.

GIS becomes part of corporate strategy

No business should use GIS unless it will contribute to the overall business, its mission, its aims – as well as its profit! GIS is no more than a tool, a business tool which uses a relatively new technology.

One of the key lessons from earlier applications of new technologies, like expert systems and office automation, is that a vision of the future (dream) is a necessary but not a sufficient condition for success. To be successful the technology needs to be integrated into the business planning process. Not just the information planning cycle but linked via a two-way bridge to the corporate plan (Earl 1989). More organisations will see GIS as a technological opportunity that can be brought into the business to make a significant impact on profit. The question of how this can be done was discussed in Chapter 3. The underlying trend, for which evidence was discussed in Chapter 3 and in the case study chapters, is for GIS to be increasingly considered as part of the information strategy of the organisation.

During the next decade, business will be confronted with tough challenges to maintaining market share, and IT will be viewed as the means to attain and increase competitive advantage. Specifically, it is likely that GIS will rise to dominate as a key tool for strategic planning. All technologies can be seen as contributing efficiency, effectiveness or strategic transformation depending on the stage of growth attained in a particular organisation (see Chapter 3). What we will see in the period of the early 1990s is GIS technology maturing so that its application moves from one of achieving efficiency benefits to one of achieving strategic benefit.

High-level decision making can be facilitated by GIS, helping to ensure the integrity and survival of the organisation, particularly as competitive pressures increase. There are two main areas in which GIS technology is likely to have a major impact upon business strategies – competitor analysis and branch rationalisation. In addition, GIS provides a means of examining, in detail, the market share a competitor enjoys.

From the viewpoint of the private sector GIS applications are currently of an *ad hoc* nature, supporting decision making in functional areas (say) marketing. The major business justifications for developing and using such systems will typically have been to enhance the productivity or effectiveness of the functional area rather than to contribute to the business as a whole. The initiators of early GIS projects would typically be functional specialists. The trend will be for GIS projects to be introduced into companies via a 'top-down' process.

The central concerns of both public and private sector users and potential users of GIS are now beginning to turn towards the corporate needs of the organisation (Maynard and Pearce 1990). At this important stage of thinking the central concern becomes strategic. Managers begin to look for real business reasons for justifying an investment in GIS. The potential of hitherto neglected data sets are realised as data is now regarded as a true corporate resource.

GIS unlocks spatial data

Bringing GIS into the business involves releasing the potential of spatial data already locked away in company databases, purchasing data where relevant and using it to enhance the business. The estimates of the proportion of spatial data contained in business databases range up to 90% of all company data (Moloney *et al.* 1993). Chapter 4 looked at how that data could be unlocked and transformed into useful information. It is a truism to say that business requires information in order to make decisions. Some of the problems with this simplistic view were examined in Chapter 5. But it fundamentally remains true that the demand for geographic data by business is what economists call derived demand. This idea has been well expressed by Dickinson and Calkins (1988: 317) who paraphrased Samuelson and Nordhaus (1985: 601): 'The demands for inputs of geographic information system products are derived demands. This means that when decision-makers demand a GIS product as input, they do so because that input permits the decision-maker to produce information relevant to a policy decision. The demand for the input is thus derived ultimately from the needs for policy decisions.'

The implication of this concept of derived demand for the take-up of GIS into the business is that the benefits are indirect. To unlock these benefits requires vision to understand the utility of geographic data (this point will be taken up again under the theme of GIS becoming part of the corporate strategy). Additionally it requires some practical knowledge about how to turn spatial data into information for decision makers.

The framework put forward in Chapter 4 envisages building a data architecture which will enable the business applications to thrive. The data architecture, rather like the built environment architect who works to a design brief, has to be based on an understanding of the business mission and objectives, a translation of those aims into workable assumptions, development of reasoned justification or argument, followed by actions. These ideas were conceptualised in Figure 4.1. They may be remembered as the three 'A's'.

In a similar way, there was a technology architecture framework introduced in Chapter 3 (see Table 3.1 for example). Together these architectures provide the overall environment for the development of useful information systems. They ensure that there is a consistent set of applications, standards and definitions in place at a technical level so that the benefits to the organisation may be maximised.

In Part Three of the book Chapters 9–11 discussed case studies of organisations using GIS to support decision making. The division of the chapters into levels of decision making, was to some extent artificial. In practice operational, tactical and strategic decision making is much less compartmentalised. This concluding chapter will bring some of these ideas in the case study chapters together under the theme of applications of GIS in business at the end of the chapter.

GIS helps the business focus on the customer

Many items of data collected and used by industry generally have a geographic dimension, for example customer addresses. Using this geographical dimension of data can add substantial value to information. In what way is the situation changing?

Traditionally the central accounting function of a business has been based on an accounts database. This has proved to be problematic when a business wishes to identify its customers. Consequently a great deal of effort has recently been targeted at developing good customer databases. The time is now ripe for GIS to be linked to those customer databases.

Internally held data like customer records will require the addition of a geographic reference in order to allow for the linking of data to socio-economic, demographic and other geographic data that has been extracted from public databases. The public sector needs to take on board the philosophy of seeing information as a tradable resource in order to make available geographic data. There is increasing evidence from a number of countries that this is indeed happening. The trend is likely to continue so that in two or three years' time the price of data will have declined considerably.

A significant trend in the GIS world has been the considerable growth of data agencies that will add value to client data. For example, suppose a company wishes to assess the market potential for a possible new product. A data agency could supply maps and potential customer addresses from an analysis of geodemographic data (see Chapter 10). As companies develop better customer databases and as the trend to cheaper geographic data sets continues, the market currently enjoyed by the data agencies is likely to decline. Organisations will bring their geographical analysis in-house as was seen in some of the case studies in Chapters 10 and 11.

Benefits management and implementation

Traditional information systems literature has viewed implementation as a *stage* in the systems development process, essentially to do with technical testing. The view presented throughout the book, and especially in Chapter 7, is that implementation is part of a wider *process* involving the management of change that is required to make an information system successful.

Linked to the idea of implementation being considered as integral to the success of an information system is the idea that benefits should be considered throughout the project. Traditional views of identifying benefits according to narrowly defined financial criteria need to be broadened to allow for contributions to the business as a whole and value-added benefits.

Applications of GIS by business

The range of applications considered throughout the book have come from a variety of different countries, each having different policies towards things like the price at which digital data is sold and transferred. The applications considered in Chapters 9–11 were discussed in relation to the stages of growth model. This model is an adaptation from the work of Galliers and Sutherland (1991) and Grimshaw (1993) to fit the particular empirical conditions found in the GIS area.

The main exciting finding is that GIS is being applied in a range of different industries, to a range of different business processes. The overall pattern of the way in which GIS is started in organisations, then develops further, is in accordance with the stages of growth model. This shows that those organisations with loose, *ad hoc* strategies, informal structures and existing information systems that generally support operational decision making are likely to ask, 'What is GIS?' Partly because the appropriate skills in-house will be in short supply, such organisations are likely to 'opt out' and purchase GIS services from a data agency or consultancy. See Table 8.4 for examples of such organisations.

If these GIS services are shown to work for the organisation there is evidence from the case studies that systems will be brought in-house, most often in a 'stand-alone' capacity by some enthusiasts doing their own thing on the basis of strictly controlled financial benefit criteria.

Those organisations, and there are many examples, who take a strategic approach to adopting GIS are likely to have fairly well-developed information systems generally, with well-developed partnerships between business and IT staff. The benefits looked for may well be effectiveness, not just simple efficiency. Project management skills will be evident throughout the organisation and GIS will be seen as 'linking' to other information systems. The benefits are likely to be wide-ranging rather than narrowly functional. These are organisations who have already taken on board many of the messages inherent in the completeness paradigm.

There is some evidence amongst the case study organisations that GIS has been spotted as a 'new' technology by technology planners in the business. There has then been an opportunity to use the technology for strategic business reasons. Finding out exactly which comes first – the identification of the technology presenting the opportunity, or the identification of a business need – is difficult. Perhaps it is a result, on many occasions, of some process of serendipity.

A final stage identified in the model is the so-called 'corporate' stage. Before engaging in the research it seemed likely that utility companies would be at this stage. This was borne out by the case study organisations. However, a surprising finding is that there are examples of the corporate stage of GIS being reached by manufacturing, mining, transportation and retail organisations. These are all companies who have thought through their strategies from first principles and found opportunities to use GIS to assist in the achievement of those strategies.

The application of the adapted stages of growth model shows that some business uses of GIS have reached a very sophisticated stage, that there is a pattern to the way in which most organisations have adopted GIS, and therefore there is the potential for organisations to learn from each other. In some small way it is hoped that this book will make some contribution to achieving that potential.

Summary

Traditionally, single functional areas, like marketing, have been responsible for introducing GIS. Yet the potential applications in many businesses go beyond marketing (or indeed any single functional area). In the future the opportunities offered by GIS technology need to be realised by the business as a whole. When this happens the GIS 'island of technology' will become part of the corporate-wide information systems infrastructure. This can be seen as a natural progression of IT usage in any business organisation resulting in business strategy having strong links to information strategy.

As a further spin-off from the integration of GIS technology with other corporate information systems two things will happen. Firstly, the spatial analysis capabilities of GIS will improve; and secondly, geographical outputs will become recognised as just one more business graphic. These two steps will help each business to explore the geographical dimension of their existing data in addition to the more obvious exploitation of specially purchased geographical data.

The geographical data required by business will become cheaper as state and private agencies cooperate on data standards and pricing according to a national strategy. For example the Spatial Data Transfer Standard (SDTS), ratified in the USA as a Federal Information Processing Standard on 29 July 1992, is being adopted in many other countries. Software vendors as well as data vendors will adopt such standards in the near future.

This chapter has concentrated on identifying some of the major organisational and geographical data trends that will have an impact on the application of GIS in business. Currently seen as a specialised tool, GIS is about to become just another business tool as it moves into mainstream information systems. A greater business focus on the customer will result in improved customer databases that will benefit from being linked to cheaper spatial data available in an internationally agreed standard format. One of the major challenges ahead is to ensure that GIS enters the consciousness of those responsible for information systems planning in their business.

References

ALIC 1990 *National Strategy on Land Information Management* Australian Land Information Council, Belconnen, Australia

Betak J, Vaidya A 1991 On becoming an information-based company: a role for GIS. *GIS World* **4**: 44–7

Dickinson H J, Calkins H W 1988 The economic evaluation of implementing a GIS. *International Journal of Geographical Information Systems* **2**(4): 307–27

Earl M J 1989 *Management Strategies for Information Technology* Prentice-Hall, London

Galliers R D, Sutherland A R 1991 Information systems management and strategy formulation: the stages of growth model revisited. *Journal of Information Systems* **1**(2): 89–114

Grimshaw D J 1989 Geographical information systems: a tool for business and industry? *International Journal of Information Management* **9** (July): 119–26

Grimshaw D J 1991 GIS – a strategic business tool? *Mapping awareness and GIS Europe*, **5** (2) (March 1991): 46–8

Grimshaw D J 1993 Corporate GIS stage by stage. *Proceedings of the GIS in Business '93 Conference* Boston, Mass, 7–10 March, GIS World Books Inc, Fort Collins, Colo, 133–7

Maynard J C, Pearce N J 1990 GIS as part of a corporate IT strategy: a practical approach. *Proceedings of the European Conference on Geographical Information Systems* Vol. II, Amsterdam, April, pp 729–36

Moloney T, Lea A C, Kowalchuk C 1993 Manufacturing and packaged goods. In *Profiting from a Geographical Information System* GIS World Books Inc, Fort Collins, Colo, pp 105–29

Rhind D W, Goodchild M F, Maguire D J 1991 Epilogue. In Maguire D J, Goodchild M F, Rhind D W (eds) *Geographical Information Systems* Vol 2 *Applications* Longman Scientific & Technical, Harlow, pp 313–27

Samuelson P A, Nordhaus W D 1985 *Economics* McGraw-Hill, New York

List of acronyms

ACM	Association of Computer Machinery
ACORN	A Classification of Residential Neighbourhoods
AGI	Association for Geographic Information (UK)
AHS	American Hospital Supplies
ALCOA	Aluminium Corporation of Australia
ALIC	Australian Land Information Council
AM/FM	Automated Mapping/Facilities Management
ANZLIC	Australia New Zealand Land Information Council
AS	Australian Standard
ATM	Automatic Teller Machine (Hole in the Wall)
AUSDEC	Australian Spatial Data Exchange Centre
BS	British Standard (UK)
CAD/CAM	Computer-Aided Design/Computer-Aided Manufacture
CASE	Computer-Assisted Software Engineering
CALM	Department of Conservation and Land Management, Western Australia
CD-ROM	Compact Disc-Read Only Memory
CEO	Chief Executive Officer
CRA	Community Reinvestment Act (USA)
DBMS	Database Management Systems
DCDSTF	Digital Cartographic Data Standards Task Force (USA)
DCF	Discounted Cash Flow
DoE	Department of the Environment (UK)
DOLA	Department of Land Administration
DOS	Disk Operating System (standard for IBM-PC)

DP	Data Processing
DSS	Decision Support System
DXF	Drawing Exchange Format (Autodesk)
ED	Enumeration District (UK)
EDI	Electronic Data Interchange
EDP	Electronic Data Processing
EGIS	European Geographical Information Systems
EIS	Executive Information System
ETHICS	Effective Technical and Human Implementation of Computer-Based Systems
EUOGI	European Umbrella Organisation for Geographic Information
FIPS	Federal Information Processing Standard (USA)
FSA	Forward Sortation Area (Canadian postcode)
GANS	Global Area Networks
Gb	Gigabyte (2^{30})
GIS	Geographic Information System
GM	General Motors
GPS	Global Positioning System
HMDA	Home Mortgage Disclosure Act (USA)
IE	Information Engineering
IKBS	Intelligent Knowledge-Based System
ILIP	Integrated Land Information Programme (WA, Australia)
IPSE	Integrated Project Support Environment
IS	Information System
IT	Information Technology
LAN	Local Area Network
LBMS	Learmouth Burchett Management Systems
LIS	Land Information System
MANS	Metropolitan Area Network
Mb	Megabyte (2^{20})
MGIS	Marketing Geographical Information System
MIS	Management Information System
MIT	Massachusetts Institute of Technology
MSA	Metropolitan Statistical Area
NCGIA	National Center for Geographic Information and Analysis (USA)
NJUG	National Joint Utilities Group (UK)
NTF	National Transfer Format (UK)

OS/2	Operating System/2 (IBM Software)
OSI	Open Systems Interconnection
OSTF	Ordnance Survey Transfer Format (UK)
RAM	Random Access Memory
ROI	Return On Investment
SAS	Statistical Analysis System
SDSS	Spatial Decision Support System
SDTS	Spatial Data Transfer Standard
SIC	Standard Industrial Classification
SIF	Standard Interchange Format (Intergraph)
SNA	Standard Network Architecture (IBM)
SQL	Structured Query Language
SSADM	Structured Systems Analysis and Design Methodology
SSM	Soft Systems Methodology
SWOT	Strengths, Weaknesses, Opportunities and Threats
Tb	Terabyte (2^{40})
TIGER	Topologically Integrated Geographic Encoding Reference File
TGI	Target Group Index
UNIX	Operating system software, running on Workstations
UTM	Universal Transverse Mercator
VAX	Operating system software (Digital)
WALIS	Western Australia Land Information System
WAWA	Western Australia Water Authority
WORM	Write Once Read Many

Index